CONTEMPORARY INDONESIAN FILM

Southeast Asia Mediated

This series considers media forms and practices, processes of mediation, and the complex evolving and intersecting media ecologies that characterize Southeast Asia whether in contemporary or historical circumstances.

Editors: Bart Barendregt (Leiden University) and Ariel Heryanto (Australian National University).

VERHANDELINGEN
VAN HET KONINKLIJK INSTITUUT
VOOR TAAL-, LAND- EN VOLKENKUNDE

277

KATINKA VAN HEEREN

CONTEMPORARY INDONESIAN FILM

Spirits of Reform and ghosts from the past

KITLV Press
Leiden
2012

Published by:
KITLV Press
Koninklijk Instituut voor Taal-, Land- en Volkenkunde
(Royal Netherlands Institute of Southeast Asian and Caribbean Studies)
P.O. Box 9515
2300 RA Leiden
The Netherlands
website: www.kitlv.nl
e-mail: kitlvpress@kitlv.nl

KITLV is an institute of the Royal Netherlands Academy of Arts and Sciences (KNAW)

KONINKLIJKE NEDERLANDSE
AKADEMIE VAN WETENSCHAPPEN

Cover: Sam Gobin

ISBN 978 90 6718 381 9

© 2012 Koninklijk Instituut voor Taal-, Land- en Volkenkunde

KITLV Press applies the Creative Commons Attribution-NonCommercial-NoDerivs 3.0 Unported License (http://creativecommons.org/licenses/by-nc-nd/3.0/) to selected books, published in or after January 2011.

Authors retain ownership of the copyright for their articles, but they permit anyone unrestricted use and distribution within the terms of this license.

Printed editions manufactured in the Netherlands

Contents

LIST OF ACRONYMS AND ABBREVIATIONS		vii
PREFACE		xiii
INTRODUCTION		1

PART 1   FILM MEDIATION PRACTICES

1   NEW ORDER AND SURFACE   25

    Production: The attempt to produce *Provokator* the New Order way   26

    Distribution and exhibition: Trade and charade in cinemas and film formats   32

    Exhibition and consumption: Film festivals as forums for national imaginations and representations   40

    Conclusion   48

2   REFORMASI AND UNDERGROUND   51

    Reformation in film production: *Kuldesak* and *film independen*   52

    Distribution and exhibition of new media formats: 'Local' *Beth* versus 'transnational' *Jelangkung*   59

    Alternative sites of film consumption: Additional identifications and modes of resistance   67

    Conclusion   76

PART 2   FILM DISCOURSE PRACTICES

3   HISTORIES, HEROES, AND MONUMENTAL FRAMEWORKS   81

    Film history: New Order patronage of *film perjuangan* and *film pembangunan*   81

    Film and historiography: Promotion and representations of New Order history   88

    'Film in the framework of': G30S/PKI and Hapsak   96

    Conclusion   103

| Contents

4 POST-COLONIAL HISTORIES, COMMON PEOPLE, AND COMMERCIAL FRAMEWORKS — 107

    Counter-history: Changes and continuities in post-Soeharto modes of engagement — 107
    Post-colonial histories and identities: *film islami* — 115
    Film in the framework of Ramadan — 122
    Conclusion — 129

PART 3 FILM DISCOURSE PRACTICES

5 THE *KYAI* AND HYPERREAL GHOSTS: NARRATIVE PRACTICES OF HORROR, COMMERCE, AND CENSORSHIP — 135

    Horror films under the New Order: Comedy, sex, and religion — 136
    Horror films for television: New narratives and debates on their bounds — 141
    Horror films for cinema and television: Developments of Reformasi — 147
    Conclusion — 155

6 THE CELEBRITY *KYAI* AND PHANTOMS OF THE PAST: TUSSLING WITH THE BOUNDS OF INDONESIAN MORALITIES, REALITIES, AND POPULARITIES — 157

    The ban on *Kiss me quick!:* The *kyai*, the foreigner, and Indonesia's morality — 161
    Censorship from the street: The authority of religion — 168
    The post-Soeharto dispute over censorship: Spirits of Reform and ghosts from the past — 176
    Conclusion — 182

CONCLUSION — 185

GLOSSARY — 203

BIBLIOGRAPHY — 205

FILMOGRAPHY — 225

INDEX — 231

List of acronyms and abbreviations

AAK	Aliansi Anti-Komunis (Alliance of Anti-Communists)
ABG	Anak Baru Gedhe (teenager)
ABRI	Angkatan Bersenjata Republik Indonesia (Armed Forces of the Republic of Indonesia)
AMAP	Aliansi Masyarakat Anti Porno-Aksi (Alliance of People against Pornographic Acts)
Asirevi	Asosiasi Importir Rekaman Video Indonesia (Indonesian Video Recording Importers Association)
BP2N	Badan Pertimbangan Perfilman Nasional (National Film Assessment Board)
BSF	Badan Sensor Film (Film Censor Board)
DFN	Dewan Film Nasional (National Film Council)
DGI	Dewan Gereja-Gereja di Indonesia (Council of Churches in Indonesia)
DVD	Digital Video/Versatile Disc
FBR	Forum Betawi Rempug (Betawi Brotherhood Forum)
FFAP	Festival Film Asia Pasifik (Asia Pacific Film Festival)
FFB	Forum Film Bandung (Bandung Film Forum)
FFD	Festival Film Dokumenter (Documentary Film Festival)
FFI	Festival Film Indonesia (Indonesian Film Festival)
FFII	Festival Film Independen Indonesia (Indonesian Independent Film Festival)
FFVII	Festival Film dan Video Independen Indonesia (Indonesian Independent Film and Video Festival)
FKLD	Forum Komunikasi Lembaga Dakwah (Communication Forum of Dakwah Institutions)
FLP	Forum Lingkar Pena (Pen Circle Forum)
FPI	Front Pembela Islam (Islamic Defenders Front)
FSI	Festival Sinetron Indonesia (Indonesian 'Electronic Cinema' Festival)
Gasfi	Gabungan Studio Film Indonesia (Indonesian Association of Film Studios)

List of acronyms and abbreviations

Gasi	Gabungan Subtitling Indonesia (Indonesian Association of Subtitlers)
Gerwani	Gerakan Wanita Indonesia (Indonesian Women's Movement),
GPBSI	Gabungan Perusahaan Bioskop Seluruh Indonesia (All-Indonesian Association of Movie Theatre Companies)
GPHMI	Gerakan Perempuan Hindu Muda Indonesia (Indonesian Young Hindu Women's Movement)
Hafsi	Himpunan Artis Film dan Sinetron Indonesia (Indonesian Film and 'Electronic Cinema' Association)
Hafti	Himpunan Artis Film dan Televisi Indonesia (Association of Indonesian Film and Television Artists)
Hapsak	Hari Peringatan Kesaktian Pancasila (Day of Commemoration of the Sacred Pancasila)
Hifki	Himpunan Film Keliling Indonesia (Association of Indonesian Mobile Cinema)
HMI	Himpunan Mahasiswa Islam (Association of Islamic Students)
HPBI	Himpunan Pengusaha Bioskop Indonesia (Indonesian Association of Movie Theatre Agents)
HT	Hizbut Tahrir (Party of Liberation, an international Sunni pan-Islamist political party)
IIPA	International Intellectual Property Alliance
IKJ	Institut Kesenian Jakarta (Jakarta Art Institute)
IMF	International Monetary Fund
Jiffest	Jakarta International Film Festival
KFT	Karyawan Film dan Televisi (Union of Film and Television Employees)
KFT-ASI	Karyawan Film Television – Asosiasi Sineas Indonesia (Film and Television Employees – Association of Indonesian Cineasts)
KISDI	Komite Indonesia untuk Solidaritas Dunia Islam (Indonesian Committee for Solidarity in the Islamic World)
Kismis	kisah misteri (mystery tales)
KKN	korupsi, kolusi dan nepotisme (corruption, collusion and nepotism)
Konfiden	Komunitas Film Independen (Community of Independent Film)
Kopassus	Komando Pasukan Khusus (Special Forces)

KP2N	Komite Peduli Perfilman Nasional (National Committee of Concern for the National Film Industry)
KPAI	Komisi Perlindungan Anak Indonesia (Indonesian Children Protection Commission)
KPI	Komisi Penyiaran Indonesia (Indonesian Broadcast Commission)
KPPU	Komisi Pengawas Persaingan Usaha (Business Competition Supervisory Agency)
KWI	Konferensi Waligereja Indonesia (Indonesian Bishops' Conference)
LD	Laser Disc
LEKRA	Lembaga Kebudayaan Rakyat (Institute of People's Culture, the key cultural mass organization affiliated to PKI
LPI	Laskar Pembela Islam (Warriors of Defenders of Islam)
LPPD	Lembaga Pengkajian dan Pengembangan Dakwah (Institute for the Study and Development of Dakwah)
LSF	Lembaga Sensor Film (Film Censor Institute)
mafin	mahluk film independen (independent-film creature)
MAPPI	Laskar Masyarakat Anti Pembajakan dan Pornografi Indonesia (Indonesian Paramilitary Unit of People Against Piracy and Pornography)
MAV-Net	Morality Audio Visual Network
MFI	Masyarakat Film Indonesia (Indonesian Film Society)
MMI	Majelis Mujahiddin Indonesia (Indonesian Council of Defenders of the [Islamic] Faith)
MPAA	Motion Picture Association of America
MPR	Majelis Permusyawaratan Rakyat (People's Consultative Assembly)
MUI	Majelis Ulama Indonesia (Indonesian Council of Muslim Scholars)
NU	Nahdlatul Ulama (Revival/Awakening of Religious Scholars, 30-million-strong Muslim organization)
P4	Pedoman Penghayatan dan Pengamalan Pancasila (Directives for Instilling and Implementing Pancasila)
Parfi	Persatuan Artis Film Indonesia (Indonesian Film Artists' Union)

List of acronyms and abbreviations

PBR	Partai Bintang Reformasi (Star of Reformation Party)
PDI	Partai Demokrasi Indonesia (Indonesian Democratic Party)
Pelita	Pembangunan Lima Tahun (Five Year Development Programmes of the state).
Perbiki	Persatuan Pengusaha Bioskop Keliling (Union of Operators of Mobile Movie Theatres)
Perda	peraturan daerah (regional regulations)
Perfiki	Persatuan Pengusaha Pertunjukan Film Keliling Indonesia (Association of Indonesian Mobile Cinema Screening Companies)
PFN	Perusahaan Film Negara (State Film Corporation)
PHDI	Parisada Hindu Dharma Indonesia (Hinduism Society)
PJKA	Perusahaan Jawatan Kereta Api (State Railway Company)
PKI	Partai Komunis Indonesia (Indonesian communist party),
PKS	Partai Keadilan Sejahtera (Prosperous Justice Party)
PPFI	Persatuan Perusahaan Film Indonesia (Indonesian Film Company Union)
PPFN	Pusat Produksi Film Negara (Centre for State Film Production)
PPHUI	Pusat Perfilman Haji Usmar Ismail (Haji Usmar Ismail Film Centre)
PPKI	Panitia Persiapan Kemerdekaan Indonesia (Preparatory Committee for Indonesian Independence)
PSA	Public Service Announcement
PSI	Pesta Sinema Indonesia (Feast of Indonesian Cinema)
PSPB	Pendidikan Sejarah Perjuangan Bangsa (Education in the History of the Struggle of the Nation)
pungli	pungutan liar (unofficial contributions)
PWI	Persatuan Wartawan Indonesia (Association of Indonesian Journalists)
QFF	Queer Film Festival
RCTI	Rajawali Citra Televisi Indonesia (Indonesian Hawk Image Television)
RUU APP	Rancangan Undang Undang Anti Pornografi dan Pornoaksi (Anti-Pornography and Porno Action Bill)

SARA	suku (ethnic groups), agama (religion), ras (race), and antar-golongan (class)
SCTV	Surya Citra Televisi (Sun Image Television)
sinetron	sinema elektronik (soap)
TPI	Televisi Pendidikan Indonesia (Indonesian Education Television)
Trans TV	Transformation Television
TVRI	Televisi Republik Indonesia (Indonesian Republic Television)
UMM	Universitas Muhammadiyah Malang (Muhammadiyah University in Malang)
USIA	United States Information Agency
VCD	Video Compact Disc
warnet	warung internet (internet stalls)
YFI	Yayasan Nasional Festival Film Indonesia (National Foundation of the Indonesian Film Festival)
YMMFI	Yayasan Masyarakat Mandiri Film Indonesia (Independent Society of Indonesian Films)

Preface

The research for this dissertation was carried out under the auspices of the Indonesian Mediations Project, part of the Indonesia in Transition programme (2001-2005), funded by the Royal Netherlands Academy of Arts and Sciences (KNAW). I would like to thank the School of Asian, African, and Amerindian Studies (CNWS), and the Netherlands Organization for Scientific Research (NWO) for their financial support.

There are so many people both in my professional and in my personal life who have contributed to this book that the list is too long to mention them separately. I owe them my sincerest gratitude. In particular, I am indebted to all the persons in the Indonesian film scene, who supported me in so many ways. A special word of thanks goes out to the filmmakers for allowing me to use their work in the DVD that formed part of the thesis on which this book is based.

Introduction

The contemporary media shape identity; indeed many argue that they now exist close to the very core of identity production. In a transnational world typified by the global circulation of images, sounds, goods, and peoples, media spectatorship has a large impact on national identity, communal belonging, and political affiliations. By facilitating a mediated engagement with distant peoples, the media 'deterritorialize' the process of imagining communities. And while the media can destroy community and fashion solitude by turning spectators into atomized consumers or self-entertaining monads, they can also fashion community and alternative affiliations (Shohat 2003:74).

The audio-visual mediascape in post-Soeharto Indonesia is very dynamic; it is marked by a great variety in film formats, genres, and styles, and entrenched by a host of discussions and activities. All sorts of films can be found in cinemas, at cultural centres and in galleries, in cinema clubs at universities, and in other public or private places. Indonesian independent film productions, documentaries, auteur films, popular films, and gay and lesbian films are just some examples of what is on display. National television is also animated by numerous programmes, such as soaps, infotainment programmes, game shows, and reality shows. At first glance, many Indonesian films and television programmes make use of styles, genres, and formulas that are similar to those that can be found all over the world. Even so, all films and programmes which are produced, distributed, screened, or watched in Indonesia are part of a specific complex of discourses and mediation practices. This setting suggests particular ways of reading and understanding film texts. Consequently, notwithstanding the effects of globalization and transnational media flows, similar genres, styles, programmes, and formulas engage in representations and interpretations which tap into Indonesian imaginations of community and nation.

In *Virtual geography*, a book about the media coverage of the First Gulf War, McKenzie Wark wrote about a staged media appearance by Saddam Hussein. Filmed with Western people whom he had taken hostage, Hussein gently ruffles the hair of one of them, a little boy. Wark asserts that in doing so Saddam Hussein was making use of, and performing, a well-known and widely accepted Iraqi generic style: to give the impression of 'the noble and respected elder'. In the West, however, that same image had a totally different affect as it tapped into other 'confounded and most cherished beliefs about genres of television and the kinds of stories they legitimately tell us'. Viewers in the West, raised on 'Orientalist' media literacy, responded with disgust on seeing a vile Arab who harassed a little boy (Wark 1994:4). Wark comments on how people brought up in different cultural frames are geared to other ways of handling information, and have a repertoire of quite different stories with which to filter events. As he phrases it: 'How could we claim to know what goes on at the other interzones, in quite other spaces where different flows from different vectors meet quite other memories and experiences of everyday life?' (Wark 1994:19). In other words, how do we make an image of and imagine the other, and how do they make an image of and imagine themselves?

In any nation, the significance and possible interpretations of images and media texts are based on both discourses that circulate in society as well as mediation practices. In this book, I situate film as a social practice within the shifting political and cultural frames of the Indonesian nation.[1] Exploring historically emergent forms of representation and imagination of communities in the Indonesian audio-visual mediascape, I address the impact of discourses and film mediation practices on the production of collective identities and social realities. My account ranges from discussions on the 'idealized Indonesian self in television discourses' (Kitley 2000:12) and film (Sen 1994) under the New Order, to a topsy-turvy heated debate about the representation of the Indonesian nation and the daily lived reality of the people in film and on television in 2007.

'Discourse' is a prominent concept in this book. Along the lines of Norman Fairclough's media discourse analysis, I use the term in a combination of two senses. I use it in the sense which is prevalent in language studies: 'discourse as social action and interaction, people interacting together in real social situations' (Fairclough 1995:16). In addition, I use the term in the sense in which it is prevalent in post-structuralist social theory, as propounded by Foucault: 'a discourse as a social construction of reality, a form of knowledge' (Fairclough 1995:16). Discourses appertain broadly to knowledge and knowledge construction. In a combination of these two senses, a dis-

---

1 Other authors who discuss film as a social practice include Friedberg 1993; Stacey 1994; Staiger 1992; Turner 1992; Wasko 1994; Willemen 1994.

course is the language used in representing a given social practice from a particular point of view. For instance, the social practice of politics is signified differently in liberal, socialist, and Marxist political discourses (Fairclough 1995:18, 56). In addition, film mediation practices are defined here as the practices of film production, distribution, exhibition, and consumption. The use of language studies or literary theories to analyse audio-visual media is not uncommon. Here I would like to mention two constructive studies in which the research of this book can be placed. The first is a more general study on film by Robert Stam, professor of cinema studies at New York University. Stam uses Mikhail Bakhtin's literary theories drawing on key concepts associated with Bakhtin's works such as dialogism, heteroglossia, the carnivalesque, and chronotope. Through these concepts, Stam (1989) presents a 'translinguistic' critique of Saussurean semiotics and Russian formalism. Furthermore, he addresses the question of language difference in cinema, analyses issues of national culture in Latin America, and considers 'the carnivalesque' in literature and film. The second commendable study of audio-visual media that uses a critical discourse analysis approach concentrates on Indonesian television: Klarijn Loven's research (2008) on the popular television serial *Si Doel*.

There is no one-to-one meaning which clings onto media (McLuhan's 'the medium is the message' (1995)); rather, different, culturally imbued practices, mechanisms, and politics lie at the base of all meaning. This is not to say that politics and mechanisms of mediation practices are the key to how a text is read, for it is up to the audience 'to decide whether to read the image in terms of 'our' frame of reference, or in the frame of what we know about the other' (Wark 1994:5), and there are many other ways of reading from which to choose. Prevailing discourses and film mediation practices disclose competing forms of representation and the imagination of specific identities, as well as the construction of social realities. In my account of the construction of social realities, I draw on the Foucauldian idea that each society has its own regime or general politics of truth. This refers to the types of discourse that a particular society harbours and causes to function as true: which facts, narratives, myths, or representations are acknowledged to function as true in a society. Rather than focusing on audience research, I concentrate on the broader mediation practices and discourses about films. This account will be interspersed with the opinions and comments of film-makers, journalists, academics, film fans, or other people who participate in the filmmaking process or who explicitly discuss the films or developments in the Indonesian mediascape that are analysed here.

| *Introduction*

Even though audience research has not been the main focus of my investigation as such, I can make a few general remarks based on my personal experiences watching films in Indonesian movie theatres, at various film festivals, and at the homes of Indonesian friends. For those not familiar with Indonesia it may be useful to mention that like other parts of Asia in the 1980s-1990s, Indonesia experienced a rapid process of industrialization and economic growth in the three decades of New Order rule. In a relatively short period various groups of people, among them bureaucrats, manufacturers, traders, and entrepreneurs, accumulated wealth and began to enjoy much higher levels of prosperity. The Asian economic boom led to the rise of an affluent middle class and the so-called New Rich, who engage in new lifestyles and new forms and patterns of consumption. Many of the affluent middle classes now live in residential estates, purchase international designer brands, eat out, and seek entertainment in luxurious shopping malls; depending on their level of wealth, they also travel around the world. The Asian New Rich, increasingly preoccupied with lifestyle and consumption, emerged, in the words of Michael Pinches, in contexts of 'substantial material inequality and social tension', whose characteristics 'are changing rather than disappearing' (Pinches 1999:7).

Generally speaking, Indonesian films are hardly, if ever, watched by my upper-middle-class and middle-class friends who are not part of the Indonesian film scene. They only watch transnational productions, mostly from the US but also art house movies from all over the world. Generally they watch films and transnational TV series at home on transnational cable networks such as HBO, Star Movies, Cinemax, E, and so on. Another option is pirated DVDs. If my friends watch a film in a movie theatre, it is because they want to have a nice night out, or the special effects of the film are deemed significant enough to watch them on the big screen. My film-maker and independent-film friends, who are mainly middle-class, watch both transnational and Indonesian film productions. The Indonesian films they watch are primarily the ones produced by their network of colleagues and friends. Mostly they watch these films at the premieres or at film festivals. Less often they watch Indonesian commercial films in movie theatres. Only if there is some sort of buzz about a commercial film they may want to see it. As a rule my film-maker friends ignore the Indonesian cliché horror, teenage, slapstick films. But if these films are so bad that it makes them excel in inferiority some film-makers will buy the pirated version of these films for fun. The people that I know who do watch commercial Indonesian films are lower-middle-class and lower-class audiences. Some of the staff of the shops I regularly visit, waiters in my favourite restaurants, my construction worker friends, and hairdressers from beauty salons have told me they like to go to movie theatres to watch commercial Indonesian films. They also rent VCDs of Indonesian films or buy the pirated versions to watch them at home. The household staff in the houses of my friends mostly watch TV, in particular soaps and reality shows. They say they never go to a movie theatre, believing it not to represent value for money. Apart from these fragmented observations, in this book the audiences 'just do it': they watch, or do not watch, the films, and appreciate or dislike them, or both at the same time.[2]

Central discourses, such as those about the ethical values of a nation, resound in discourses on film and permeate the discourse practices and narrative practices of film texts, television programmes, and soaps. The term 'discourse practice' is a concept within Fairclough's discourse analysis theory. Discourse analysis 'is concerned with practices as well as texts, and with both discourse practices and sociocultural practices'. With discourse practice Fairclough (1995:16) means 'the ways in which texts are produced by media workers in media institutions, and the ways in which texts are received by audiences [...], as well as how media texts are socially distributed'. Sociocultural practice refers to 'the social and cultural goings-on which a communicative event is part of' (Fairclough 1995:57). Thus discourse practice is media text production and consumption, and sociocultural practice is mass communication as a particular type of situation, the economics of media, the politics of the media, and the wider cultural context of communication in the mass media. Discourse practices and sociocultural practices intermix, since there are various levels of sociocultural practice that may constitute parts of the context of discourse practice (Fairclough 1995:57). Film discourse practices entail the merger of societies' discourses with mediation practices. In discourse practices, discourses are put into practice in the production, distribution, and consumption of film texts; in other words, discourses materialize in film texts. An example of a discourse practice is the production of historical films and documentaries and their mode of distribution. In Chapter 3, I show that the production of these genres represents prevailing concepts of historiography and the nation-state, and that

---

[2] I use the phrase 'Just do it' as it refers to a slogan in both the Indonesian and Malaysian independent-film scene. In Indonesia 'Just-do-it-(yourself)' was first used to encourage aspiring independent film-makers to start making their own films. Later, the phrase was used as the slogan to get beyond the complicated discussions that had emerged about independent film and its makers' identity, legitimacy, and aspirations. For more about the Malaysian independent-film scene, see Khoo Gaik Cheng 2004.

| *Introduction*

their mode of distribution ties in with the endeavour to direct discourses on historiography.

Film narrative practices are a component of discursive practices; they relate to the form and content of film texts. Narrative practices are about stories and the way in which these are told in audio-visual media within the context of power relations. Power relations involve both the actual power of the state in controlling the mass media through censorship and broadcasting and press policies, and through the possession and control of private national and transnational media industries and institutions.[3] These elements coalesce to shape the form and content of domestic audio-visual products. Powerful as they may be, the state and public and private media industries and networks are not alone in shaping the form and content of film; audiences and pressure groups are also important in defining these. Audiences can decide if they want to watch a film or not, and even though rating polls have been criticized for their inaccuracy, they guide advertisers who in turn influence private media industries.[4] Furthermore, state censorship is not the only force delineating the margins of the form and content of media productions. Pressure and protests from audiences, mass organizations, or communities of conviction can lead to self-censorship on the part of film-makers and even to the banning of films and television programmes. The form and content of audio-visual media, in conjunction with the questions of power, authority, and access to resources, impinge on what representations of the nation, communities, and social realities circulate in society. Social truths or realities are not stable, but are constantly defined and re-defined in competing discourses. Fairclough (1995:52) argues that '[c]hanges in society and culture manifest themselves in all their tentativeness, incompleteness and contradictory nature in the heterogeneous and shifting discursive practices of the media'. Particularly after the resignation of President Soeharto, the Indonesian mediascape has been marked by a wide range of discourses in which different communities compete for representations of the Indonesian nation and its social realities. Contemporary imagined community in Indonesia is pluralistic, diffuse, and not easily tied to place. It is formed around a range of social and cultural concerns, not simply political ones (Kitley 2002:211).

3   Abu-Lughod 1993; Croteau and Hoynes 1997; Dasgupta 2007; Harbord 2002; Hong 1998; Lull 1991; Shohat and Stam 1994, 2003.
4   Ien Ang (1991, 1992), among others, has argued that the rating institutions do not really measure the 'audience', but rather create and manage an image of it to bind advertisers. For more on the corporate practice of 'audience measurement' and its pitfalls, see Ang 1991, 1992.

Benedict Anderson's idea (1983) of imagined communities, a phrase he coined to draw attention to the imagined rather than experienced character of communities, is one of the key concepts in my research. Anderson showed how new media technologies contributed to the formation of nations by enabling imaginations of the nation as a sovereign and territorially bounded community. He argued that with the rise of print media, the wide circulation of newspapers and novels written in national languages induced readers to imagine themselves as being part of a vast community, one not based merely on face-to-face encounters between its members. Whilst the imagination of communities can be connected to consumption of media technologies and discourses, Anderson's notion of imagined communities has been criticized. As Philip Kitley (2002:211) has argued, the totalizing, unifying ideas suggested by Anderson were an intrinsic part of post-colonial national communities, and are no longer applicable to contemporary imagined communities. These are far more pluralistic and diffuse, and often transcend the boundaries of the nation. Several others have also criticized Anderson's theory. Criticisms leveled at Anderson include that he fortuitously strengthens a Eurocentric argumentation while de-legitimizing Third World nationalisms as Western constructs (Desai 2009). Some condemn his shortfall in addressing wider connections and a central dynamic between particular aspects of nationalism, in particular with regard to the spread of capitalism (Davidson 2007) and globalization (Hamilton 2006). Others point to the 'missing analysis' of why some national myths are successful while others are not (Haesly 2005). For a critical assessment of various individual points of critique on Anderson's theory, see Özkırımlı (2000).

In the last decade scholars have questioned the capacity of the nation-state in the post-colonial world to bind its citizens in the same way as this was achieved in Western history.[5] In film and cultural studies, the crisis of the nation-state, which is central to current debates as well as to actual power struggles, led to a shift in focus towards transnational formations. Extensive circulation of transnational mass media and a growing access to these media through new technologies have led to an expansion of constructions of new shared worlds, and in imaginations of distinct communities of sentiments, which are no longer confined by national borders.[6] In this context, the nation-state and national identity are no longer recognized as the privileged

---

5   Meyer 2000. See also Bayart 1993; Chabal 1996; Mbembe 1992; Taussig 1997; Van der Veer 1994; Werbner 1996.
6   Appadurai 1996; Garnham 1993; Gillwald 1993; Shohat 2003; Sen 2003.

space and form for the imagination of communities.[7] Nevertheless, notwithstanding a globalizing world, the state is still important in shaping political realities (Baumann 1996; Duara 1999, 2008; Shami 1999). Moreover, the state can be important in defining the shape of cinema. As Wimal Dissanayake has argued, cinema in Asian countries was closely allied to the nation-state for the simple reasons of economics and exercise of content control. In Asian cinemas, assistance from and co-ordination by the government was imperative as film corporations, script boards, training institutes, and censorship panels in Asia were mostly supported or supervised by the state (Dissanayake 1994:xiv). Krishna Sen (2003:147) emphasized this point in relation to Indonesian cinema:

> At a time when the border zones of the Indonesian nation are being violently tested by ethnic, religious and regional differences, when in fact it has contracted in relinquishing the world's newest nation, East Timor, it may be foolhardy to speak at all of something called Indonesian cinema. But the institutional organization of films produced and consumed in Indonesia is such that it is impossible to discuss these except as 'national cinema'.

Now the tide has turned and in the past decade, it would be hard to speak of a 'national cinema' – not only in the context of Indonesia, but possibly also with reference to other Southeast Asian countries that have experienced similar developments in their access to new media technologies. In Indonesia, particularly after the stepping down of President Soeharto, several changes have occurred in the constitution of power relations and the discourses which define Indonesian cinema. The resignation of Soeharto on 21 May 1998 marked the commencement of the era of Reformation (*Reformasi*). The slogan Reformasi – reform of Indonesian politics, economy, and legislation – reigned supreme.

Before Soeharto decided on the wisdom of retirement, Reformasi in politics had meant the demand for a new president, free general elections, the freedom to found political parties, and the annulment of five political acts from 1985 which lay at the core of the deficiencies in the formal political system. Economically, those in favour of Reformasi demanded an end to crony-capitalism, monopolies and cartels,

---

7   See Birgit Meyer's research project 'Modern mass media, religion and the imagination of communities; Different postcolonial trajectories in West Africa, Brazil, and India' (2000-2006). This project investigated the shift from the nation-state as the privileged space for the imagination of identity to the genesis of new publics in a pluralist public sphere in which the role and place of the state is called into question, and in which religion often plays a crucial role.

and the dominant role of the big conglomerates. Supporters of Reformasi also called for a strong legislative power, a bureaucracy and judicial power which were not at the beck and call of the ruling elite, and an end to corruption, collusion, and nepotism (*korupsi, kolusi* and *nepotisme*, KKN) (Van Dijk 2001:114-5). After the fall of Soeharto, the bid to introduce reform affected every possible field and led to a negotiating and redefining of all kinds of issues.[8]

Besides being stirred by the euphoric atmosphere of Reform, which induced a new-found freedom of expression as opposed to the hegemonic narratives of the nation-state, an important part of the changes in Indonesian film mediation practices and discourses can be traced to the circulation of new audio-visual media. Many new activities and developments in Southeast Asian cinemas were made possible by the growing and widespread availability of such new technologies for film production and exhibition as digital video cameras, computer editing programmes, and digital video projectors. Digital video, for instance, presented 'the ability to construct and transform meanings and practices' (Ukadike 2003:128), which challenged the dominant cinematic practices and film culture. Both Indonesian film-maker Garin Nugroho and film-maker and academic Gotot Prakosa asserted that because of the new video technologies virtually everyone in Indonesia was given access to audio-visual media. In their opinion, the advance of new technologies has definitely shaped democratization processes in film production and creativity in Indonesian cinema.[9] It must be noted, however, that while the availability and relatively low costs of new media technologies indeed have broadened the access and possibilities to produce films, a majority of Indonesians still cannot afford to purchase a computer and broadband internet or to buy a video camera. The 'democratization' process is mainly within the reach of the New Rich and middle classes. Internet and movie cameras are not restricted to the richest of middle classes. Many members of the middle class own computers, laptops, and smartphones. Moreover, if you cannot afford a computer there are lots of warnet (*warung internet*, internet stalls) where you can rent a computer for around Rp 4,000 per hour to surf the internet. However, the further away one goes from the capital and city centres, the slower the connection will be. The same goes for video cameras. A rich

---

8 For more details about Reformasi, see for example Van Dijk 2001; Emmerson 1999; Schulte Nordholt and Abdullah 2002; O'Rourke 2002; Samuel and Schulte Nordholt 2004; Schulte Nordholt and Hoogenboom 2006.
9 'Eforia film generasi digital', *Kompas*, 4-11-2001; Gotot Prakosa 2005:10-1. For another reference to democratic grassroots media, see Peter Manuel 1993.

youth in the metropolitan Jakarta will perhaps easily buy the newest camera and gadgets. A middle-class adolescent in, for example, the Central Javanese city of Cilacap will probably rent a seventh-hand one consisting of spare parts from a variety of other cameras. New media technologies and its developments affect different people in different regions and different classes in different ways.

Both political change and the 'democratization' of Indonesian cinema in the wake of new film technologies have given rise to discourses which have opposed the concept of national cinema '[to privilege] ideas of coherence and unity and stable cultural meanings associated with the uniqueness of a given nation' (Dissanayake 1994:xiii). Instead, post-Soeharto new and oppositional film mediation practices and discourses have supported the premise that in today's transnational world, national identities are transformed or substituted by identities which transcend the purely national and are based on social, political, or religious sentiments. The post-1998 generation of film-makers is very aware of developments in cinemas worldwide and is inspired by foreign film movements. For example, in 1999 thirteen film-makers formulated an Indonesian version of the Danish Dogma '95 Manifesto, which they dubbed I-Sinema (see Chapter 2). They turn to foreign films to reproduce particular styles; *Kuldesak* and Quentin Tarantino's *Pulp fiction* (see Chapter 2) or replicate parts of scripts, just as *Virgin* did with David McNally's *Coyote ugly* (see Chapter 6). Moreover, they foster contacts and interaction with film-makers all over the world through online media networks such as YouTube and live events as international film festivals. However, at the same time post-Soeharto practices and discourses have underscored that contemporary processes of imagining communities are increasingly accentuating local identities. Commenting on cultural production and transnational imaginary, Rob Wilson and Wimal Dissanayake (1996:1) have called attention to the interplay between globalism and localism:

> Postmodern cultural workers, on the verge of becoming 'symbolic engineers' and critical self-consciousness of global capital, stand at the cross-roads of an altered and more fractal terrain everywhere we guess at century's end: a new world space of cultural production and national representation is simultaneously becoming more *globalized* (unified around dynamics of capitalogic moving across borders) and more *localized* (fragmented into contestory enclaves of difference, coalition and resistance) in everyday texture and composition.[10]

10 For a more elaborate discussion of these issues, see Wilson and Dissanayake 1996.

Elsewhere Dissanayake has proposed dealing with the dialectic of the local and the global through an examination of the production of newer localities, that is, to focus on the production of the local and its constantly changing contours in response to the demands of the global. As he phrased it (Dissanayake 2003:216-7): 'How the symbolic forms and modalities of association of Western capitalism are transformed, localized, and legitimized in most countries in relation to their historical narratives and changing lifeworlds is at the heart of the discourse of localism.' In discourses of localism, the simultaneous process of transnationalization and deterritorialization of consciousness does not primarily have to lead to new, shared cultural imaginaries of transnational identities alone; rather, it could also engender the formation of hybridized local ones. Furthermore, in the view of Arif Dirlik (1996:35), the re-emergence of 'the local' can be seen as a site of resistance and struggle for liberation:

> It is the struggle for historical and political presence of groups suppressed or marginalized by modernization [...] that has dynamized this postmodern consciousness and has produced the contemporary notion of the local, which must be distinguished from 'traditional' localism if only because such struggles are themselves informed by the modernity that they reject. This is the local that has been worked over by modernity. It finds expression presently in the so-called 'politics of difference' that presupposes local differences (literally and metaphorically, with reference to social groups) both as a point of departure and as a goal of liberation.

Although Dirlik and Wilson and Dissanayake do not explicitly differentiate between the local and the national, Krishna Sen, with reference to Dirlik, has drawn attention to the difference between the two. She has argued that a few years before the fall of Soeharto, local culture in Indonesia was mobilized in the cultural discourse to oppose the dominant rhetoric of national culture and nationhood propounded by the New Order state. In Indonesia, notions of localism as a figurative site of resistance were often not defined in opposition to transnational culture or globalism, but rather in terms of the political constellations within the nation (Sen 2003:147, 155-6). It is along these lines that I address Anderson's concept of imagined communities.

Treating film as part of a complex semiotic field which foregrounds formations of social identities and realities, I focus my account on three main themes. Firstly, I examine discourses on particular audio-visual media formats and genres that lend themselves to the imagination of identity and community formation. Secondly, I query the processes of empowerment which are entailed by the consumption of these media formats and genres. Thirdly, I explore the impact the circulation of particular genres and formats has on public debates.[11] Questions that will be addressed in this context include: How is one to characterize the Indonesian film industry before, during, and after the fall of Soeharto? How has the spirit of Reformasi altered Indonesian film mediation practices, and what was the significance of new technologies that were available around the same time? What representations of history were screened during the New Order, and to what extent did notions of 'truth' and 'reality' determine the critical discourses surrounding Indonesian media? What was the role of Islam in film mediation practices before, during, and after the Reform era? To what extent did secular and religious discourses clash in defining the moral bounds of mainstream film and television productions? In what way did such discourses shape social realities?

This book is divided into three parts, each consisting of two chapters. The first chapters in the first two parts outline New Order film discourses and practices. The chapters discussing the New Order era heavily rely on Krishna Sen's research (1994) on Indonesian cinema. In each case the chapters are followed by a second chapter in which the developments, continuities, and changes in these discourses and practices in post-Soeharto Indonesia are set out and discussed. In the third part, New Order and post-New Order developments are incorporated in both chapters.

The first part contains an analysis of film mediation practices; the second is about film discourse practices, while the third studies film narrative practices. Investigating film mediation practices, I dissect specific practices of film production, distribution, exhibition, and consumption and describe the discourses surrounding these practices. These discourses disclose a series of representations of divergent imagined communities. When I turn to film discourse practices, I concentrate on the use of narrative tropes, rhetorical strategies, and modes of film distribution and exhibition during the New Order and Reform era which are connected to historiography. The choice to focus on historiography is founded

---

11 My analysis of these three elements is inspired by Birgit Meyer's approach taken in her PIONIER research programme 'Modern mass media, religion and the imagination of communities', as specified in her research proposal to the Netherlands Organization for Scientific Research (NWO); see Meyer 2000.

on the general view that history is the essential basis of the narrative of nation-states. History provides the foundation for a nation's unity and the state's legitimacy to rule (Anderson 1983; Hobsbawm and Ranger 1983). Another reason for this focus on historiography is that film discourse practices under Soeharto rule which related to history were immersed in New Order politics and policies of national myth-making and the production of ideology. In my exploration of film narrative practices, I study the composition of film narratives in the context of power relations. I examine to what extent the form and content of narratives depend on censorship, commerce, and ideological or political motives. The central point here is the impact these power relations have on debates and representations of realities and the moral bounds of the Indonesian nation and society.

In the first part I contrast New Order mainstream film mediation practices to post- Soeharto alternative, underground mediation practices. I show that in discourses and film policies, different film formats and festivals represent imaginations of different audiences and communities. In Chapter 1, I discuss policies whereby the 16 mm format represents national lower-class audiences, while 35 mm film stands for transnational middle-class audiences. I also analyse New Order film festivals and give details of particular representations of audiences and the nation, conventions and motives for film showings, as well as discourses about participation in these festivals. In Chapter 2, I examine the changes and continuities in post-Soeharto film mediation practices. I discuss new mediation practices and the rise of new film genres and festivals. I demonstrate that in the post-Soeharto-era discourses, mainstream 35 mm film is connected to New Order domination and transnational identities. Conversely, alternative independent film, which uses the digital video format, is seen as an oppositional cinema, representing local identities. I furthermore discuss the emergence of film festivals during Reformasi, examining how these are connected to supranational identities. I end the second chapter with an analysis of the circulation of pirated films as an oppositional media practice.

In the second part, I elaborate on the conception and use of particular discourse practices, focusing on what I call specific 'modes of engagement' in relation to discourses about history, historiography, and events in society. Modes of engagement consist of dominant representations or ways to address certain topics, which are part of the central discourses of a society. Modes of engagement reach beyond particular modes and styles of film production (Nichols 1991:22-3) in that they encompass the ways in which particular topics in society are represented across all kinds of media. In film, modes of engagement materialize in the use of particular generic features, narrative styles, and conventions. I also identify through what kinds of discourse practices particular film genres reach Indonesian audiences, and investigate the practice of 'framing' film texts. Chapter 3 is devoted to the way in which the New Order state seized upon particular film genres in order to promote its own model of national history and identity, legitimizing its mandate to rule the nation. I give an account of discourses on the production of history, development, and propaganda films and on the particular modes of engagement which these films tap into in relation to historiography. Taking it further, I examine the practice of screening these films as part of a special framework: a New Order memorial day. In Chapter 4, I reveal in what way dominant modes of engagement and generic conventions in film changed or continued to exist after the stepping down of President Soeharto. I discuss the production of counter-histories and the emergence of alternative genres and new practices of framing during the era of Reform. One of the focal points in this chapter is the rise of Islam in the post-Soeharto mediascape. I address the founding of the new genre of Islamic film, and the interconnected formation of the Islamic film community, which sees itself as an oppositional, post-colonial cinema, based on Islamic ideology. Once again I tackle the practice of framing, and the growth of images of Islam in mainstream post-Soeharto audio-visual media, as part of the commercialization of the Islamic fasting month of Ramadan.

The last part of this book discusses narrative practices. I examine the circulation of popular genres and the composition of stories within film genres, such as the use of particular generic formulas, in connection with power relations. This leads me to address the margins of possible narratives and the basis of socio-political power relations. I sift through debates on particular narrative practices, seeing how far they can go morally before they are obstructed by the boundaries set by the state and religious pressure groups. In this context, I address the tussling of realities constructed on competing worldviews and truth claims, and the role of real and imagined Islamic figures of authority in delineating film narrative practices. Chapter 5 considers the connection between film and television formats of horror, generic formulas, and imagined audiences and communities. On another level, the chapter seeks to explore how discourses about the formulas of horror films can be related to debates on what constitutes the modern Indonesian nation. In Chapter 6, I delve deeper into discourses on representations of modern Indonesian realities. I discuss recent debates about the moral bounds of narrative practices in the post-Soeharto Indonesian mediascape, demonstrating in what ways commerce and censorship, both from the state and the street, define the film texts produced. Subsequently I examine debates about which narrative practices are perceived to be fitting modes of representation of Indonesian society. These debates are related to divergent worldviews derived from religious and secular realities. They are part and parcel of the struggle about who and what shapes and decides on national popular discourse and what realities are included in modern Indonesian society.

It must be noted that quite a few developments in the practices and discourses of Indonesian audio-visual media are not unique. The content, style, and formulas of narratives to be found in Indonesian horror and history films, documentaries, infotainment, quiz shows, or reality TV programmes appear worldwide. All over the world gossip shows feature and discuss celebrities. Films in all locations are about fictional or real heroes. Preachers in the United States, Brazil, and Egypt have their own programmes and talk shows. Horror films thrive in Hollywood, Africa, and Asia. Common people are the focus of various national and transnational reality TV programmes and quiz shows. Everywhere victims are seen in fiction films, documentaries, and daily news programmes. Still, most images of, and pre-occupations in, Indonesian audio-visual media can be related to socio-political developments in that country in particular and the Southeast Asian region in general. For the most part, the cinemas of the various countries in the Southeast Asian region share similar social and political concerns.

In his keynote speech at the Sixth Southeast Asian Cinemas Conference in Vietnam in July 2010, film scholar Adam Knee identified comparable issues and developments in cinemas throughout the region. He pointed out several parallel phenomena in Southeast Asian cinemas that are induced by interconnections in geographical, historical, political, economic, and social terms. Knee highlighted the impact of the 1997 Southeast Asian economic crisis on film-making in the region, as well as the significance of changing moving-image technologies in shifting modes of production, distribution, consumption, and aesthetics. Knee (2010:4) also emphasized the active networks of Southeast Asian media-makers in an increasingly globalized media industry. Film-makers communicate and meet at various Southeast Asian film-specific fora and festivals within the region, such as Cinemanila in the Phillipines, Jiffest in Jakarta, and the Singapore or Bangkok international film festivals. In addition, they meet internationally and participate in, for example, the Southeast Asian film programme of the International Film Festival Rotterdam in the Netherlands, or the Berlinale in Germany. Southeast Asian film-makers moreover engage in co-productions and make use of the same industrial services in the region. Thailand in particular functions as the regional hub for post-production and the processing of print, but Singapore is now developing a production services industry with government monies able to compete directly with Thailand's facilities (Knee 2010:4). In addition to sharing experiences in economy, technology, and connection to regional and transnational networks and media industries, the different cinemas across the region denote similar paradigms in socio-political terms. Among these are the debate on mainstream versus independent film, dealings with censorship, the impact of religious influences in film and film production, issues of ethnicity, problems of gender and sexuality, rural versus urban concerns, as well as the impact on society of political and traumatic events.

To briefly illustrate some corresponding themes: The Indonesian, Malaysian, and Philippine independent film scene mostly operate in comparable ways and often produce films that are similar in content and style. Particularly issues of race, ethnicity, gender, and sexuality are addressed in these films in such a critical way as could never be done in mainstream productions. Censorship is a central concern of all film-makers across Southeast Asia. In Vietnam and Singapore state censorship is particularly strong, but also in the other countries it is a force for film-makers to reckon with. Religion is or has become a popular theme in Southeast Asian films: Catholicism resounds in many Phillipino films, Islamic film is increasingly on the rise in Indonesia, and Buddhist monks, like Islamic preachers in Indonesia and Catholic priests in the Philippines, are often a main character in Thai horror movies. In fact, horror films – which, as Knee (2010:8) emphasizes, have a strong regional perspective and a substantial overlap from country to country with their cast of supernatural characters – as well as action, comedy, and melodrama genres thrive in all countries in the region. At times the horror films, but also other genres like historical dramas, refer to shared political or traumatic events. According to Knee (2010:8), historical dramas have a strong regional import in the issue of how to represent the problematic or traumatic local pasts which, again, links various Southeast Asian films and in fact transcends the genre. A recurring traumatic theme across the region and across genres is the red scare of the 1960s and its implications for the present. To give a few examples of films addressing this theme: from Indonesia *The poet* (*Puisi tak terkuburkan*, Garin Nugroho, 2000) and *Lentera merah* (Red lantern, Hanung Bramantyo, 2006); from the Philippines *Snatch* (*Dukot* (*Desaparecidos*)), Joel Lamangan, 2009); from Malaysia *The last communist* (*Lelaki komunis terakhir*), Amir Muhammad, 2006); from Thailand: *Lung Boonmee raluek chat* (*Uncle Boonmee who can recall his past lives*, Apichatpong Weerasethakul, 2010). Other shared, regionally inflected and prevalent themes are the local experience of, and response to, modernity and globalization, addressing tensions between urban and rural lifestyles as well as tensions between old values and new and/or foreign ones (Knee 2010:9). Another point of reference in cinemas across the region is the role in film industries of Chinese entrepreneurs, as well as the representation of ethnic Chinese characters and communities in films produced in the different Southeast Asian countries (Knee 2010:10-1). Lastly, Southeast Asian cinemas all encounter the same problem in film archiving and preservation. They share a climate that hastens the deterioration of films; moreover, government funding is lacking in all countries.[12]

A final note on methodology. In February 2001 I joined the Indonesian Mediations Project (IMP), part of the larger 'Indonesia in Transition' research project, to study post-Soeharto Indonesian audio-visual media. Back then my only references were books written around ten years earlier by Salim Said (1991), Karl Heider (1991), and Krishna Sen (1994). These studies were all set in the context of Soeharto's New Order. In the meantime, in 1999, I had come across new phenomena in the world of film. One of the most conspicuous new developments was the energetic promotion of *film independen*. Only a few months after the resignation of President Soeharto, groups of young people in Jakarta, Bandung, and Yogyakarta began to bolster the production of independent films and to organize independent screenings and festivals. At one of these screenings, held at the Japan Foundation in Jakarta in 1999, I was amazed by the passionate discussion about and content and style of the short film *Revolusi harapan* (Revolution of hope, Nanang Istiabudi, 1997). It was very critical of the New Order and had a stylized and rather surreal tone. Such a film could never have been openly shown during the New Order. In order to grasp the changing nature of the post-Soeharto film scene, I set out to conduct my first round of fieldwork research in August 2001. I deliberately did not centre my research on any theoretical premises. Ella Shohat

---

12 Knee 2010:8. For in-depth information on past and future Southeast Asian Cinema Conferences and different Southeast Asian Cinemas, see http://seaconference.wordpress.com (accessed 19-12-2011).

| *Introduction*

and Robert Stam's critique (2004) on the excessive inclination of film studies to take up a Eurocentric angle greatly influenced my approach. I was particularly aware of my background – a Dutch (which means both from Europe and former colonizer) academic analysing Indonesian cinema, and was open to all aspects of the world of audio-visual media in Indonesia.

Because all participants of the Indonesia in Transition research project were to meet in August 2001 in Yogyakarta for a first shared conference, I began my research there. Earlier that year, in May, I had met some students from the Yogyakarta Muhamadiyah University film club, who had told me they were organizing a national independent-film festival in June. In August I again met the students, who told me that in a few days' time there would be an independent-film festival at the Muhammadiyah University in Malang, East Java. After the festival, they would organize a meeting in Batu, a resort in the mountains near Malang, which would be attended by a variety of independent film communities from all over Indonesia. I joined the festival and stayed with the participants during the overnight meeting and discussion in Batu. It much helped me to accumulate data and acquire contacts from independent-film communities, film-makers, and festival organizers from all over the country – though the large majority came from Java.

Two weeks later, when I was still in Yogyakarta, going around town to meet all kinds of film-makers and film communities and attending their discussions and watching their films, the Twin Towers in New York were hit. The television in my cheap hotel room could only receive local news programmes, and in the first days after the attack I saw little else than the almost stylized images of the planes crashing into the towers; hardly any discussions were broadcast about the assault. It was only a few days later, when I visited a five-star hotel to go to the gym there, that I saw the devastating images broadcast by transnational news networks CNN and BBC World. Seeing the destruction in such detail gave an entirely different perception of the event than the mere clean-cut crash of the planes. I was very aware that having access to different images formed the way in which I, and with me other people from different social classes and plausibly different nations too, could or would interpret the events. I was not as much emotionally affected by the attack as such when I only had access to national Indonesian media networks. Rather, in the days before my encounter with the transnational broadcasts I had shared a notion of awe and amazement at the event, which nearly all film-makers and members of independent-film communities had expressed in their comments. Some had even made cold remarks that the United States had it coming to them because of their government's arrogance, their conceited hegemony of the world, and their hypocritical and harmful intrusion in world politics aiding or empowering corrupt regimes. It was around the same time that discussions began to flare up about CIA involvement in the Indonesian coup of 1965, and its compliant support of the violent aftermath in which hundreds of thousands of 'communists' were killed and imprisoned. The flux of the categories victim-perpetrator or hero-villain; the existence of different levels of access to and different images in the media; the impact of the socio-political background in which the images and their framing take place – these were all at the heart of why I decided to analyse contemporary Indonesian film with a focus on discourses and media discourse analysis. To me it was important to explore the setting and make-up of Indonesian audio-visual media and to render as much as possible the way in which Indonesians who are involved in the world of film themselves reflect on contemporary developments in their mediascape and society.

During the first half year of fieldwork research in 2001-2002, and again in later stages between 2002 and 2005, the methodological approach of my research encompassed extensive attendance of film screenings, film festivals, and discussions about Indonesian cinema. I watched numerous films in bigger and smaller cities in Java and Sumatra, and at bigger and smaller events. I attended the annual glamorous Jiffests, the energetic independent festivals by Konfiden, and abundant Q festivals in Jakarta, and visited different film screenings and discussions in Bandung, Purwokerto, Semarang, and Yogyakarta. I trailed the 'roadshows' of some of Aria Kusumadewa's films via alternative networks across Java, followed the setting-up and wrapping-up of a rainy and muddy mobile cinema screening at a circumcision ceremony in Bojong Gedhe, a remote village near Bogor, and came across an Islamic film festival in Jayapura, Papua. I moreover observed the shooting of films on the sets of independent and commercial film and television productions. I followed the production of the Yogyakarta independent film *Sangat laki-laki* (Very manly, Fajar Nugroho, 2004), with their self-made lamps, props, and other equipment, and the shooting of the commercial television soap *Three in one* (Nanang Istiabudi, 2003). Furthermore, I searched in detail through film archives and collected early and contemporary articles on film in newspapers and magazines. I found and photocopied hundreds of clippings of newspaper articles in the PPHUI film archive in Jakarta concerning a wide range of subjects such as, for example, film reviews, articles on film laws, clashes in film organizations, problems with pirated films, censorship, and pornography. In addition, I interviewed both young and upcoming as well as established film-makers, producers, members of film communities, festival organizers, journalists, actors and actresses, and artists. Over the years I became friends with students who wanted to become independent film-makers or festival organizers 'from scratch', as well as connecting with more established film people. Some of them, who were not successful at the time, have now become renowned producers, directors, or editors. Others have quit film-making, particularly when they had to find a more substantial and certain source of living after graduation or marriage. Some remained loyal to their 'independency', others now produce soaps and other programmes for commercial television.

The voices and premises that are raised in this book are to a large extent based on those that circulated in discussions at the film screenings and festivals, on opinions in newspapers and magazines, and on statements in personal interviews and communication by film people, artists, intellectuals, and others talking about film. To name a few examples: as mentioned earlier, Garin Nugroho and Gotot Prakosa speak of a 'democratization' of Indonesian cinema with the rise of new audio-visual media. In Chapter 1 and Chapter 6, film-makers and journalists refer to '*festival arisan*' to describe state supported film festivals. In Chapter 4, members of *film Islami* groups refer to 'Hollywood hegemony' and Third Cinema theories, and post-Soeharto documentary film-makers claim to raise 'the voice of the voiceless' in their productions. Others, like Lulu Ratna in Chapter 2 and Aulia Muhammad in Chapter 4, respectively promote their own ideas on festivals below the radar' and the 'voidness of outward appearances of Islam' in Ramadan programmes. In Chapter 3, I applied Umar Kayam's assertion about the New Order inclination to perform 'art in the framework of' particular events. In addition to rendering Indonesian theories and points of view, I applied some theories from history and media studies. For example, in Chapter 2 I refer to the way in which Third Cinema theories relate to discourses about the case of *Beth*, and in what way these discourses reflect Indonesian power relations in national and local politics of identity formation. In Chapter 3, I consider theories on documentary film-making (Nichols 1991) and media events (Dayan and Katz 1992). In Chapter 6, I cite Prasenjit Duara (2008), historian of modern nationalism in East Asia, who discerns that nationalism in each nation encompasses different 'nation views' and 'regimes of authenticity'. Furthermore, I customized a few theories to explain the working of particular media formats or genres in Indonesian mediation and narrative practices. In Chapter 2, I draw on Shohat and Stam's theory (2004) of 'media jujitsu' with regard to pirated films. In Chapter 5, I expand on Anderson's concept (1983) of the novel and newspaper as a form of imagining and as a technical means, probing to what extent a film genre can be seen to 're-present' elements of what constitutes the nation.

Apart from exposing or applying Indonesian voices and premises in Indonesian film and media discourses, and raising or modifying existing theories to compare or explain the Indonesian setting, I added two new concepts to media discourse analysis theory to assess the particulars of the Indonesian situation. The first is the notion of *praktek miring* (skewed practices, henceforth: cursive practices). This concept primarily denotes the widespread, unauthorized practices that constitute an important part of the complex of Indonesian film mediation. For example, it can be applied to the unofficial levies that film-makers need to pay to local authorities or *preman* (thugs) to carry out shooting at a location, or to the widespread circulation of pirated films. On a different level the concept of cursive practices also defines the unsolicited complement of conceptual discourses. I deliberately use a literal translation of the Indonesian term *praktek miring* for 'cursive' practices in order to position it against the 'dis-cursive' practices of film policies and media ownership officially endorsed by the state. The illicit practices transcend state power relations, yet at the same they can be part of them, as the distinction between official and unofficial practices or policies is often blurred. For example, police officers who, in return for some payment, turn a blind eye to the sales of pirated films, or politicians who pay groups of people or assailants to boycott the production of a film. But the off-key notes within discourses on how it is and how it should be are also part of the cursive practices. They form the specific yet illegitimate complement to conceptual rules and regulations. The second new concept relevant to media discourse analysis and the Indonesian condition is the notion of 'modes of engagement' mentioned earlier, which encompass the ways in which particular topics in society are typically represented across all kinds of media.

Because I choose primarily to expose the discourses expressed by those involved in Indonesian society and film and build on their premises and opinions, in this book the debate between the power relations of Islam and 'secular' individual universal rights gets ample attention. This is of course not to say that this is the only debate and issue in contemporary Indonesia and its audio-visual media; in fact, there are many more and other competing voices in politics, society, and film. Nonetheless, this heated

| Introduction

debate clearly was at its height during my research. In this book, I aim to show in what way this particular debate harks back to representations of Indonesia in an intermixture of tangible policies – a new pornography law and deliberations on a new film law – and notional claims to the truths and realities of the nation. This intermixture positions the spirit of Reform amidst the lingering ghosts from past New Order ruling, and also dealings with Islam in media and politics.

PART 1

Film mediation practices

1

New Order and surface

In the second week of May 1999, a little van toured around West Java hunting for a location to shoot the film *Provokator* (Provocateur). As it entered Cigosong, a village in the district of Majalengka, the vehicle was attacked by an angry mob. The van was attacked because the title of the film had been written in large letters on the van's windows, and members of the rural community thought that the team consisted of '*provokator*' – a label given to unknown forces which had been stirring up eruptions of violence in the country since the mid-1990s. To save themselves, the production team, led by the film's producer Sonny P. Sasono and its director Mardali Syarief, quickly wiped the word *provokator* off the van's windows. After this rather upsetting experience, Sonny decided to postpone the shooting of his movie until after the general elections of 1999, when, he hoped, emotions would be running less high. He believed that after the elections the shooting of the film in Majalengka would present no difficulties. By means of a judicious payment his party had already secured the 'protection' of the local police force; it had arranged with local authorities that there would be no interference during the shooting of the film, and had obtained the support of one of the regents (*bupati*) of the Cirebon district to help provide facilities for shooting the film.[1] The decision to postpone the production of *Provokator* was the third hindrance the film encountered in its pre-production process; before production stopped completely four months later, it would face even more.

In this chapter I explore different aspects of film mediation practices during the Soeharto era. In each section I discuss a particular example which illustrates the situations and conditions in which the different mediation practices took place. As several discourses involve imaginations which address inequalities on the social and material level, it may be useful to call attention to Michael Pinches'

---

1 'Saat mencari lokasi syuting untuk film Provokator produser & sutradara nyaris diamuk massa', *Pos Kota*, 25-5-1999.

| *Contemporary Indonesian film*

analysis (1999:9) of the rise of affluent middle classes in Asia in the 1990s: 'The positions occupied by Asia's new rich are not simply to be understood in reference to the internal class relations and social organization of the nation-states to which they belong. Their existence is premised on the structures and growth of capitalism, which are global as well as local. Thus, the new rich are also uniquely positioned in a global and international context, in which their societies have long been subjugated and disadvantaged.'[2]

PRODUCTION: THE ATTEMPT TO PRODUCE PROVOKATOR THE NEW ORDER WAY

About a year after the stepping down of President Soeharto, the pre-production of *Provokator* commenced. In April 1999, the new film production house PT Mutiara Industri Perfilman Rakyat (Pearl People's Film Industry) planned to produce two new films. PT Mutiara was owned by Sonny Sasono, who was also head of the new mobile cinema organization Himpunan Film Keliling Indonesia (Hifki, Association of Indonesian Mobile Cinema) and Komite Peduli Perfilman Nasional (KP2N, National Committee of Concern for the National Film Industry). The films were meant to revive the film industry, which had been losing ground from the beginning of the 1990s. One of the films, entitled *Bonex*, was going to be about hooligans on a train, while the other, *Provokator*, was based on the issue of 'provocateurs' who had incited riots on various locations in Indonesia in the past few years.

The story of *Provokator* is about a girl who has an illegitimate son by a man of Chinese descent. After the child is born, he is placed in a foster home. As he grows up it appears that he is a very clever boy. Because of his intelligence he is sent to school abroad, but there he is taught to become a provocateur. No explanation of how this works is given. When the boy returns to Indonesia he is constantly engaged in acts of provocation, and at some point in the film he will even rape his stepmother. It was estimated that the film would be finished in one month and then distributed to middle- and lower-class cinemas by Himpunan Pengusaha Bioskop Indonesia (HPBI, Indonesian Association of Movie Theatre Agents) and Hifki (*Calon bintang* 1999). The production costs of the film were estimated to be around

---

2   For more on the structural and symbolic transformations in Asia that occurred during the emergence of the New Rich, with a focus on their social and cultural identities, see Pinches 1999. For particular case studies of Indonesia, see Heryanto 1999; Antlöv 1999.

Rp 13 billion (US$ 928,571).[3] According to Sonny his production house deliberately set out to make a film about the inciters of chaos and riots in order to give the Indonesian public an insight into what was happening and into aspects behind issues of provocation which were left unsaid. He believed that while it was public knowledge that all riots were deliberately staged, none of the reports in the written or electronic media made clear who the provocateurs actually were. The fictional film *Provokator* would provide a picture of the lives and backgrounds of real-life provocateurs, whose names would be concealed to avoid the protests of family members or NGOs. To ensure the film would be as real as possible, the plan was to insert stock material in the film of riots which occurred between 1997-1998 in Ambon, Sambas, Banyuwangi, Kupang, and Ketapang, and of the 'Semanggi tragedy' in Jakarta in which police and armed forces used excessive violence to combat students.[4]

The first hurdle in the production process of *Provokator* which had to be overcome was to obtain permission from Direktorat Pembinaan Film dan Rekaman Video (Guidance Council of Film and Video) of the Department of Information to register for production. The registration request was almost turned down, on the grounds that the film contained elements of the SARA law (an abbreviation of *suku* (ethnic group), *agama* (religion), *ras* (race), and *antar-golongan* (class) differences; one should refrain from these subjects as insensitive representations of group differences may incite violence). New Order censorship prohibited the mass media to address any of these subjects. With such a controversial theme, there were real fears that the production of the film would result in protests and new riots. After a fortnight, when there had still been no answer from the Department of Information, Sasono guaranteed that the film would not contain anything which could give rise to anxiety.[5] When the Department of Information finally did grant permission to register the film for production, a new complicating factor presented itself: the Department of Information sent the Lembaga Sensor Film (LSF, Film Censor Institute) a memo requesting them to pay special attention to *Provokator* after production.

After the aforementioned third impediment, which postponed the film's production until after the 1999 elections, the next complication the film encountered in the pre-production stage concerned registration of the film crew, actors, and actresses with official film organizations. The production team had decided to use a new

---

3 'Hifki garap film kolosal "Provokator"', *Harian Terbit*, 21-5-1999.
4 'Provokator diangkat ke layar film', *Pos Kota*, 22-4-1999.
5 'Provokator diangkat ke layar film', *Pos Kota*, 22-4-1999.

approach: they would not draw on established actors and actresses to play in the film, but instead give new or aspiring stars, recruited by the newly established Himpunan Artis Film dan Televisi (Hafti, Association of Film and Television Artists), an opportunity. At the film's *selamatan* (ceremonial meal, which in the context of film is commonly held at the beginning and end of production in order to pray for a successful outcome), director Mardali Syarief frankly admitted that the production team had neglected to acquire 'recommendations' of the Persatuan Perusahaan Film Indonesia (PPFI, Indonesian Film Producers' Union), the Ikatan Karyawan Film dan Televisi (KFT, Union of Film and Television Employees), or the Persatuan Artis Film Indonesia (Parfi, Indonesian Film Artists' Union).[6] In the past, film producers had been required to work with members of these organizations, which entailed arranging payments for assistance at several stages of film mediation. Mardali's new approach appeared to have overstepped the mark. About two weeks later, aspiring actors and actresses who had signed on for the film complained that they were asked to pay a levy of Rp 30,000 (US$ 2.14) to the Himpunan Artis Film dan Sinetron Indonesia (Hafsi, Indonesian Film and 'Electronic Cinema' Association) for a membership card, and another Rp 70,000 (US$ 5) for the costs of training. Producer Sonny acknowledged that it was mandatory for all aspiring actors to join Hafsi and obtain a membership card. However, his production house did not know anything about other charges and Sonny assumed that the training costs were part of a deal with the agency managing the artists.[7] The initial plan to start the shooting of *Provokator* on 10 July 1999 was postponed so that the actors and actresses could be registered. Another reason for postponing the shooting was that there were still some problems with determining the location.[8]

Around a month later shooting had still not commenced as there was now a fifth hurdle to be faced. This time the delay was caused by the subject of the film. Because the story touched on several political conflicts which had occurred in Indonesia, it was decided that direct permission from the army was needed if the movie were to be shot. The letter of permission from the headquarters of the Tentara Nasional Indonesia (TNI, National Army of

---

[6] 'Dalam selamatan 'Provokator' dan 'Bonek' artis pemula banyak yang kecewa', *Pos Kota*, 3-7-1999.
[7] 'Karena dipungut Rp 30 ribu untuk kartu HAFSI pemain film Provokator & Bonek mengeluh', *Pos Kota*, 17-7-1999; 'Main film malah bayar', *Harian Terbit*, 24-7-1999.
[8] 'Karena dipungut Rp 30 ribu untuk kartu HAFSI pemain film Provokator & Bonek mengeluh', *Pos Kota*, 17-7-1999.

Indonesia), which the producer was still waiting for on 30 August 1999, was also to allow the use of 1,200 fake firearms, which were barely distinguishable from the real weapons used by the army and police force. The fake firearms were going to be used in a scene in which the police defuses the demonstrations by students in several areas of Jakarta, depicting among other unrests the Trisakti and Semanggi affairs: bloody interventions by police and armed forces against demonstrating students in 1998, resulting in severe casualties and loss of life on the part of the students in both incidents. To make these scenes as realistic as possible, miniature replicas of the Trisakti University in Jakarta, where four students were shot by the army on 12 May 1998, and Semanggi Bridge were built on the terrain of a sugar factory in Majalengka, West Java.[9]

Another month later, on 25 September 1999, there were plans to start the production of *Provokator* in two weeks' time and to screen the film on the private television channel TPI. By this time, it emerged that the theme of *Provokator* had somewhat changed and it would now be packed with social messages. Instead of showing the background of a provocateur, *Provokator* was to portray how the violent behaviour of disaffected masses was destructive to the nation. It was hoped that the film would teach people not to be easily provoked to act destructively, and thereby harm the nation.[10] Three weeks later, however, there was a new obstacle for *Provokator* in its pre-production process: a lack of funding. Even though the United Nations Development Programme had provided Rp 4.4 billion (US$ 314,285) for the production of both of the films PT Mutiara Film wanted to produce, it turned out this was not enough. Whereas the film *Bonex* received extra financial support from the Perusahaan Jawatan Kereta Api (PJKA, State Railway Company), for which it had to change its initial story into one which celebrated the PJKA, *Provokator* was not able to obtain additional funding.[11] This latest problem in the pre-production process could not be overcome, and the attempt to produce *Provokator* stopped there.

Even though the endeavour to get the production of *Provokator* under way began about a year after the stepping down of President Soeharto, it transpired that virtually all New Order rules and practices in film production were still valid. The obstacles strewn in the path of the production team of *Provokator* at different stages of its pre-production process offer an apt illustration of how film produc-

9 'Film Provokator tunggu izin mabes TNI', *Sinar Pagi*, 30-8-1999.
10 'Pesan film Bonek dan Provokator rakyat jangan brutal!', *Sinar Pagi*, 25-9-1999.
11 'Karena kekurangan dana untuk produksi pembuatan film Bonek tertunda', *Pos Kota*, 19-11-1999.

tion under the New Order was carried out. The pre-production process of *Provokator* reveals several essential issues. Firstly, most of the hindrances the production team encountered relate to different aspects of official censorship, mainly pre-censorship, in film production. In her book on Indonesian cinema under the New Order, Krishna Sen (1994) noted that the role of the Badan Sensor Film (BSF, Film Censor Board, after 1992 LSF) was only one part of the New Order censorship pertaining to domestic film. Even before a film reached the censor board, it had first passed several stages of pre-censorship. For example, it was a common procedure under the New Order to refer a scenario on to other departments with responsibility for the issues and subjects addressed in the film. Sen (1994:66) specifies that this worked as a discreet kind of censorship affecting fewer people and causing little open friction between the government department and those involved in the industry.

The requirement that the approval of the Guidance Council of Film and Video of the Department of Information be obtained before the shooting of *Provokator* could start and the examination of the screenplay of the film by the headquarters of TNI are examples of such pre-censorship measures. Another example is the obligation for aspiring actors and actresses to join Hafsi or Hafti, if they wanted to play in a movie. In 1976, six professional film organizations were officially endorsed as the only lawful organizations of particular functional sectors of cinema. Besides the KFT, the union for all those employed in film production (technical, artistic, and unskilled staff of the film industry, excluding actors), these were: the Persatuan Artis Film Indonesia (Parfi, Indonesian Film Artists' Union) for actors; the Persatuan Perusahaan Film Indonesia (PPFI, Indonesian Film Producers' Union) for producers; the Gabungan Perusahaan Bioskop Seluruh Indonesia (GPBSI, All-Indonesian Association of Movie Theatre Companies) for cinema owners; the Gabungan Studio Film Indonesia (Gasfi, Indonesian Association of Film Studios) for the half dozen studio owners; lastly, for those working in subtitling, the Gabungan Subtitling Indonesia (Gasi, Indonesian Association of Subtitlers). Membership of the professional film organizations was compulsory for anyone who wished to work in the film industry, and no one could participate in film production without prior approval of the relevant functional organization (Sen 1994:56). Hafti, newly founded during Reformasi, instantly gained a reputation for applying the same procedures as Parfi during the New Order: aspiring actors and actresses were to make a payment in order to obtain a recommendation.[12]

12 'Main film malah bayar', *Harian Terbit*, 24-7-1999.

Besides these formal bureaucratic hurdles, the outline of the pre-production of *Provokator* gives an indication of the widespread unauthorized practices in film production. I call these, in a literal translation of *praktek miring* (skewed practices), the 'cursive practices' of film mediation. The account of *Provokator* shows such straightforward cursive practices as the payment of unofficial contributions (*pungutan liar* or *pungli*) to parties which were either related to official institutions of film production or were part of unofficial yet institutionalized conventions. In the case of *Provokator*, Sonny hinted at the payment of *pungli* in his comment that he had secured safety from the local police in Majalengka. Another example of *pungli* is the ambiguous mandatory payment of a levy of Rp 70,000, beyond the accountability of the producer, for 'training costs' for participating actors and actresses. More examples of *pungli* and other stratagems in different New Order film mediation practices will follow in the next section of this chapter.

The outline of the production process of *Provokator* also gives an insight into the choices in film themes and into the common practice of revising scripts to satisfy censors or sponsors during a film's pre-production process. In his position as a film producer who was simultaneously head of the new mobile cinema organization Hifki, Sonny wanted to make two commercial films which would be distributed to middle-class and lower-class cinemas.[13] Consequently, these films should cater to the tastes of middle-class and lower-class audiences. In order to attract a large number of viewers from this audience segment, both *Provokator* and *Bonex* were to represent real-life issues of provokers and riots, and also hooligans. Probably to avoid taking any censorship risks, the themes were transformed into stereotypical stories, similar to the stories found in popular films or television soaps which were produced in Indonesia during the New Order. Such themes as the illicit affair, rape, and violence, which were to be addressed in *Provokator*, had been a mainstay of hundreds of films produced in Indonesia since the 1970s.[14] Another aspect of changes made to the film's initial story was the revision of the script

---

13 Hifki was a post-Soeharto organization for mobile cinemas, which competed with Perfiki, the official organization for mobile cinemas established in 1993.
14 See Kristanto 1995, 2005. Another element in the story of the film – the fact that the boy who turns into a bad guy was of Chinese descent – is related not only to customary type-casting in film scripts, but also to a particular stereotypical image of people of Chinese descent existing in Indonesian society. The industrious Chinese population, although small in number, is mainly involved in the money and trading segments of the local economy. By virtue of their success in these areas and because some powerful Chinese businessmen were linked to Soeharto crony capitalism, Chinese Indonesians have unwittingly created a negative image of themselves with the majority of the Indonesian population.

in response to the wishes of either the authorities (censorship) or sponsors (financial backing). After examination by the headquarters of TNI, the story of *Provokator* was altered from being an account of 'who were responsible for issues of provocation preceding the resignation of Soeharto' to a social edification for the people warning 'how violent behaviour of the angry masses damages the nation'. In the case of *Bonex*, the story was altered to please its sponsor, PJKA.[15]

While in many aspects the story of the pre-production process of *Provokator* shows the workings and legacy of the New Order system, conventions, and practices of film production, it also gives a subtle insight into New Order mediation practices in relation to film distribution and exhibition. Both the establishment of the new mobile cinemas organization Hifki as well as Sonny's intention to distribute his films to middle-class and lower-class cinemas can be seen as attempts to tackle profound problems in film distribution and exhibition, the structure of which had been implemented during the New Order. These problems are inextricably linked to New Order business deals and political manoeuvring, which shaped both the organization of film distribution and exhibition, and normative discourses about different film media and formats.[16]

DISTRIBUTION AND EXHIBITION: TRADE AND CHARADE IN CINEMAS AND FILM FORMATS

After the resignation of President Soeharto on 21 May 1998, Indonesia was intensely caught up in the spirit of Reformasi. Reform was either negotiated or forcibly implemented in every possible field. In this setting, the make-up, and at times even the existence, of some of the professional film organizations was called into question. Depending on their records of internal disputes, some organizations were

---

15 'Dengan suntikan dana dari UNDP dan PJKA film Provokator & Bonex digarap', *Pos Kota*, 19-11-1999. For details on the financing and sponsoring of film production during the New Order, see Sen 1994:41, 65. During the Reformasi, filmmakers still respected the position of authorities. For example, in 2001 film director Slamet Rahardjo first paid a 'respectful visit' (*sowan*) to the Governor of East Java and high ranking members of the military and police there. Only after their consent he started with the production of *Marsinah*, a film about the rape and murder in 1993 of a woman labour activist in Sidoarjo, East Java, which allegedly was committed with the participation of the military and police.

16 For newspaper cartoons referring to film production during the New Order, see Disc One 1.1. Here and below, when I refer to Disc One, Two or Three, the reference is to the set of DVDs published with my PhD thesis, which forms the basis of this book. Both thesis and book can be hired from academic libraries around the world, among others the library of KITLV, Leiden, the Netherlands.

reformed by replacing the former top with new leaders. In other cases, organizations were divided into different alliances, mostly consisting of those supporting the old system versus those wanting to reform it. Hifki was an example of such a new division founded during Reform, forged in a crucible of internal disputes and personal interests. Hifki was a secession from the Persatuan Pengusaha Pertunjukan Film Keliling Indonesia (Perfiki, Association of Indonesian Mobile Cinema Screening Companies) to which Sasono had been appointed the Secretary General in 1996. Mobile cinemas, called *layar tancep* (literally 'screens stuck in the ground'), were open-air film screenings which usually operated in villages at the fringes of cities or in remote areas. People hired *layar tancep* to enliven all kinds of festivities, for example wedding parties or circumcision ceremonies. Because mobile cinemas were able to reach remote areas, they were also used to convey public service announcements or make known government political policies. The original mobile cinema organization was founded in 1974 and before 1993, when it was granted official recognition as one of the New Order professional film organizations, it was mostly disregarded by the state.

Despite many years of official disinterest on the part of the government, mobile cinema was an important part of the system of film distribution and exhibition in Indonesia, particularly given the share of film audiences which were reached by this medium. Krishna Sen mentions a sample survey of thirteen provincial capitals in 1971 which showed that 11% of those surveyed had seen films at mobile cinemas. It was estimated that by the late 1970s, mobile cinemas were regularly visiting at least 80% of villages in Indonesia (Sen 1994:72). The mobile cinema organization Perfiki had branches and representatives in sixteen regions, mostly situated in Java. According to Perfiki data, in 1993 there were around 200 to 300 *layar tancep* companies with approximately 500 to 750 film units (car, screen, generator, and projector). Many of the *layar tancep* companies had their own film copies, which were stored in depots. In 1993 the number of films owned by the companies was estimated to be around 40,000. There was a wealth of varying types and genres of domestic, Indian, Mandarin, and Hollywood films to choose from (Marjono 1993; My 1993; Kartika Sari 1993). Nevertheless, with *layar tancep* audiences, domestic films, in particular those with comedy and action as their themes, were most popular. Because of the setting in which *layar tancep* was operated and the taste of its audiences, it was perceived to be a medium most likely to appeal to lower-class and village people.[17]

---

17 'Menpen kukuhkan Perfiki, pengedar film nasional', *Harian Ekonomi Neraca*, 28-9-1993; Rianto 1993; Kartika Sari 1993.

The fact that mobile cinema was seen as lower-class and rural entertainment may be one of the reasons why it had been mostly disregarded by the New Order state. Before 1993, there had been no specific government policy for mobile cinema, nor was it ever included in the National Film Development Programme. In its operations, *layar tancep* dealt mostly with regional authorities, for example to obtain permission to screen films and pay levies and viewer taxes. Inevitably, before Perfiki was acknowledged as an official organization some rules and regulations for mobile cinema screening were enforced. For example, at the first Perfiki congress, organized in 1983, decisions were made about some organizational matters. Most of these arrangements related to market segmentation. One of these was that the GPBSI and, as it was called at that time, the Persatuan Pengusaha Bioskop Keliling (Perbiki, Union of Operators of Mobile Movie Theatres) agreed on an action radius for mobile cinemas. These were only allowed to operate in an area which was situated at a distance of at least 5 km from the location of a movie theatre. It was emphasized that mobile cinemas were only to screen domestic films, a rule which had already been in force since 1974.[18] With one stroke of the pen the market segment of mobile cinema was clearly defined: it was to cater to people in rural areas and viewers of domestic films.[19]

In 1993, the same year in which the production of Indonesian films declined significantly, *layar tancep* was officially acknowledged by the state. It was said that the reason for authorizing Perfiki as its official organization was that the government was aware of its value in facilitating the distribution of Indonesian films and purveying the development messages of the government to remote areas. At the same time, the late recognition of *layar tancep* was closely linked to a new law on film issued in 1992. The State Policy Guidelines of the Majelis Permusyawaratan Rakyat (MPR, People's Consultative Assembly) in particular played a role in the sudden spate of attention paid to mobile cinemas. This law enshrined the aspiration that the position of national film needed to be improved by means of establishing a 'cultural fence'. The MPR formulation of the 1992 Bill No. 8 on Film stated that a solid cultural fence was needed to diminish the danger of contagion by the spread of information technologies caused by globalization. It was planned to establish this cultural fence by building around 500 small cinemas screening exclusively domestic films, and spread these out over different remote areas. The idea was to use *layar tancep* as a starting point to reach 'blank-

---

18   'PERFIKI dan segmentasi pasar film', *Harian Ekonomi Neraca*, 28-3-1994; Sen 1994:72.
19   'Menpen kukuhkan Perfiki, pengedar film nasional', *Harian Ekonomi Neraca*, 28-9-1993.

spot areas' which had no cinemas. Perfiki was to be the facilitator for a chain of semi-permanent movie theatres, which would later be transformed into permanent theatres. The motivation behind this policy was the perception that village people were not ready to be confronted with foreign culture. Through the erection of a cultural fence they were to be shielded from foreign values and conduct, which could be transmitted by, for example, Hollywood films.[20]

The idea to build 500 new cinemas in remote areas was launched at a time when hardly any domestic films were being produced and 12.5% of regional cinemas was forced to close their business.[21] The most important cause of the downfall of the national film industry and the related closure of cinemas was the rise of private television stations which began in the late 1980s. Between 1988 and 1995, five new channels were permitted to broadcast alongside the state television channel TVRI.[22] Because of the ambiguous censorship regulations for film production and the related unstable income, many film producers turned their backs on the production of films for the silver screen, and began producing films and soaps for television. Now Indonesian films could be watched on TV, and people did not need to leave their homes and pay to watch a film. Some producers who still produced films for the cinema tried to attract audiences by making films which were liberally dosed with erotic and violent scenes, which could not possibly feature on television. However, confronted by an overall lack of film stock, many of the regional, middle-class, and, in particular, lower-class theatres, whose audiences favoured domestic films, were not able to survive.

The already weak position of these cinemas was aggravated by the grip on film distribution and exhibition of the Subentra group, which possessed both the distribution rights of Hollywood films in Indonesia and a franchise of top-end movie theatres. Subentra was owned by President Soeharto's foster brother, Sudwikatmono. Through some crafty political manoeuvring, the group had become the sole distribution channel for all imported films throughout Indonesia by the end of the 1980s (Sen 1994:62). Although this monopoly was established by means of crony capitalism, it was admittedly made possible because of the large investments of the Subentra group in a new type of luxurious cinemas, called 'Sineplex' (Cineplex).[23] Commencing in 1986, the Subentra

---

20 For pictures of mobile cinema, see Disc One 1.2.
21 'Perfiki', *Harian Ekonomi Neraca*, 19-5-1999.
22 For more details on the privatization of Indonesian television, see Sen and Hill 2000:111-3.
23 For details concerning the Subentra group creating a monopoly in film distribution, see Sen 1994:58-62.

group began to invest heavily in the renovation of older theatres into new-style Cineplex cinemas, called Cinema 21. By 1989 the franchise (generally known as the 21 Group) owned 10% of the approximately 2,500 screens in Indonesia, and a much larger proportion of the top-quality theatres in major cities (Sen 1994:62). Because of the international standard of the Cinema 21 movie theatres and the market position of the 21 Group, in 1991 Subentra secured the exclusive distribution rights for films imported from the United States to Indonesia. The Motion Picture Association (MPA), which represented such major Hollywood studios as MGM, 20th Century Fox, Warner Brothers, Universal, United Artists, and Disney, appointed three companies which were run under PT Subentra Nusantara as the sole distributors of films produced by major American film studios.[24] Consequently, three different constituents of the film industry – import, distribution, and exhibition – ended up in the hands of one business syndicate. As the 21 Group controlled both the imports and distribution of American films and their exhibition theatres, it prioritized the screening of American films over other film productions at the Cinema 21 theatres.[25] At a time when television definitely prevailed over domestic films in Class-C cinemas, Hollywood ruled in Class-A cinemas, and Class-B cinemas were either turned into Cinema 21 theatres or filed for bankruptcy, the government planned to build 500 new film theatres in remote areas.

Alongside the goal of establishing a cultural fence, the motivation behind this plan to transform the semi-permanent theatres of Perfiki into permanent cinemas, was prompted by another reason. It was a specific step towards applying article 28 of Bill No. 8 1992, which stated that the screening of films could only take place in a building or place designated to show films.[26] The new rule was devised to increase control over the screening of films, in particular *layar tancep*, which had acquired a reputation of causing upheaval during screenings. There were a number of reasons for such accusations. *Layar tancep* screenings were a magnet for all kinds of activities besides watching film, such as trade and small-scale gambling. Often around or after midnight some brawl would erupt over gambling or the film being screened. Besides this, it was an open secret

---

24   Joko Anwar 2002a; Sen 1994:64. For a discussion of the economic and political background of the Subentra monopoly, see Sen 1994:62-5.
25   In 1992 the stronghold of Hollywood films in Indonesian cinemas was reinforced by a trade deal with the US in which the number of American film imports was increased in return for an extension of Indonesian textile exports to the US (Sen 1994:157).
26   'Pertunjukan film hanya dapat dilakukan dalam gedung atau tempat yang dipertunjukkan bagi pertunjukan film.'

that at many mobile-cinema screenings the rules for film screening as set out by the New Order government were simply ignored. For example, at *layar tancep* screenings often uncensored films or individually re-edited films, consisting of an amalgam of attractive scenes from different films, were shown. Moreover, Hollywood and other imported films were on show, as were films which were still playing in regular cinemas.

The latter practice was called the 'fast-track film' (*film pelarian*) process (Firman Syah 1997; Adityo 1997). It was a rule of film distribution under the New Order that *layar tancep* was the last in line to screen films. Films were first distributed to Class-A cinemas of Subentra 21 in major cities, and a few weeks later to its cinemas in smaller cities and regional areas. After the popularity of the films and the quality of the copies had faded, these were then distributed to non-affiliated Class-B cinemas, and later to the lower-class C cinemas. Officially, the films would eventually trickle down to mobile cinemas. This was the theory, but in practice screenings at *layar tancep* frequently showed the newest films. Cinema owners, particularly the Subentra Group, complained about substantial losses because of fast-tracked films. The plan to change mobile cinemas into permanent ones was drawn up with such practices in mind. It was much easier for the government to monitor film screenings in permanent cinemas than to try to control mobile cinemas in the field and force these to abide by its rules for film screening – especially so since officials who were supposed to monitor such illegal practices were simply paid by film-operators to turn a blind eye. By becoming an official organization, Perfiki hoped to acquire government protection against the demand for the payment of many types of unofficial contributions at *layar tancep* screenings. As an official film organization, it expected to be exempt from paying 'cigarette' money to, for example, members of the Department of Information, village heads, members of the police, and other official or unofficial parties who happened to turn up before, during, and after the event. It was a forlorn hope. As soon as Perfiki was given the status of an official film organization, it became part of a world of slogans and empty policies. Those *layar tancep* companies officially acknowledged were not only required to pay various official and semi-official levies to the bureaucracy; Perfiki members were also trapped in a maze of all kinds of new rules and regulations.

Besides the ambitious plan to transform mobile cinemas into a cultural fence of permanent movie theatres, a new policy was set up to regulate the distribution and screening of films by mobile cinemas. In 1983, the segmentation of the market for movie theatres and *layar tancep* was based on a division between cities and rural areas, and between upper-class and lower-class film audiences. In 1993 this division was expanded by linking the system of film distribution and exhibition to film formats. A new policy was launched which announced that mobile cinemas were no longer allowed to screen films of the 35 mm format. All *layar tancep* units were compelled to use the 16 mm film format, and units which used 35 mm equipment were given a period of three years to convert to 16 mm. Moreover, as part of the rhetoric of mobile cinema forming a cultural fence, it was emphasized once more that members of Perfiki were only permitted to screen domestic films. Imported (read: Hollywood) films were linked up with movie theatres, which in practice meant primarily those affiliated to the 21 franchise.[27] The aim of having all units operate the 16 mm film format was essentially to prevent mobile cinemas from screening Hollywood or other imported films, which were generally distributed in the 35 mm format. The restricted allocation of local, 16 mm films to mobile cinemas would particularly benefit Subentra 21's grip on distribution and exhibition of mainly imported films. Partially for this reason, government policies on film distribution and exhibition were alleged to favour the business interests of Soeharto cronies.

The policy of linking formats to either imported or domestic films also exposed state views about identity formation. Between 1993 and 1998, the issues of identity formation and politics of representation surfaced in discourses which linked specific formats to particular spaces of exhibition. In the burgeoning discourses, different film formats began to represent different film genres and/ or places of exhibition. Generally, in normative discourses about the new regulations the formats were linked to certain genres and places of exhibition and particular imaginations of local audiences and communities. Top-end cinemas were associated with modern urban upper-class to middle-class audiences. Mobile cinemas were associated with traditional rural lower-class audiences. The mission to form an Indonesian cinematic cultural fence within whose boundaries only cultural-educational films designed to preserve Indonesian culture would be promoted, threw into sharp relief the

---

27 In an interview, Hidayat Effendi of Perfiki emphasized that the 500 new small cinemas were not to compete with top-end cinemas. Rather, they were meant to become the partners of the top-end cinemas by serving the market segment of lower-class audiences only. Effendi believed that it would be a good idea for Perfiki to copy the arrangement of film distribution and exhibition of the 21 Group as soon as mobile cinemas were turned into permanent ones, with the market for domestic films as its focus. 'Perfiki harus jadi pagar budaya', *Harian Ekonomi Neraca*, 1-2-1993.

division between the two different imagined audiences. Traditional rural lower-class audiences were perceived not to be 'ready' yet to watch and identify themselves with imported films containing depictions of foreign culture. As the 35 mm films consisted mainly of imported film productions from the United States, the format policy reinforced the divide by imagining domestic films as belonging to mobile cinemas and foreign film productions as belonging to 'proper' cinemas. The division between 16 mm and 35 mm film prescribed that audiences of either format had access to a different source of representation and identification.

However, the 1993 New Order format policy and its ideas about preserving Indonesian identities and culture were a far cry from reality, given the advance of new media technologies. The policies and discourses were outdated first and foremost by the advent of parabola antennas. The installation of parabola antennas, which began around 1983 and enabled people to receive overseas programmes, the discourse that lower-class/village people should be protected against the pernicious influences of foreign culture could not be upheld. In many remote areas, in particular those that were faring well economically, parabola antennas were installed, allowing people to receive uncensored foreign programmes, including South-East Asian public broadcasts and broadcasts of international operations such as NBC, STAR, and CNN (Sen and Hill 2000:117). In 1993, when Perfiki was employed by the Centre of Information of TNI to screen domestic, mainly propaganda, films in remote regions and villages in the province of East Timor, the units climbing the mountain tops of the most remote areas discovered that even there people could receive and watch foreign television shows without difficulty (Rianto 1993). The 21 Group also entered into fierce competition with television after the setting up of parabola antennas and by 1996 was forced to shut some of its cinemas.[28]

Another important influence greatly affecting the cinema business and making New Order discourses redundant, was the rise of video cassettes and, later, laser discs. Since the beginning of the 1990s, video rentals and video shops started mushrooming everywhere in Indonesia. At these outlets a wide variety of films was on offer, including films which never reached domestic television or cinemas. Importantly, many banned and uncensored films were also available in these formats. Consequently, the state's endeavour to control the unruly mobile cinema through sweeping policies and discourses on media, film formats, and places of exhibition,

---

28 'Kelompok 21 alami kerugian, televisi dianggap sebagai penyebab', *Pikiran Rakyat*, 29-8-1996.

was hindered by the new video format, which emerged as a new 'uncontrollable' medium, disrupting everything all over again.

EXHIBITION AND CONSUMPTION: FILM FESTIVALS AS FORUMS FOR NATIONAL IMAGINATIONS AND REPRESENTATIONS

In the first and second sections, I highlighted mediation practices in film production and distribution. Here I turn to practices, conventions, and motives for film exhibition under the New Order. I look only at film festivals which were acknowledged by the state. Other alternative sites for film exhibition, are discussed in more detail in Chapter 2. The first formal film festival of the New Order, the Festival Film Indonesia (FFI, Indonesian Film Festival) was organized in 1973. With the Festival Film Asia Pasifik (FFAP, Asia Pacific Film Festival), this was the most important film festival of the regime, bolstering the concerns of the government. In fact, two years before FFI first took place, the film section of the Persatuan Wartawan Indonesia (PWI, Association of Indonesian Journalists) had already started a small-scale festival, handing out awards for best actors and actresses. Between 1973 and 1975, both the Citra (the Indonesian equivalent of the Oscar) of FFI, and the PWI awards were handed out to winning contestants. In 1975, however, the state requested PWI to stop its event. The reason was that some of the awards for the same categories of FFI and PWI were given to different winners. Instead of allowing for different assessments at two different festivals, the government wished to limit the evaluation of films to an official (state) jury. Since then FFI has always included a selection of journalists in its jury (Ardan 2004:27-8). After PWI stopped organizing its event in 1976, there was only one other officially acknowledged film festival during the New Order, which was, however, not allowed to call itself a festival. This festival, which was held for the first time in 1988, selected and handed out awards to both foreign and domestic films which were screened in cinemas in Bandung. Because the government did not permit the event to be called a festival, in 1988 its founders changed the original name Festival Film Bandung to Forum Film Bandung (FFB, Bandung Film Forum).[29]

Until 1980, when the Department of Information took over, FFI was managed entirely by the Yayasan Nasional Festival Film Indo-

---

29 For more details on Forum Film Bandung, see Ardan 2004:156-66.

nesia (YFI, National Foundation of the Indonesian Film Festival). YFI was founded on 30 October 1972 by PPFI, Parfi, KFT, and Gasfi. Later, GPBSI also joined. In 1973, YFI was officially inaugurated by the Minister of Information. The foundation was established in order to stimulate the growth of film, increase the quality of Indonesian film productions, and strengthen the appreciation of Indonesian film, both in Indonesia and abroad (Ardan 2004:79, 99). FFI was organized on an annual basis. Each year new members of the jury were selected by the festival's organizing committee and appointed by the Minister of Information. Until 1986 the festival was organized in turn in one of the provincial capitals and the national capital in co-operation with local governments. As the organization was carried out in different cities across Indonesia, the organizational structure and scale of FFI changed from year to year (Sen 1994:53). In addition, the management of the festival's organizing committee also rotated. Every year an executive of one of the film organizations which constituted YFI was appointed to lead a new organizing committee.

The organization of FFI was big show business. Particularly in the provincial capitals, the celebration of FFI was a huge public event. Despite the fact that the character of FFI was different in every city, some standard elements were part of all festivals. One of these was that famous actors and actresses came over from Jakarta and drove around the cities in open jeeps, acknowledging the acclaim of thousands of people. Every year people also flocked out the evening before the ceremony to attend meet-and-greet sessions with some of the nominated artists.[30] However, regardless of the enormous appeal of FFI in the provinces, in 1988 it was decided to stop the rotation of the festival and confine it to Jakarta. In fact, even before this curtailment occurred FFI had featured in Jakarta more often than in other cities. Above all it was organized in the capital in the years in which the Indonesian elections were taking place. The decision to restrict future festivals to the national capital was partly prompted by the unpleasant reality that almost every year the organization of FFI in provincial capitals resulted in 'issues'. Most of these contretemps consisted of disputes and quarrels within local boards or committees, or between local officials from executive boards, organizing committees, and members of the jury. The different backgrounds and ambitions of the parties concerned with the organization of FFI often clashed, causing a myriad of frictions. Quite apart from circumventing such problems, another reason for organizing the festival only in Jakarta was

30 'FFI; Masa pesta-pesta itu di mana sekarang...', *Kompas*, 5-12-2004; Sen 1994:52.

to stop the competition in the extravagance of the event in which the different provinces vied to outdo each other. In the provinces, the festival was perceived mainly as a display case in which the organizational skills, development, and assets of the different provinces could be exhibited. Over the years, this resulted in a huge explosion in the funding spent on hosting FFI. Even though the event was organized only in Jakarta since the late 1980s, it still reached different parts of Indonesia through the state television channel, TVRI.

The award system of FFI developed over the years. As the festival was organized by a different organizing committee and executive board each year, new rules were introduced almost on a yearly basis. As Sen has suggested, the award system of FFI formed part of a selective process which determined who participated in Indonesian film-making. According to Sen, the festival award represented the values, ideas, and interests of the urban intelligentsia under New Order rule. In most cases the films which were selected for nomination and which won a Citra were the same that had received positive reviews in elite national publications (Sen 1994:54-5). In her description of domestic films, Sen addresses the juries' evaluations of these films, which reinforced certain New Order representations and imaginations of Indonesian society. Sen's remarks about the assessment of films by different FFI juries reveal the juries' support of three principal themes. In order of precedence, these were: films which juxtaposed 'science' against 'rural beliefs', whereby science wins (Sen1994:124); films which focused on the mediating role of the middle class, standing between the high and mighty and the poor – these films were particularly in favour with festival juries during the 1970s and much of the 1980s (Sen 1994:128); narratives about the countering of corruption and the restoration of femininity (Sen 1994:148). In contrast to these themes, FFI juries largely rejected films which tackled unconventional social commentaries.[31]

In a nutshell, the evaluations of the films nominated and given awards at FFI show that these reinforced representations of New Order norms about development (the victory of modern science over traditional beliefs), the valued position of middle classes, and

---

31   Sen 1994:121, 124, 127-8, 148. See, for example, Sen's account of the FFI jury's rejection of the corroboration of Javanese mysticism in the film *Rembulan dan matahari* (The moon and the sun, Slamet Rahardjo, 1979) (Sen 1994:124-8). For an example of the FFI jury's endorsement of mainstream gender constructions, see its evaluation of *Bukan isteri pilihannya* (Not the wife of his choice, Eduart P. Sirait, 1981) (Sen 1994:148). For more on the content of films that won Citra between 1973 and 1992, see Seno Gumira Adjidarma 2000.

mainstream gender constructions. A Citra was not an indication of the popularity of a film with the audiences. On the contrary, most audiences preferred watching popular action films, slapstick comedies, cheap dramas, teen flicks, horror, and other kinds of films that hardly ever entered the FFI competition. Nevertheless, as a symbol of prestige the Citra was an important goal for film professionals, in particular those who wanted to go international. Inevitably films that scooped a Citra were followed by other films constructed on similar formulas (Sen 1994:54). This practice of copying certain formulas only served to strengthen the role of FFI in reinforcing New Order values and ideas about representations and imaginations of Indonesian culture and society.

Although initially FFI was run by YFI, over the years the organization of the festival was increasingly absorbed into the matrix of New Order political considerations. In 1981-1982, official parties connected to the Department of Information were systematically involved in FFI events (Ardan 2004:79-81). The control of the Department of Information over the organization of the festival was gradually solidified under the auspices of Minister of Information Ali Murtopo (1978-1982). In 1978, at the FFI in Ujung Pandang, Murtopo launched the first FFI motto coincident with New Order politics: 'Cinema as a powerful means of communication for the sake of national development.'[32] A year later, in 1979, at the FFI in Palembang, Sumatra, a new slogan was launched: 'We decree that the character of Indonesian film should be cultural-educational.'[33] At the FFI in Surabaya in 1981, Murtopo voiced the new task of FFI as follows: 'Socialize and unite Indonesian cinema in national development.'[34] Gradually, the festival was turned into an event which represented the state's considerations. Under the next Minister of Information, Harmoko (1983-1998), FFI was even more deeply allied to New Order political concerns. At the opening of the festival in Yogyakarta in 1984, the new motto for FFI ran: 'Intensify the role of Indonesian cinema as a medium of communication and information in order to contribute to the success of the fourth *Pelita* [abbreviation of *Pembangunan Lima Tahun*; Five Year Development Programmes of the state].'[35] In the first year following the appointment of Harmoko as Minister of Information, the

---

32 'Perfilman sebagai sarana komunikasi yang ampuh demi pembangunan nasional.'
33 'Kultural edukatif kita jadikan watak film Indonesia.'
34 'Memasyarakatkan dan memanunggalkan perfilman Indonesia dalam pembangunan nasional.'
35 'Meningkatkan peranan film Indonesia sebagai sarana komunikasi dan informasi dalam ikut mensukseskan Pelita IV.'

custom of transmitting FFI's award ceremony as a live broadcast on TVRI was initiated to 'enable the entire nation to participate in that important event'.[36] Sen (1994:53) noted that some people perceived FFI as nothing more than publicity stunts for successive information ministers and provincial governors.

A new executive board responsible for the organization of FFI was installed in 1988, the year that a decision was taken to organize the festival only in Jakarta. With great ceremony this new board was appointed for a period of five years, until 1994; however, as mentioned earlier, from the beginning of the 1990s onwards the production of Indonesian films had strongly declined. As the remaining small number of film productions consisted mostly of popular, erotic, horror, slapstick, or action films, there was a huge lack of films which were considered suitable to enter the FFI competition. Given the lack of 'quality films' in 1992, FFI was shelved temporarily. At first the organization wanted to postpone the festival for a year. This was extended by another year, and then again by another year. Later, the 1991 edition of FFI proved to have been the last one organized under New Order rule. Only in 2004, circa six years after the fall of President Soeharto, was the festival organized again. In 1992, with the run of film-makers to television, the first television-film festival, Festival Sinetron Indonesia (FSI, Indonesian 'Electronic Cinema' Festival), was organized instead. This festival replaced FFI as a New Order forum for domestic film productions. The motivations for the awards presented to films at FSI were not much different to the assessments which were valid during the last years of FFI. Both festivals had the mission to 'instruct the world of Indonesian film' and 'uplift the Indonesian people' by handing out awards to those films which endorsed New Order rhetoric, politics, and ideals. The only key difference between the FFI awards and their FSI counterparts was the consideration that the medium of television reached broader audiences.[37]

Another important film festival held during the New Order era was the transnational film festival FFAP. This pan-Asian festival was organized for the first time in Tokyo between 8 and 20 May 1954. At the time it was called the Southeast Asian Film Festival. In 1957 the word 'Southeast' was removed, and in 1983 the word 'Pacific' was added. FFAP was organized by the Federation of Motion Picture Producers in Asia, the FPA. This federation was founded in

---

36 Ardan 2004:80-1. '[M]emungkinkan peristiwa penting itu dapat diikuti oleh seluruh bangsa.'
37 For more on Indonesian television, see Kitley 2000; Loven 2008; Veven Wardhana 2001a.

Manila on 17-19 November 1953. Its founding fathers were Manual de Leon (the Philippines), Masaichi Nagata (Japan), Run Shaw (Hong Kong), and two Indonesian film- makers, Usmar Ismail and Djamaluddin Malik.[38] By 1994, FPA consisted of fourteen members; besides the Philippines, Japan, Hong Kong, and Indonesia, these were India, Thailand, Vietnam, Malaysia, Singapore, South Korea, Australia, Taiwan, New Zealand, and Kuwait.[39]

Twice Indonesia did not participate in the festival for political reasons. At the first Southeast Asian Film Festival in Tokyo in 1954, Indonesia was not present because it could not produce a film for the event. At the time the Indonesian government had prohibited the Indonesian production company Perfini-Persari to complete a joint production with a Japanese company because of the frosty diplomatic relations between the two countries (Ardan 2004:8). The second time Indonesia did not participate in the festival was in 1968, this time due to the internal political situation. As an after-effect of the alleged coup in 1965 and the ensuing chaotic political situation, no film could be produced to be presented at FFA.[40] Indonesia's request to organize the festival was turned down twice, in 1956 and 1960. It was not honoured because of President Soekarno's contemporaneous political stance, this being his support of communism. If the organization of FFAP had taken place in Indonesia, this would have meant that both South Korea (Indonesia supported North Korea) and Taiwan (Indonesia supported China and refused to acknowledge Taiwan) would have either declined or been unable to participate in the festival. In both instances the festival was organized on more neutral soil in Hong Kong (1956) and Manila (1960) respectively (Ardan 2004:22). The first time Indonesia organized FFAP was from 15 to 19 June 1970.[41] Indonesia hosted FFAP five times in total until the demise of the Soeharto regime. Besides in Jakarta, it was also organized in Yogyakarta and Denpasar.

Under the New Order, FFAP was seen as a prestigious festival, and to a certain extent as a festival representing inter-Asian relations, connections, and diplomatic affairs. Indeed, particularly in the early years of the festival, both the choice which country was to organize the event and the system of handing out awards was strongly linked to political considerations. Awards were regularly

38 'Sejarah festival film Asia Pasifik', *Suara Pembaruan*, 7-10-2001; Ardan 2004:7.
39 'Festival Film Asia Pasifik Ke-39 di Sydney dibuka', *Suara Pembaruan*, 29-8-1994.
40 'Sejarah festival film Asia Pasifik', *Suara Pembaruan*, 7-10-2001.
41 At the time, Ali Sadikin, the governor of Jakarta, linked the festival to the anniversary of the national capital on 22 June. In June 1975, Sadikin sponsored FFAP a second time, again in the framework of the anniversary of Jakarta (Ardan 2004:28).

handed out to films of the host countries, and often every country received at least one award. Hence, in some Indonesian reviews about the festival FFAP was simply written off as a *festival arisan*: a regular social gathering whose members contribute to and take turns at winning a collective sum of money.[42] An *arisan* film festival was seen as a party organized for the sole purpose of establishing and maintaining harmony among its participating members. Another element of FFAP was the very glamorous and sumptuous organization of the event. The host countries always did their utmost to entertain guest officials, artists, and film-makers as lavishly as possible. At most FFAP, shows were organized during which traditional dances of the host country were performed. Excursions and all types of other tourist attractions were also provided to promote the host countries. Sometimes the film screenings and the award ceremony at FFAP seemed to be of less importance than the fringe events.[43]

The prestige of having a film screened at FFAP and, more importantly, the winning of an award was highly valued by the Indonesian government. Apart from the relations, connections, and diplomatic affairs for which FFAP stood, it was also seen as a forum which spread 'ideal' images of Indonesia to the outside world. Reaching audiences beyond the Indonesian nation, the films screened at FFAP were deemed to present images of what constituted Indonesian culture, people, and society. This resulted in the production of *film festival* (festival films), that is, films produced exclusively to compete in film festivals abroad. For example, and particularly because Indonesia was to host FFAP in 1995, the directors Garin Nugroho and N. Riantiarno both received funding from the government to produce *film festival* to represent Indonesia. They made the films *Bulan tertusuk ilalang* (The moon pierced by a blade of grass, internationally distributed with the title: *And the moon dances*, 1994), and *Cemeng 2005 (The last prima donna)* (Black 2005 (The last prima donna), 1995) respectively, but neither of these films received an award.

As FFAP formed a forum for political relations between Asian nations and perhaps even more because it was labelled an *arisan* film festival, many film people in Indonesia shrugged it off as an inferior film festival compared to other international or regional

---

42 'Sineas Indonesia harapkan FFAP '95 momentum kebangkitan film nasional', *Merdeka*, 14-6-1995; 'FFAP, masihkah sebagai festival "arisan"', *Merdeka*, 2-7-1995; 'Festival Film Asia Pasifik ke-46; Ajang bergengsi, minim promosi', *Suara Pembaruan*, 7-10-2001; Susanti 2001.
43 'Anggota delegasi FFAP pun asyik poco-poco', *Warta Kota*, 18-10-2001; 'Ramai2 gaet pemirsa; Televisi bersaing tayangan Ramadhan', *Warta Kota*, 2001.

film festivals. Others, in particular members of official film organizations and New Order departments related to film, rejected such assertions. They came up with different examples to prove that FFAP was not just an *arisan* festival, mentioning several instances where Indonesia did not receive any awards. Apparently these examples were given to suggest that if FFAP was indeed a festival of diplomatic affairs, it would not be likely that Indonesia would have been passed over so often in receiving an award.[44]

In sum, both at domestic and transnational festivals, films which participated were perceived as representations of their nations' cultures, and, in particular at FFAP, seen as representations of the participating states themselves. For this reason, in 1995 the New Order government supported the production of special 'festival films', so as to present 'proper' representations of Indonesia at the FFAP in Jakarta. In contrast, popular Indonesian films featuring action, sex, comedy, or horror neither participated in FFI nor in FFAP. Only films which provided authorized representations of Indonesian culture were submitted to the FFAP jury, and awarded with Citra at the FFI.[45]

---

44 'FFAP, masihkah sebagai festival "arisan"', *Merdeka*, 2-7-1995; 'Festival Film Asia Pasifik ke-46; Ajang bergengsi, minim promosi', *Suara Pembaruan*, 7-10-2001. An informative article covering some elements of both FFAP and FFI is a report by film journalist Rosihan Anwar of the 37th FFAP in Seoul in 1992. Anwar mentions the involvement of political issues at the festival. This covered both the question of whether or not Moscow should be accepted as a member of the festival, and the politically informed choice of Seoul handing out the award for Best Film to Taiwan. Taiwan felt offended by South Korea, as the latter maintained diplomatic relations with Beijing. Furthermore, as the Indonesian film *Cinta dalam sepotong roti* (Love in a slice of bread, 1991) by Garin Nugroho won an award for best new director at FFAP, Anwar recalls the process of how the film was chosen as Best Film during the 1991 edition of FFI. *Cinta dalam sepotong roti* won a Citra only after heated debates among the jury members. Much of the controversy arose from the question of whether the rules of the Department of Information, or the guidelines written down in the ministerial order of the standing committee, should prevail. After this account, Anwar comments on the FFAP film market. He briefly mentions that the festival programme is so packed with visits to tourist sights that the delegates, including those who want to buy and sell films, were hardly able to watch any films. He ends his report with the remark that FFAP was defunct and a festival devoid of any significance (Rosihan Anwar 1999:204-18). Two other informative articles about FFAP are Anwar's reports of 1988 and 1994. The first reveals the large extent to which FFAP functions as a tool for (tourist) promotion of the country hosting the festival (Rosihan Anwar 1999:124-9). The 1994 report exposes transnational politics at the 39th FFAP in Sydney. During the award ceremony the representative to New Zealand raises the issue of the Indonesian occupation of East Timor, much to the dismay of the Indonesian delegation (Rosihan Anwar 1999:232-6).
45 For pictures of the festival jury and awards, see Disc One 1.3

CONCLUSION

The examination of the different stages of film production, distribution, and exhibition in this chapter yielded an outline of different aspects of New Order mediation practices. All the practices involved specific discourses and policies, which had in common that they pertained to New Order national and transnational politics of representation and imagination, as well as strategies designed to produce economic benefit. Besides the three main lines of inquiry – pre-censorship and other hurdles in the production process of films, the political and economic motivation to identify specific audiences and formats with specific film media, and the politics of representation at film festivals – two additional themes ran through this chapter. These were, firstly, the magnitude of *praktek miring*: the semi-official or illegal 'cursive practices' in film mediation, and secondly, the importance of glamour in official film policies and festivals. The substantial influence of cursive practices in Indonesian film mediation practices emerged most clearly in my account of the pre-production of the film *Provokator*, and in the section about *layar tancep*. The production process of *Provokator* revealed how its makers juggled with deep-seated cursive practices and the semi-official rules of New Order film mediation practices. The team could not escape the purchase of the certified recommendations and the need to obtain official status for its actors and actresses, but it was also obliged to secure covenants with 'third' parties, who may otherwise at some stage have obstructed the film's production. This entailed paying semi-official or unofficial (*pungli*) fees in order to get their 'recommendations' or 'protection'. Moreover, to satisfy the semi-official conventions of pre-censorship control, and after 'consultations' with members of the police and military, the producers felt compelled to change the film's storyline.

The new, politically and economically informed film distribution and exhibition policy of mobile cinemas, too, was principally created to try to control the widespread cursive practice of screening fast-track films and non-censored or self-engineered films at *layar tancep* screenings. It was believed that the format policy was the best instrument to control these illicit activities effectively. Another reason underlying the new policy was to respond to the emergence of parabola antennas and new video technologies, which opened the doors to the circulation of video cassettes and laser discs. However, with the steady growth of free access to the new technologies and bogged down in the quagmire of conflicting state policies, the discourse about the need for the protection of Indonesian culture and the rural lower classes against the effects of globalization proved to be nothing but a charade.

This example of window-dressing introduced the second additional theme in this chapter, exposing the importance of woolly rhetoric and artificial facades in New Order film policy and formal mediation practices. The artifice consisted in part in the conflicting state policy of supporting, on the one hand, economic deals to import films and new media technologies, and on the other hand, of upholding the 1992 Film Law, which aimed to protect the masses from foreign influences and culture. Also at the film festivals which were acknowledged by the state, outward appearances reigned supreme. In 1988 the idea of organizing the Indonesian Film Festival in different provinces was discontinued because the event had deteriorated into a competition in extravagance in which the different provinces vied to outdo each other. The Asian Pacific Film Festival was also renowned for its glamour and sumptuousness. From time to time the film screenings and the award ceremony at the festival seemed to be of less importance than the lavish feasts, excursions, and tourist attractions offered to promote the host countries. Perhaps the clearest articulation of the meaning of film festivals during the New Order was expressed in the notion of *festival arisan*: a social get-together in which the focus lay on harmonious relations, glamour, and fame, instead of film.

All in all, the cursive practices and charade of official film policies were important ingredients in the complex of Indonesian film mediation practices. Charade, affectation, and glamour were the chosen vehicles for the ambitious propagation and representation of New Order values, state politics, and the idealized Indonesian nation. The cursive practices were their concrete complement.

2

Reformasi and underground

After May 1998, the bid to introduce reform was felt in every possible field. The spirit of Reformasi instigated a negotiating and redefining of all kinds of issues, and the term reformasi was rather ubiquitous. All types of groups and organizations were inspired to use the word in their names. Nor did it stop there. The popularity of the slogan cast a wider net and spread to advertisements in which everything was transformed into a product of reform: 'reformation apartments' were on sale; special reformation religious journeys to Mecca (*umroh reformasi*) were promoted, and special offers for office space were advertised as a 'Reformation Package' (Van Dijk 2001:208-9). Indonesian cinema was not immune to Reform and various changes inevitably occurred at that time.

In the first chapter I discussed mainstream New Order film mediation practices and discourses which disclosed the politics of representation and imagination of Indonesian communities. This chapter is its antithetical image in that it presents post-Soeharto alternative, underground, or, as Gotot Prakosa (2005:3) has called them in English, 'side-stream' channels of film mediation practices and discourses. This is not to deny that also under the New Order alternative film productions and underground or side-stream modes of distribution and exhibition did exist. In the 1980s, experimental short films shot with 8 mm video or 16 mm film cameras were produced under the banner of 'street act cinema' (*sinema ngamen*), and 'guerilla film' (*film guerilla*). Such films were taken from one district to another and screened on walls, or sometimes bed sheets, which explains one of the nicknames given the cinema movement: 'drying [laundry] cinema' (*sinema jemuran*).[1] Because this type of film existed outside mainstream channels for film production, distribution, and exhibition, however, it barely ever received a mention in Indonesian media.

1 Prakosa 1997:116-8. For more on sinema ngamen and 'side-stream' film, see Prakosa 1997.

After the resignation of Soeharto, side-stream cinema cultures and practices had the chance to gain visibility. The rise of new, alternative film genres and channels of distribution and exhibition transformed discourses on representations and imaginations of Indonesian communities. Many discourses, which were connected to comparable concerns in Third Cinema theories, evolved around themes of domination and resistance in post-Soeharto film mediation practices and society. Third Cinema theories addressed discourses on political and economic domination, and the global distribution of power of neo-colonialist First Worlds over Third Worlds. The theories on Third Cinema will be further explained below. In this chapter, I refer to Third Cinema on two different levels. In the first two sections, I allude to Third Cinema because comparable concerns were part of the post-Soeharto mediascape. In the third section, I broaden the analysis of discourses and use of Third Cinema theories. Here I connect discourses on representations of dominance and resistance to other post-Soeharto alternative channels of film distribution and consumption: side-stream film festivals and pirated Video Compact Discs (VCDs).

REFORMATION IN FILM PRODUCTION: KULDESAK AND FILM INDEPENDEN

The voice of an old man singing a song recalls the time of the struggle for Indonesian Independence; it is a song of pride, hope, and great expectations for the future.[2] His singing is accompanied by an image of the Indonesian flag, the symbol of the nation's pride and glory. Yet, the flag is not blowing bravely and proudly in the wind, but is flapping weakly around the flagpole – a symbol of the confusion and disappointment of so many in an unstable Indonesia three years after President Soeharto had resigned. This shot was the last scene of the short independent, or *indie*, film *Kepada yang terhormat titik 2* (To the esteemed:). The film was produced by Dimas Jayasrana and Bastian, students at the Jenderal Soedirman University in the rural town of Purwokerto, Central Java. It had its premiere there on 18 January 2002. The film shows how the common people of Purwokerto perceived their municipality. It captured urban life, and deliberately added a gritty touch by showing an impression of the lives of street vendors, street children, and farmers. At the end of the film, an old peasant recounts that throughout his life those

---

2 Part of this section was published in *Inside Indonesia* (Van Heeren 2002).

in power never spared a thought for the meagre livelihood of the farmers of Purwokerto.

The production and screening of this film represented new developments in Indonesian cinema which emerged at the beginning of Reformasi. Between 1999 and 2001, in the midst of the euphoric atmosphere of reform and the seemingly limitless freedom of expression, film-making became a very popular activity in Indonesia. The widespread availability of new audio-visual technologies such as digital video cameras and projectors, liberally dosed with the spirit of Reform that permeated the Indonesian film scene, instigated the start of a new film movement. This new movement incorporated an array of new activities in film mediation practices and discourses on the subject. One element was the introduction of the label of independence, which gave birth to the new genre of independent film. Indonesian *film independen* should not be confused with the Euro-American meaning of 'independent' film, which stands for a movement which opposes the mainstream, mainly Hollywood, studio system. In Indonesia this genre became a model and banner for many young people who set out to make their own films. The scope of *film independen* transcended the production of independent films; it fostered the formation of a new community of *mafin* (an abbreviation of *mahluk film independen*, independent-film creatures). These *mafin* established their own channels of film distribution and exhibition through independent-film festivals. Looking beyond the temporal limitations of a festival, they created their own forums to exchange thoughts on the subject of film on the Internet and by arranging regular meetings.

The incentive to undertake activities in the field of *film independen* really commenced with the production of the film *Kuldesak* ('Cul-de-sac', or Dead-end street), an anthology of four short features about such problems of the middle-class youth of the city of Jakarta as drugs, homosexuality, and the feeling of absolute desolation. *Kuldesak* was made by four young film-makers who decided to produce it 'underground' in 1996, breaking all the rules of film production of the New Order. The directors, Mira Lesmana, Riri Riza, Rizal Mantovani, and Nan Achnas, had a background in producing films, series, documentary-soaps, or music video-clips for television. Inspired by the cheap independent film production *El-Mariachi* (1992) by Robert Rodriguez and his book on the film's production process, *Rebel without a crew* (1996), they decided to take the plunge and jointly produce a film for the silver screen.

Between 1996 and 1998, the four directors produced *Kuldesak* behind closed doors. To save energy, time, and money, they abandoned the beaten track of New Order film production. To start with, they did not register the production plan of *Kuldesak* at the Guidance Council of Film and Video of the Department of Information. In addition, as the film's directors, they neither obtained the mandatory membership of the KFT, nor did they follow the conventional New Order system in which it was only possible to become a film director after having been an assistant film director five times. As *Kuldesak*'s producers, the four did not join PPFI. Finally, they did not force their amateur actors and actresses to register as members of Parfi. Eschewing all the formal channels, the directors and production team paid for the production costs of *Kuldesak* themselves, and were helped by actors and crew who joined the project for free. To distribute the film, they applied for foreign film funding.

Unexpected changes in the political situation enabled *Kuldesak* to reach the screens of the cinemas throughout Indonesia in November 1998. Many rules and restrictions for film production and exhibition of the New Order were dissolved by the process of Reformasi, which was at its peak at that time, and were applied less strictly. Apart from a mandatory last-minute registration with KFT, the team was excused for not having registered at the other official film organizations. Another hurdle was cleared when *Kuldesak* passed the censor. However, despite the freer political climate, one of the most radical scenes of this film – that of two boys kissing in a bus – was censored. Apparently this scene was too revolutionary even for Reformasi. *Kuldesak* reached the theatres of Cinema 21, and was highly successful among young audiences. In different cities, queues at the ticket office stretched outside the cinema buildings. Touching on controversial issues and filmed in an MTV-style, the film showed a departure from both films produced by the earlier generation of Indonesian film-makers and from the everyday *sinetron* (soaps) on television. The press labelled *Kuldesak* the first-ever Indonesian 'independent' film, and often highlighted its 'non-Indonesian' features.

Kuldesak, made by four film-makers who 'just went for it', triggered a euphoric energy among other aspiring young Indonesians. In 1999, the Komunitas Film Independen (Konfiden, Community of Independent Film) began to hold a series of 'travelling' film screenings (*film keliling*) and discussions in the bigger cities in Java. These were organized at cultural venues, educational institutions, and foreign cultural centres. The objective of the travelling screenings and discussions was to introduce the concept of independent film to a wider public. They were also a warm-up for the first Festival Film dan Video Independen Indonesia (FFVII, Indonesian Independent Film and Video Festival) held in Jakarta at the end of

October 1999. This festival was designed to provide independent film-makers with a forum in which to screen their films. More ambitiously, it fostered a hope of reviving Indonesian film as a whole, an industry which had virtually died in the last decade of New Order rule. Besides organizing the annual FFVII between 1999 and 2002, Konfiden also published a monthly bulletin and commenced organizing workshops for film-making.

With the Jakarta-based Konfiden about to organize its third independent film and video festival in 2001, other parties in other cities (mainly in Java, but also in Sumatra, Sulawesi, and Bali) formed their own Indie film communities. These communities assumed the task of organizing independent-film festivals with discussions, workshops, and their own bulletins. Generally speaking, the independent films screened were rather unsophisticated and unprofessional. The majority consisted of short films made by young people in their early twenties who had no real background in film-making. This did not prevent them from broaching subjects which were often thought-provoking. Many included maverick ideas and depicted issues in the daily lives of the young, their interests, and sense of humour. Sometimes the films (indirectly) revealed issues of cultural, social, and political criticism. Some examples of films which circulated at the Konfiden festival and other film festivals of the time are: *Revolusi harapan* (Revolution of hope, 1997), by Nanang Istiabudi – a surrealistic story about a gang of thugs who go out on orders to kill and pull the teeth of artists, students, and others who are in any way critical; *Dunia kami, duniaku, dunia mereka* (Our world, my world, their world, 1999), by Adi Nugroho, which narrates the life of a transvestite in Yogyakarta; and *Kameng gampoeng nyang keunong geulawa* (The village goat takes the beating, 1999), by Aryo Danusiri, a chilling testament to the survivors of torture inflicted by the Komando Pasukan Khusus (Kopassus, Special Forces), filmed in Tiro, northern Aceh. These films were also screened at international film festivals and on other occasions.

As members of the various communities started to communicate on the Internet and visit each other's festivals, it did not take them long to begin to think about a coalition. About a hundred people from all over Indonesia, mainly film buffs and students from art academies and Muhammadiyah universities, came together in Yogyakarta for the National Indie Film Festival (Festival Film Indie Nasional) in late May and early June 2001. At the end, after much deliberation, they decided to form a national affiliation of independent-film communities. The next step was to establish an Information Centre (ICE), which operated an Internet mailing list called Forum Film, co-ordinated from Yogyakarta. The film communities also planned to hold a national meeting every two months. On 26 August 2001, during the Indie Film-Maker Meeting in Batu (a resort near Malang in East Java), the various communities tried to formulate a collective vision. They wanted to set up a programme to acquaint a broader public with the medium of film in general, and *film independen* in particular. After an all-night debate, three new ICE divisions were set up. Supplementing the earlier Forum Film mailing list, a web-site was to be co-ordinated from Malang, and an archive and a publication division were to be set up in Jakarta. The four ICE divisions would each remain autonomous bodies, standing for the same ideal but free to formulate their own policies.

The allotment of different divisions to different cities and their autonomy was a crucial issue during the debates. One reason the independent-film movement took on the form of a national alliance, in which the different communities remained 'independent' and retained an equal say, was the fear of domination by Jakarta. This was a legacy of New Order rule, when the Jakarta-based government officials and politics controlled the regions. Presumably not entirely coincidentally, at the same time that film communities were talking about independent divisions within a national alliance, on the political stage parties were engaged in fierce debates on a Bill that would give regional autonomy to the different provinces of Indonesia. Another spin-off of this reinforced commitment to regional autonomy in post-Soeharto film was that many new independent films made concerted efforts to reflect the characteristics of their home region. The film-makers wanted to produce a movie which differed in every sense from a film that would have been produced in Jakarta – something imbued with local pride and joy. For example, *Topeng kekasih* (English title: *Dearest mask*, 2000), by Hanung Bramantyo, is entirely in Javanese and revolves around the Oedipus complex, while *Di antara masa lalu dan masa sekarang* (Between the past and the present, 2001), by Eddie Cahyono shows the reflections of an old man about the guerrilla struggle for Independence. Both films depicted a typically Yogyakartan atmosphere. Another example of a film that explicitly reflected local culture is *Peronika* (Veronica, 2004), directed by Bowo Leksono from Purbalingga. This film is about villagers being baffled with technologies which are mainly used in the city. All dialogues are in Banyumas dialect.

The movie *Kepada yang terhormat titik 2* alluded to earlier was another creative manifestation of this emphasis on locality. Both the film's contents and its production and screening in Purwokerto epitomized the re-invigorated expression of local identities in Indonesian film and on the political stage. By 2003 the euphoria of Reformation had passed its peak, and so had the *film indie* movement. Several ICE divisions had stopped operating because of a chronic lack of funding, the dim prospects for turning the coalition into an official organization, and internal private conflicts. These conflicts revolved around questions of leadership, disputes over what direction to take, clashing personalities, and, at times, envy and distrust. By 2003 it was increasingly unclear exactly what Indonesian independent film was supposed to stand for. For some, independent film meant just any film produced outside the New Order system of film production. To a few, it also meant that films had to be produced for less commercial motives. In their opinion commercial film was contaminated by the New Order politics of economic growth, and a derivative of its structures of crony capitalism.[3] They believed that because the New Order had treated film as a commercial commodity, it had crippled the production of domestic films with the exception of cheap commercial films filled with sex, violence, or slapstick humour. In their eyes, the combination of film and commerce implied structures of New Order domination. Others believed that independent films tackled daring subjects, broached innovative subjects, and depicted the film-maker's free artistic expression. Yet others thought that independent film meant the production of low-budget, technically inferior, (short) films, filmed by unskilled film-makers with a digital camera. Some people even thought the term stood for the production of films about the Indonesian struggle for Independence in 1945.

Another reason why the use of the term *film independen* had lost its appeal, was that within the broader context of Indonesian film the label was connected to too many different groups. Broadly speaking, these groups could be divided into two factions. In mainstream media, the four directors of *Kuldesak* and nine other directors who produced music videos, soaps, and documentaries for television, were said to represent independent film. In October 1999 these directors had formed a movement based on a manifesto called 'I-Sinema'. I-Sinema was inspired by a movement of avant-garde Danish film-makers who in 1995 had drafted a manifesto called Dogme 95. The 'I' in 'I-Sinema' had different meanings – it stood for the words 'Indonesian', 'Independent', and also other terms like the English 'eye' or even 'I' (Sharpe 2002). The I-Sinema film-makers were not overly concerned about whether they were called independent film-makers or not. The main point

---

3   See, for example, Prakosa 2001:3-4, and Chapter 1 of this book.

of I-Sinema was to find new ways to produce films for the silver screen in order to revive the Indonesian film industry. In the manifesto, the use of digital technology was mentioned specifically as a new tool allowing the film-makers the opportunity to work more freely and independently (Sharpe 2002). On the other hand, the label of 'independence' was used by members of the above mentioned different *film indie* communities across Indonesia. These communities consisted of amateur film-makers, the majority of them students, who tried to produce films on a shoestring budget, borrowing money and film equipment from friends and family. In these communities, there was plenty of discussion about what independent film really meant. In their opinion, in comparison to themselves, the I-Sinema film-makers were well-established film directors who had easy access to film equipment, funding, and even the theatres of Cinema 21. Some members of the *indie* groups were of the opinion that if the I-Sinema film-makers were seen as independent film-makers, everyone producing a film in Indonesia could be labelled independent, particularly since there was no real film industry to speak of anyway.[4]

When in 2002 and 2003 the private television station SCTV began organizing an independent-film-festival competition, members of these more 'hardcore' *indie* film communities decided to drop the term. They were convinced that the label of independent film had now been hijacked by the commercial television industry, and therefore was not worth holding onto. Despite the wrangling, SCTV's Festival Film Independen Indonesia (FFII, Indonesian Independent-Film Festival) was a big success. In the first year, 1,071 short films were submitted to the festival committee, of which 836 qualified to enter the competition. In the following year this number rose to 899 films (Prakosa 2005:81). The films were from all over Indonesia – places as far afield as Berau (a city on East Kalimantan), Banyuwangi (the outermost point of East Java), Mataram (a town on the island of Lombok), the island of Batam (off the coast of Sumatra), the Sumatran cities Medan and Padang Panjang, as well as such smaller Javanese towns as Wonogiri and Cilacap. They were made by a variety of people ranging in age from nine to seventy. Among those who registered their films at the SCTV festivals were primary school students, bureaucrats, housewives, journalists, and police officers (Prakosa 2005:7-9). In particular after the SCTV festivals, the label 'independent film' often tended to fall by the wayside. As the term was burdened with too many dif-

---

4 Personal communication with members of Konfiden, Kine Klub UMY, Bulldozer, and other independent film communities in Jakarta, Yogyakarta, Malang, and Surabaya in 2001 and 2002.

ferent definitions, and represented too many different groups of film-makers, the *indie* communities decided to forget about debates to find a single definition for *film independen*. They decided that no matter what format, formula, subject, or label was used to describe their movement, it was best just to focus on the goal of bringing domestic film back to the people of Indonesia.

DISTRIBUTION AND EXHIBITION OF NEW MEDIA FORMATS: 'LOCAL' BETH VERSUS 'TRANSNATIONAL' JELANGKUNG

When the production and screening of *film independen* was at its height in 2001, discussions on film distribution and exhibition began to cover the problems of access of domestic films to the top-end cinemas of Cinema 21. These discussions were fuelled by the case of *Beth* (Aria Kusumadewa, 2001), a domestic film scheduled for screening in one of the theatres of Cinema 21 at the end of November 2001. This screening did not materialize, however, as negotiations between the film's director and bookers of Cinema 21 failed and the film was withdrawn from mainstream channels of film exhibition. Instead, it was distributed and screened through alternative networks set up by *film independen* communities. The failure of *Beth* to reach Cinema 21 theatres prompted discussions about existing power structures in Indonesia in relation to film and local and national/transnational identities. Particularly in the discussions about *Beth* held at *film indie* meetings and on mailing lists on the Internet, the Cinema 21 network was made to epitomize entrenched New Order structures. Allegedly, the network gave access only to those Indonesian film-makers or films representing upper-middle-class transnational identities, meaning well-to-do people who can afford schooling at universities in Indonesia or abroad.

Only a few months after the resignation of President Soeharto, Indonesian film productions began to reach the screens of Cinema 21. Most films were made by film-makers who had received their film education at the Faculty of Film and Television at the Institut Kesenian Jakarta (IKJ, Jakarta Art Institute), but now others who had mastered the technical aspects of film-making abroad also began to produce films for domestic audiences. In 2001 two digital films, made by semi-professional film-makers who had received film education in the United States, were screened in Cinema 21 in Pondok Indah, South Jakarta. Including these two productions, around ten domestic films were screened in Cinema 21 between

1998 and 2001. The growing number of domestic films, both in 35 mm and in digital video format, reaching Indonesian top-end cinemas prompted discussions in national media on 'the birth of a new generation of Indonesian film-makers' and 'the revival of Indonesian cinema'. Even though most films were art movies which were not enormously popular with a broad audience, the mere fact that they were produced and reached Indonesian cinemas seemed to offer a source of hope for the future of Indonesian film.

In October 2001, the film *Jelangkung* (Rizal Mantovani, 2001) was released, which was a huge success in theatres belonging to the 21 Group.[5] With the unexpected success of *Jelangkung* the future for Indonesian film in domestic cinemas seemed brighter than ever. *Jelangkung* was directed by music-video director Rizal Mantovani, and produced by soap actor and producer Jose Poernomo, who had recently founded his own production company, Rexinema. The film was made purely with commercial objectives. The producers stated they wanted to make a film that would simply entertain, and not in any way deal with any moral or social messages, or other, often incomprehensible, 'heavy stuff' (Agustin 2002; Sitorus 2001). *Jelangkung* was produced in two weeks and shot on digital video format. The film is about a group of teenagers who set out to trace ghosts based on legends of haunted places in Jakarta. The director and producer of *Jelangkung* were inspired by two popular American horror films, *The Blair Witch project* (Daniel Myrick and Eduardo Sànchez, 1999) and *Fright night* (Tom Holland, 1985). They used a combination of elements from these two films and translated this into an Indonesian setting using urban legends of Jakarta.

Jelangkung was initially screened in only one of the movie theatres of Cinema 21 in Jakarta. This theatre in Pondok Indah Mall was the only theatre in which a video-projector could be operated for the preview of films or presentations. However, as were other Cinema 21 theatres, it was equipped only with standard 35 mm projectors. For that reason, the producers themselves had to supply the video projector to screen the film. Because of word-of-mouth promotion, which praised the film's story and its musical score, as well as the gossip that a real ghost had slipped into the film during recording, *Jelangkung* became a real hit, initially among teenagers whose enthusiasm passed on to other categories of audiences. People were queuing for hours at the Pondok Indah box office to obtain tickets which were sold out in only a few minutes. Because the film was such a success, in December 2001 the producers

---

5   A *jelangkung* is a doll made out of a coconut shell and some wooden sticks, which is used as a medium to invite spirits to possess it.

decided to make copies of *Jelangkung* in Singapore, 'blowing it up' to the 35 mm format. This way the film could be screened in different cinemas. To illustrate the huge popularity of the film: at that time the costs of transferring digital film to 35 mm were approximately Rp 400 million (US$ 32,000), plus an extra amount of Rp 13 million (US$ 1,040) per copy. By February 2002, twenty-four Cinema 21 theatres all over Indonesia screened *Jelangkung* (Agustin 2002). In January 2002 *Jelangkung* attracted even more viewers than the just released *Harry Potter and the sorcerer's stone* (Chris Colombus, 2001), which was a worldwide success. The enormous success of the film attracted the attention of some American film companies, such as Miramax and Vertigo Entertainment, which expressed an interest in previewing the film and perhaps turning it into an American version.[6]

With both the rise in production of domestic films and their unproblematic distribution to prestigious cinemas, it seemed that after the fall of Soeharto domestic film had met a more conducive environment. When *Jelangkung* became a box office hit, film producers and journalists started to believe that Indonesian cinema had been successfully 'reformed', but this optimistic idea was questioned by the case of *Beth*. *Beth*, a film directed by Aria Kusumadewa, was an independent production. The idea of producing the film was born out of nightly conversations of the director with artists, famous local actors, actresses, and other individuals from various backgrounds frequenting Bulungan in South Jakarta. This group, which called itself Komunitas Gardu (Security Post Community), wanted to make a film that criticized the contemporaneous Indonesian socio-political situation. The story of *Beth* is about a forbidden love between a boy and a general's daughter, who meet each other again in a mental institution. But, the director argued, the film is actually a comment on Indonesian society, in which there is a thin line between sane and insane behaviour. In *Beth*, the mental institution and its inhabitants form a representation of Indonesia in miniature, exposing characteristics of different members of Indonesian society. Here, no one really is what he or she seems to be. The mad really are sane, the sane really are mad, and almost everyone can be bribed. The director, crew, actors, and actresses financed the production of *Beth* themselves, but a lack of funding meant its completion took a few years. To save production costs *Beth*, as was *Jelangkung*, was shot on digital video.

It was planned to have the national premiere of *Beth* at the Jakarta International Film Festival (Jiffest) in October 2001. Jiff-

---

6 'Produser AS tertarik pada film "Jelangkung"', *Pos Kota*, 27 January.

est was organized for the first time in November 1999, as a forum to screen both international and Indonesian films which were not likely to enter mainstream channels of distribution and exhibition. After Jiffest, *Beth* would be distributed to Cinema 21 in Jakarta, and thereafter to other cities in Indonesia via alternative networks. This was not to be, however, as the screening of *Beth* at Jiffest turned into a controversy. When the director discovered that the organizers of Jiffest paid a screening fee for some foreign films, he demanded the same treatment for his film. In a discussion between Aria and the organizing committee of Jiffest, it was explained that screening fees were only charged for some of the films entered in the festival. These were films that had been very successful abroad and were likely to attract large audiences at the festival. The committee assumed *Beth* could never compete with these films, and even considered its screening at the festival a complimentary promotion. Moreover, since Jiffest would require a digital video projector to screen it, the committee saw no need to pay extra for its screening. Frustrated, Aria felt that his film was not valued as much as foreign films, and he decided to cancel the screening of *Beth* at Jiffest. In the local mass media, he voiced the criticism that Jiffest favoured foreign films above domestic productions, and thereby showed contempt for Indonesian film.

Although there was no premiere of *Beth* at Jiffest, other options for screening the film were still open. A few days before *Beth* was withdrawn, a message had already been posted on the Internet stating that Aria was looking for partners outside Jakarta to screen his film. Soon after this posting, various *film indie* communities from different regions showed their interest in collaborating with Aria. Besides these alternative offers, Aria had settled with the management of Cinema 21 that his film was going to be screened in the Pondok Indah theatre at the end of November. But here the screening of *Beth* ran into another problem, leading to a second controversy. Riding the crest of its unexpected success, *Jelangkung*, which had only been expected to last ten days at the most, was still being screened in the Pondok Indah theatre in November. As the Pondok Indah theatre was the only cinema where films in digital video format could be operated, the screening of *Beth* was initially postponed to the first week of December, and thereafter indefinitely.

This was a huge problem for Aria. He had to rent a digital video projector (LCD), at that time around Rp 2.5 million (US$ 200) for one day up to Rp 6 million (US$ 480) for seven days, and pay for film posters and other promotion material for screening at Cinema 21. To cover these costs, Aria needed sponsoring, but to obtain funding from a potential sponsor, he needed to know the exact screening schedule. Several times he tried to obtain a fixed schedule from the management of Cinema 21 but did not succeed. Instead, he was told that the policy of Cinema 21 did not permit two Indonesian films to be screened at the same time. As long as *Jelangkung* was still popular, *Beth* would be put on hold. Due to the uncertainty of the film's screening schedule, it was impossible for Aria to negotiate with sponsors. At the end of December 2001, out of sheer frustration and disappointment, he withdrew the proposed screening of *Beth* from Cinema 21. Instead, Aria decided to focus fully on distributing and screening the film via alternative channels.

The discord between Aria Kusumadewa and Cinema 21 erupted into a controversy in the Indonesian mass media. In entertainment and celebrity infotainment television programmes Aria and two of the leading actresses of *Beth*, Lola Amaria and Ine Febriyanti, spoke their minds about what they perceived to be the unfair treatment of Indonesian film by the management of Cinema 21. They suggested that Cinema 21's policy of not screening two Indonesian films at the same time was related to business deals on film distribution and exhibition between the Subentra 21 Group and the American Motion Picture Association. Hollywood films were scheduled months in advance and entered many different cinemas simultaneously, whereas Indonesian films had to line up to be screened one at the time. The case of *Beth* led to heated debates about the position of domestic film in Indonesian cinemas and even drew the attention of the non-governmental organization Media Watch, resulting in an investigation into an alleged monopoly on film distribution and exhibition in Indonesia by the 21 Group.[7]

Hindered by accusations of nepotism, the theatre management of Cinema 21 blamed the failure to screen *Beth* in its theatres on problems of adaptation to new media technologies. With the exception of one Pondok Indah theatre, all other cinemas could operate the 35 mm film format only. As such, the case of *Beth* could basically be perceived as a problem of adjustment of conventional technologies of film exhibition to new film media and formats. The problem of the adaptation of established cinemas to new audio-visual media technologies was not a problem of Cinema 21 alone. All over the world cinemas equipped with 35 mm projectors for film exhibition

---

7 In the light of these discussions, in July 2002 Media Watch came up with a report which noted nine violations of the Indonesian anti-monopoly law of 1999 by the 21 Group. Media Watch filed a complaint with the Komisi Pengawas Persaingan Usaha (KPPU, Business Competition Supervisory Agency) alleging unfair business practices by Subentra 21. The case was taken to court. In April 2003 the verdict handed down was that there was neither proof of monopoly, nor of unfair business practices by the 21 Group.

had difficulties adapting to the new developments in film productions in digital video format. In most cases digital films were first transferred to 35 mm before they reached the screens of cinemas or film festivals. Nevertheless, discussions about *Beth*'s failure to reach Cinema 21 tended to overlook this point. Instead the discourse focused on issues raised before, such as the link between trade and power, structures of nepotism, and the domination of the Indonesian film industry by the middle classes.

The failure to distribute *Beth* through mainstream distribution channels was a particularly hot topic in discussions about film on the Internet and at gatherings of *film independen* communities. Here, many discussions again emphasized that it was imperative to set up a diverse and competitive system of film distribution and exhibition, free of business interests and state control. The growing appeal for alternative networks which would show a diversity of films in opposition to the uniformity on offer in Cinema 21 fuelled discussions about the potential of local film productions. As mentioned earlier, the idea was that local films could articulate free artistic expressions and specific local identities. Learning from the distribution problem experienced with *Beth*, members of *film indie* communities developed this idea further into the concept of creating regional cinemas (*sinema daerah*). In regional cinemas, the production of local films would challenge what Yogyakarta film-maker Doni Kus called 'the colonization of [film] aesthetics' ('*penjajahan estetis*') by Jakarta and the rest of the world. Kus' point was that regional cinema had the potential to be individual, original, and resistant to both Hollywood mass products imported into Indonesia, and commercial films and television soaps produced in the Jakarta-based film industry.[8] The hope was that the potential rise of regional cinema would produce a break with the policy of the 21 Group, which prioritized the screening of films in Jakarta before distributing these to the regions.

The issues raised in discussions on *Beth* correspond with themes found in Third Cinema discourses. The goal of Third Cinema was to raise questions about domination and resistance in 'non-Western' film cultures. The political disposition of economic domination, and concomitantly the global distribution of power of First over Third Worlds, was an important aspect of its theories. Ella Shohat

---

8 Kus' statement about 'the colonization of aesthetics' by the Jakarta-based Indonesian film industry was made at a *film indie* meeting in Yogyakarta in December 2001. At that meeting local film-makers were talking about founding a Yogyakarta-based film industry. This industry was to be supported by the local government and the Sultan of Yogyakarta, and would be called Mataram film.

and Robert Stam identified forces of neo-colonial globalization and domination by a group of powerful nation-states consisting basically of Western Europe, the US, and Japan. This domination, they argued, was economic ('the Group of Seven', IMF, the World Bank, GATT), political (the five veto-holding members of the UN Security Council), military (new 'unipolar' NATO), and techno-informational-cultural (Hollywood, UPI, Reuters, France Presse, CNN). Neo-colonial domination, Shohat and Stam (1994:17) asserted, was 'enforced through deteriorating terms of trade and the "austerity programs" by which the World Bank and IMF, often with the self-serving complicity of Third-World elites, imposed rules that First-World countries would themselves never tolerate'. Challenging such hypocrisy, they addressed the unequal terms of exchange and global distribution of cultural productions, pointing out that the economic dependency of Third World countries made their cinemas vulnerable to neo-colonial pressures. Hollywood films that had covered their costs in the domestic market could profitably be 'dumped' on Third World markets at very low prices. When dependent countries tried to strengthen their own film industries by setting up trade barriers for foreign films, First World countries could threaten retaliation in some other economic area, such as the export or pricing of raw materials (Shohat and Stam 1994:30).

As in the case of Third Cinema, the majority of discourses about *film independen* and post-Soeharto film mediation practices during and after the case of *Beth* addressed the position of nationally hegemonic dominant film practices and the modes of resistance open to minoritarian regional cinemas. Discussions about the position and treatment of non-commercial domestic film in the Indonesian mediascape (mainly in cinemas, but also at Jiffest and on national television), and the need for oppositional regional cinemas and alternative distribution and exhibition networks, revealed the efforts made to shed the legacies of New Order hegemonic rule in film and society. Several discourses implied that the post-Soeharto mediascape was a post-neo-colonial setting. In film, the New Order was marked as an imperialist force in its own right, a part of a process of neo-colonization of hegemonic Western culture through the connections and business deals of Soeharto cronies with transnational media corporations.

In Indonesian studies, the idea of the New Order as neo-colonizer is not new. Benedict Anderson has said that the struggle for independence and the years that followed represented the defeat of the colonial state by a newly imagined nation. Soeharto's New Order, on the other hand, 'is best understood as the resurrection of the State [founded in Dutch colonialism] and its triumph vis-à-vis society and nation' (Anderson 1990:109). Speaking of Third Cinema theories, Krishna Sen also treated the New Order as a neo-colonial force that disseminated national culture in the same way as neo-imperialistic forces distributed global Western culture. Sen (2003:156, 163) argues that under the New Order, local or global culture rather than hegemonic national culture could be perceived as modes of resistance.

Sen (2003:147) felt that 'the globalist paradigm of Third Cinema theorizing [did] not quite capture the radical drives within Indonesian cinema'. Instead, she argued, Indonesian cinema's radicalism needed to be defined in terms of the political constellations within the nation and could not be read in any generalized way in relation to Hollywood, global culture, or capitalism (Sen 2003:147). There is more than a grain of truth in this, but in discourses on the case of *Beth*, Hollywood was equated with political constellations within the nation. Hollywood and concomitantly the domination of global culture were seen as examples of the structures of New Order rule that supported crony capitalism. A tangible example of this was the involvement of Soeharto cronies in import and export deals with the US. The most glaring case in point was that Soeharto's foster brother Sudwikatmono, owner of Subentra 21, had secured the exclusive distribution and exhibition rights of imported US films. Another such link became apparent when Soeharto's business partner Bob Hassan was involved in a deal between Indonesia and the US at the beginning of the 1990s. In exchange for Indonesia importing Hollywood films, the US agreed to import batik and timber from Indonesia. In this light, the representation of *Beth* and its connection to alternative film cultures and side-stream, independent, or underground networks of film distribution and exhibition can be seen as part of Third Cinema discourses, which set minority oppositional cinemas against their dominating counterparts. In the post-Soeharto mediascape, the mediation practices of *film independen* as a movement of oppositional cinema were perceived to be a counterpoise to the enduring structures of the New Order and its incorporation of Hollywood/First World domination in Indonesian cinema. In post-Soeharto cinema, 'Third' as a denominator of opposition stood for local Indonesian film cultures and identities, whereas 'First' represented hegemonic global and national culture.

The emphasis on the local as subversive or oppositional to national or global culture and identities in post-Soeharto cultural discourses can be linked to Arif Dirlik's views about the re-emergence of the local as a site of resistance and struggle for liberation. While Dirlik (1996:35) notes that such struggles are informed by the modernity that groups suppressed or marginalized by modernization reject, the local *film indie* communities felt that they were neither suppressed by modernization, nor were they rejecting it. Instead, in step with movements of Third Cinema, the communities highlighted localism as a point of departure and goal of liberation, which questioned and opposed the imbalanced access to national and transnational film distribution and exhibition networks.

ALTERNATIVE SITES OF FILM CONSUMPTION: ADDITIONAL IDENTIFICATIONS AND MODES OF RESISTANCE

In the years following Reformasi, film festivals began to proliferate everywhere in Indonesia. Besides the movement of *film independen* with its various film screenings, discussions, workshops, and festivals, after 1999 other groups and communities also undertook the organization of film festivals. Some festivals with special themes saw the light of day only once, for example the 2002 Festival Film Perdamaian (Peace Film Festival), which screened domestic and international films about human rights issues. Other festivals were held annually. Most festivals emerged from communities which either drew on or 'claimed' particular film genres or formats. Sometimes new genres were formed or co-opted – 'peace' or 'gay and lesbian' films spring to mind – or concepts of existing genres changed. Documentary film, which was equated with propaganda under the New Order, was now transformed into a genre which epitomized the advocacy of human rights issues and the deconstruction of New Order narratives on history and society. The various new film festivals catered to different imagined audiences and were connected to a new set of discourses, related to concerns in society or daily life.[9] Besides the specific choice for a film genre or format, another important feature of the new festivals was that nearly all of these combined the screening of domestic and foreign films.

The most important post-Soeharto festival on a national scale was Jiffest, Jakarta's international film festival. Jiffest was organized for the first time from 20 to 28 November 1999, a month after the first independent-film festival by Konfiden. Two women, the Indonesian producer and documentary film-maker Shanty Harmayn and the Franco-American festival organizer Natacha Devillers, founded the festival to provide audiences with foreign films

---

9   At SCTV's FFII in 2002 and 2003, Prakosa (2005:83) noticed that the main themes of films at various film festivals, including SCTV's, were: love, drugs, *togel* (abbreviation of *toto gelap*, illegal lottery), dreaming or daydreaming, and homosexuality.

and art films, which were hard to find in Indonesia. In his review of the first Jiffest, cultural critic Seno Gumira Adjidarma spoke of the rise of a new generation of film-makers and film audiences.[10] Over the years Jiffest grew into a big event that screened all kinds of classic, modern, short, and experimental films and documentaries, both from Indonesia and abroad. Alongside its annually changing theme, different workshops and discussions were also organized during the festival. After 2001, a section of Jiffest travelled throughout Indonesia to screen part of its film programme in cities across the country. In its fourth year, Jiffest expanded this section by having local film-makers in each city enter their own films and screen these alongside the regular programme.

Another new Jakarta-based film festival which was held annually and which also travelled to other cities was the Queer Film Festival (QFF). The QFF was organized for the first time by the 'Q-munity' in September 2002. Q-munity was a community which consisted of gays and lesbians and other people with an interest in film and arts. The QFF was the first Indonesian film festival to cover the genres of gay, lesbian, and Aids films. The festival was non-competitive and screened both international and domestic productions. Beyond its core screenings, at the fringes of the festival there were discussions with film-makers, photo and painting exhibitions, and seminars about such topics as Aids. QFF tried to keep a low profile because various groups in Indonesia do not accept homosexuality. To reduce the focus on homosexuality, the committee strategically tied its festival to campaigns about Aids awareness and the dangers of free sex. Despite such manoeuvres, Q's director John Badalu regularly received threats from Muslim fundamentalists who tried to stop the event each year.

Other recurring film festivals which were tied to either a certain format or a particular genre included the Pesta Sinema Indonesia (PSI, Feast of Indonesian Cinema), the Festival Film Dokumenter (FFD, Documentary Film Festival) and Hello;fest. From 2001 to 2005, PSI was held each June in Purwokerto. It was organized by a group of students who formed a community called Youth Power, which was also active in the field of theatre, arts, and photography. The festival exclusively covered the screening of films produced in video format. These films consisted of domestic as well as foreign films. In 2005 the PSI added a 'one minute film' competition for local Purwokerto film-makers to its programme. Since 2002, the *komunitas film dokumenter* (documentary film community) has organized FFD each year in December in Yogyakarta. This festi-

---

10   Personal communication with Seno Gumiro Adjidarma, Jakarta, November 2001.

val has screened both international and domestic documentaries, and organized a competition for documentaries produced by novice domestic film-makers. Besides the screening of documentary films, it has also organized workshops on documentary making and discussions. In 2005, FFD added a competition for professional Indonesian documentary film-makers to its programme. Hello;fest commenced in 2004, when it was organized by the film school Hello;Motion in Jakarta; it focused on short and animation films. Hello;fest began as a festival to screen the work of its students at the end of their four-month courses, but because many outsiders also wanted to participate in the festival it changed into an open forum. Besides the screening of films by students and outsiders, some domestic and foreign films are invited to compete for four awards each year, for which the viewers at the festival can vote (Ratna 2005).

Another alternative site of film distribution and consumption was connected to the VCD format. This format was preceded by video cassettes and laser discs (LD), and followed later by Digital Video/Versatile Discs (DVD). In Indonesia the distribution of these new film formats started in the mid-1980s under the New Order with the introduction of video players and cassettes onto the Indonesian film market. Instantly people, mainly from the middle classes, embraced the medium. In a short period of time, video began to compete with cinemas and *layar tancep*. Many retired high-ranking military officers, who had often occupied a position in local offices of the Department of Information, set up mobile video companies in provincial areas backed by the licenses they handed out themselves (Adityo 1996). At the beginning of the 1990s a new format, LD, was added to the distribution of video. In 1996 the LD format was increasingly replaced by VCD, which in 2000 was followed by the DVD format. However, in Indonesia DVDs did not immediately replace the circulation of the much cheaper VCDs.

With the introduction of video, film piracy was launched with a vengeance on the Indonesian market. Pirated films were very popular. Apart from their low price, about one-half to one-third of the price of original products, pirated films often circulated before the original film reached Indonesian cinemas. Unquestionably, part of their popularity was that pirated films were not censored.[11] Compared to films in cinemas and the original products sold in shopping malls, which mainly consisted of the same Hollywood and local

---

11 'Akan dicari sampai ke akarnya', *Suara Pembaruan*, 11-12-1997; 'LD/video beredar mendahului film impor terbaru di bioskop', *Harian Ekonomi Neraca*, 24-1-1996; 'VCD hasil bajakan dijual sangat murah; LSF berperan menegakkan UU Hak Cipta', *Pikiran Rakyat*, 10-9-1999.

products, the variety obtainable in pirated films was much more diverse. Pirated films included classic and art house films, Mandarin, Hong Kong, and Bollywood film productions; many productions moreover consisted of pornographic or semi-pornographic films. The piracy of films in video, LD, and later VCD and DVD format launched an extensive underground economy (F.Y. 1993). In August 1997, Wihadi Wiyanto, Secretary General of the Asosiasi Importir Rekaman Video (Asirevi, Indonesian Video Recording Importers Association), stated that 90% of the VCDs circulating in Indonesia were illegal copies.[12]

VCD was perceived as a medium and format accessible to all people. Even though the quality of VCD was second rate compared to videotapes and LD, it was cheap. Because of their price and quality, videotapes and LD were perceived as formats used by the middle classes (Nurhan and Theodore 1999a). In contrast, especially because of film piracy, even the poorest people could watch a VCD. Indeed pirated VCDs were even cheaper than their originals, though often of inferior quality. With the exception of fairly professional reproductions of a master copy, many pirated films had indistinct, blurred images and sound. Some of these pirated films were digital video recordings of films screened in cinemas or on videotape or LD at home. This was betrayed by the fact that movie theatre audiences could be heard commenting on the film; other nuisances which had been inadvertently recorded included people walking by the screen, kitchen noises, the crowing of a cock, or children playing in the background. Because of their inferior quality it was said that pirated VCDs had their own market segment, consisting mainly of the lower classes.[13] It was asserted that the number of pirated products circulating in rural areas was much higher than in cities,[14] but in my experience virtually everyone, rich and poor, nearly everywhere in the city or in the countryside, consumed pirated VCDs.

Until 1997 pirated films were imported mainly through transnational underground networks operating in Singapore, Malaysia, and Hong Kong. Until 1998 most pirated films sold in Indonesia were first distributed by sea from Singapore, with a transit on the island of Batam. After transportation by boat from Batam the films were distributed over land to Medan, Jakarta, Semarang, and Surabaya, and from there to the rest of Indonesia. By 1998, not just

12 'Belasan juta VCD illegal beredar di pasaran', *Angkatan Bersenjata*, 20-8-1997.
13 'VCD bajakan punya pasar tersendiri', *Pelita*, 27-7-1999.
14 'Kaset bajakan rambah pedesaan; Lebih banyak ketimbang di perkotaan', *Sinar Pagi*, 11-3-2000.

pirated films, mostly in VCD format, were imported through these networks; the technologies to produce them were also disseminating themselves via the networks. In November 1998, it was estimated that there were approximately ten factories based in Jakarta, Semarang, and Surabaya producing pirated VCDs.[15] The production of illegal VCD copies soon expanded, eventually transforming into an export commodity for markets in Malaysia, Singapore, India, and the Philippines.[16] In the short space of a few years, film piracy was established as a substantial home industry business. In 2001, it was officially estimated that in Jakarta alone around one hundred copy machines were operating; however, in reality there were presumably many more.[17]

With the exception of pornographic films, pirated VCDs, both imported and domestically produced, were sold on the open market. The centre for pirated products in Indonesia was the Glodok area in Jakarta, but also in other cities and more rural towns pirated films were openly on offer in shops and stalls in shopping malls and on the streets. Similar to ordering a pizza, there were identical services by which pirated films could be ordered by phone.[18] Even though the government lost an estimated amount of Rp 5 billion (US$ 400,000) per year in taxes, media piracy was big business in Indonesia.[19] Besides the vendors of the illegal film copies, those benefitting from this alternative site of film distribution and consumption were producers, importers, and distributors of pirated films, not to mention the police, government officials, and Soeharto business cronies. In short, many businesses and members of official organizations and the bureaucracy in Indonesia were involved in the production or distribution of pirated VCDs. Between 1997 and 2003, Indonesian media repeatedly mentioned that producers, distributors, and importers of established media organizations were also involved in the trade in illegal copies. It was said, and sometimes proven, that factories producing original VCDs simultaneously produced copies for the underground mar-

---

15 'Benda kaca mini berdaya rusak maksi' *Media Indonesia*, 8-11-1998.
16 Tim SP (2000) wrote an article about a syndicate of film piracy consisting of Glodok (North Jakarta), Singapore, and Batam mafia.
17 'Karena terdapat 100 mesin cetak VCD di Jakarta; Aksi pembajakan terus berlangsung', *Pos Kota*, 9-9-2001.
18 'Video bajakan beredar lewat "rental berjalan"', *Sinar Pagi*, 15-12-1997.
19 This amount was estimated in May 1998 (Syah 1998). In 2003 the head of Karya Cipta Indonesia (Indonesian Intellectual Property), Rinto Harahap, stated that each year the state lost Rp 1.4 trillion (US$ 116,666,666; at the time 1 US$ was approximately Rp 12,000) on pirated music cassettes and VCDs ('Kerugian negara capai Rp 1,4 trilliun/tahun', *Pikiran Rakyat*, 10-3-2003). By 2007 this amount had risen to Rp 2.5 trillion (US$ 263,157,894; note that by then 1 US$ was valued at around Rp 9,500) (Hadysusanto 2008).

ket.[20] Certified film import and distribution networks, as well as cinema workers and staff, were rumoured to be part of the pirated-film network, passing on master copies to illegal copiers. In addition to companies, others who profited from the production and distribution of pirated VCDs were the 'rotten elements' (*oknum*) in the police forces and ruling elites. It was common knowledge that small-scale producers, distributors, and sales people regularly paid policemen a fee so as to continue their business undisturbed. Vendors of pirated VCDs were especially prone to handing out payments to pre-empt police raids, or at least to be warned prior to any police actions. Allegedly, large business empires in the illegal film industry were backed either by Soeharto cronies, high-ranking army officers, or legislative officials.[21]

Despite the fact that these goods were sold openly, piracy in Indonesia was officially illegal. Between 1993 and 1997, several new intellectual property laws and sanctions against offenders were approved in parliament. In 1997 a law on intellectual property rights was passed. Offenders against this law could be sentenced to five years imprisonment or a fine of Rp 50 million (US$ 4,000). In the same period, sporadic raids were mounted by police forces, mainly in the Glodok area in Jakarta. These raids were primarily pro-forma to show there was police action against piracy and as a reminder to vendors to continue to pay their 'safety fees' (*uang keamanan*). During these raids thousands of pirated films were confiscated, some of which were later publicly destroyed. Every few months, in a ceremony attended by members of the LSF, police, and government officials, confiscated pirated films and cuts of censored films were run over by trucks or incinerated. This sanctioned destruction was filmed and subsequently featured in news programmes on television; details were also published in newspapers. In reality the ceremony was just as much fiction as the films themselves. Only a day after piracy raids took place, if not the same evening, the same number and variety of films was again on offer and it was business as usual.[22] Occasionally producers or distributors of pirated films would be arrested. These culprits were mainly middlemen, who were back in business shortly after the payment of their bail.

20 'Bos pembajak, orang yang kebal hukum', *Warta Kota*, 18-4-2002; 'Rumah pembajak VCD di Teluk Gong digerebek', *Warta Kota*, 18-9-2002; Nurhan and Theodore 1999b.
21 See for example 'Kisruh penerbitan stiker legalisasi LD & VCD; Keluarga Cendana terlibat?', *Majalah Film* 332/298/XV, 6/19-3-1999; 'Keluarga Cendana terlibat peredaran VCD bajakan', *Harian Terbit*, 20-2-1999.
22 See, for example, 'Tanpa pembinaan, razia VCD sia-sia', *Media Indonesia*, 24-3-1998; 'VCD bajakan', *Pikiran Rakyat*, 17-5-2000; 'Polisi bakar sekitar satu juta VCD bajakan', *Republika*, 27-10-2001.

Around 1998 the raids began to increase. By then, Indonesia had achieved the third position on the 'priority watch list' of the International Intellectual Property Alliance (IIPA), an industry lobby group from the US. The principal reason for the increase in police raids against film piracy were the conditions set for foreign aid and funding by the International Monetary Fund (IMF). To facilitate loans and foreign aid after the Asian monetary crisis in 1997, Indonesia had to agree to fifty stipulations drawn up by IMF (Van Dijk 2001:82, 104). One of these demanded that the Indonesian government seriously combat offenders against intellectual property rights.[23] However, even though the number of raids increased, and concomitantly the number of films that were burned or run over by trucks at the broadcast public ceremonies, the piracy industry in Indonesia, as in other Asian countries, in no way diminished. In 2003 the Motion Picture Association (MPA), the international division of the Motion Picture Association of America (MPAA), launched an anti-piracy media campaign in eight countries in Asia. Besides Indonesia, the campaign covered South Korea, Chinese Taiwan, India, Malaysia, Singapore, the Philippines, and Thailand. MPA estimated that the US motion picture industry lost more than US$ 3 billion annually in potential worldwide revenue as a result of piracy. In 2002 six million DVDs, or 87% of pirated DVDs the world over, were seized in Asia. Hence 2003 was declared the 'Anti-Piracy Action Year in Asia', with the tagline 'Nothing beats the real thing: say 'no' to piracy' (Santosa 2003).

Both the post-Soeharto film festivals and networks of, mainly pirated, VCDs provided alternative sites of film distribution and consumption. Particularly the pirated VCDs offered wide access to all kinds of uncensored, mainstream and non-mainstream, domestic and foreign film productions. Furthermore, the different film festivals screened various films that never reached Indonesian television or cinemas. The discourses linking local cultures to independent or 'side-stream' film and its distribution and exhibition networks cannot be applied to the alternative sites without some difficulty. The first hurdle is that the post-Soeharto film festivals and VCD networks circulated both domestic and transnational films. As such, they did not represent either domestic or transnational culture, but a combination of both. Moreover, at the new film festivals identifications and issues of representation did not spring from global, national, or local concerns or cultures. Instead, these were based on particular film genres and film formats and the domestic and transnational

---

23 It was not the first time the Indonesian government and entertainment industry were pressured to take action against piracy. For example, in 1987 the US had restricted trade in other Indonesian business sectors because of music piracy.

discourses which were linked to these genres and formats. Hence Q stood for discourses on gay and lesbian films and homosexuality, both in Indonesia and abroad; FFD represented discourses on the specificity of documentary film in Indonesia, as well as worldwide contemporary discourses on the genre; and PSI and Hello;fest were connected to discourses on the development, position, and implications of the video format in Indonesia and at other comparable festivals in the world. Jiffest, which screened all genres and formats, in this sense was all-inclusive, but through its annual changing festival theme each year it related to a specific discourse.[24]

The second problem in defining post-Soeharto film festivals and VCD networks is that it is difficult to determine which distribution and consumption channels were mainstream, side-stream, or underground. The understanding of these notions is multifaceted, as it consists of networks of distribution and consumption of original VCDs and of pirated films. Which networks represented mainstream distribution channels, those of legal films because they were legal? Or conversely, the networks of pirated VCDs? Even though piracy was an illegal activity in Indonesia, pirated films were openly on sale everywhere. Strictly speaking, from the point of view of availability and market shares, pirated films with a share of 90% against a mere 10% of legal films were more mainstream than their original counterpart. As such, the network and sales of original films could be perceived as a 'side-stream' channel of film distribution and consumption. Furthermore, because of the wide-ranging set-up of home industries producing pirated films, the vast transnational networks distributing them, the numerous vendors who sold these films all over Indonesia, and the substantial involvement of 'infiltrators' in official film production and distribution companies and organizations, police forces, and the judicial system, pirated VCDs could hardly be said to constitute an underground economy; rather, they formed a parallel economy.

Looking at film festivals the notion of mainstream versus side-stream sites of distribution and consumption is less complex in the sense that all festivals could be perceived as side-stream distribution channels because they were not initiated, supported, or run by the Indonesian state or film industry. However, on the basis of their visibility, or the amount of publicity they generated, some could be perceived as more 'side-stream' or underground than others. Instead of a division into mainstream, side-stream, or underground

24 For example, the main theme of Jiffest in 2000 was 'Issues on contemporary Islamic culture', while in 2001 it sounded 'Indonesian identity seen through film'. In 2002, the focus was 'Multiculturalism; Celebrating diversity', while Jiffest 2003 was about 'Understanding change'.

events, in this context it might be better to speak of events that were on or off the map. Or, to use a phrase coined by co-founder of Konfiden and film-maker and distributor Lulu Ratna, 'festivals below the radar'. This term refers to low-profile festivals, as opposed to festivals that were easily detectible (Ratna 2005). In this context, Jiffest was a very visible, high-profile event that generated a wealth of national publicity. In comparison, Q, which remained low profile, could be perceived as a festival that was more distinctly non-establishment. PSI, which was not of any interest to the national media, was an off-the-map, below-the-radar, underground event.

The discourses about local forms of resistance to processes of transnational cinematic neo-imperialism cannot simply be applied to the alternative sites of post-Soeharto film festivals and VCDs. However, these alternative channels of film distribution and exhibition do represent tactics which resisted or evaded hegemonic structures of film circulation. In this context, the festivals can be connected to the organization of film festivals worldwide as forums for alternative, off-beat film productions. Undoubtedly, on another level, the circulation of (particularly pirated) VCDs does represent tactics which resisted or evaded hegemonic structures of film distribution and exhibition. The circulation of pirated VCDs can be seen as a form of resistance, which Shohat and Stam (1994) call 'media jujitsu'.

As mentioned earlier, the political disposition of economic domination of First over Third Worlds and its concomitant global distribution of power was an important aspect in Third Cinema theories.[25] Assessments of Third Cinema point to various film formulas which challenged First World domination of culture and aesthetics. These included films and videos which eschewed formal conventions of dramatic realism and chose modes and strategies of alternative aesthetics rooted in non-realist, often non-Western or para-Western, cultural traditions. Among the range of modes and strategies were the carnivalesque, the anthropophagic, the magic-realist, the reflexive modernist, and the resistant post-modernist.

---

25 Shohat and Stam remarked that the global cultural situation was not as one-sided as presented in media-imperialism theories of the 1970s, but was in fact considerably more interactive. In their argument they mention that it was not a case of an active First World forcing its products onto a passive Third World. Global mass culture did not replace local cultures but co-existed with them, or was itself marked by a 'local' accent. For a similar argument, see Grewal and Kaplan's introduction (1994) to *Scattered hegemonies; Postmodernity and transnational feminist practice*. Furthermore, Shohat and Stam argued, a growing number of Third-World countries (Mexico, Brazil, India, and Egypt) dominated their own markets and even became cultural exporters. According to Shohat and Stam (1994:31) a distinction should be made between the ownership and control of the media, which is an issue of political economy, and the specifically cultural issue of the implications of this domination for the people on the receiving end.

These featured other historical rhythms, other narrative structures, and other views of collective life.[26]

Shohat and Stam indicate that many of these modes and strategies appropriated existing discourses to their own ends. In this, Shohat and Stam argue, the power of dominant First World discourses was assumed only to deploy its force through a kind of artistic jujitsu against domination. So did the Brazilian anthropophagic movement, which 'called for an art that would devour European techniques the better to struggle against European domination', most alternative aesthetics revalourized what was seen as negative, and turned tactical weakness into strategic strength (Shohat and Stam 1994:328). As mentioned above, Shohat and Stam call the appropriation of elements of dominant culture to redeploy them in the interests of oppositional praxis 'media jujitsu'.

The concept of media jujitsu can be extended to the distribution and consumption practices of pirated VCDs. Similar to strategies that appropriated dominant discourses and aesthetics only to transform these into a force against domination, the alternative site of distribution and consumption of pirated VCDs is one which incorporated First World cultural domination and supported the dissemination of its foreign hegemony, but simultaneously undermined it. Paradoxically, the networks of pirated VCDs represented the most accessible channels to hegemonic First World culture, while they simultaneously destabilized the disposition of First World economic domination. Pirated VCDs can be perceived as a form of resistance to both national control and structures of film: they evade state censorship and sidestep the lack of choice in films available via mainstream channels. These VCDs also resist the global economic domination and distribution of power of the West by undermining legal sales and copyrights. The format and its cursive practices of mediation dispersed hegemonies of leading global and national audiovisual media networks.[27]

CONCLUSION

Discourses on post-Soeharto film mediation practices depended on reconstituted frames of reference. New media technologies and

---

26 Shohat and Stam 1994:292. For a comprehensive description of these modes and strategies and their implications, see Shohat and Stam 1994:292-337.
27 For concepts on contemporary 'dispersed' and 'scattered' hegemonies in global-local cultural relations, see Appadurai 1990; Grewal and Kaplan 1994, notably the Introduction.

changes on the political scene led to new 'independent' film practices, cultures, and imaginations of identities, but old practices, cultures, and identities were not entirely disposed of. Ironically, the democratization process of audio-visual media launched by the advance in new technologies caused another divide in film formats, audiences, and communities. This time, instead of 16 mm film, the new digital video format was in conflict with Cinema 21's 35 mm format.

Since the overwhelming interest in the affair surrounding *Beth*, Cinema 21 stopped screening films in digital format. Films must now be transferred to 35 mm before they will be shown in its cinemas. The new policy strengthened the impression that the network supported long-standing power structures, as it limited the number of domestic films to reach top-end cinemas. Only film-makers or producers who could pay for the production or 'blow-up' of their film in the 35 mm format could have their films screened in Cinema 21. Consequently, film-makers with proficient business know-how and 'connections', or sufficient financial backing, had an advantage. Nevertheless, the film format alone was not the reason that few domestic films reached the Indonesian top-end theatres; the duration, content, and style of the films also had to comply with the criteria set by Cinema 21. Those who could not live up to these conditions had the old alternative of 'going international' and screening films at foreign film festivals. The new alternative was to 'go independent' and distribute and screen films via alternative networks, or to distribute them directly in VCD format.[28]

The choice for old, new, established, or alternative channels of film distribution and exhibition was based not merely on practical considerations, but also on who, and what, these channels were perceived to represent in post-Soeharto Indonesia. In debates about the failure of *Beth* to reach Cinema 21, the mainstream movie theatre network epitomized entrenched structures of domination by Jakarta related to national (New Order) and transnational (Hollywood) identities. These structures were set against alternative independent networks, which connoted local resistance. The juxtaposition of local against national and transnational identities is exemplified in the contrast between *Jelangkung* and *Beth*. *Jelangkung* stands for perceptions of power, commerce, elites, and a combination of transnational and national culture and identities. These features are pitched against *Beth*, which represents the discourses on

---

28 For details about an increase in distribution of domestic films in the VCD format in the last years of New Order rule, see JB Kristanto 2005:xiii-xiv.

a lack of power, idealism, and common people, which supposedly corresponds with local culture and identities.

The distribution and consumption of film in VCD format undermined the aforementioned connotations of mainstream, 'sidestream', and underground film mediation practices and identities. Virtually everyone – elites and common people, both in Jakarta and in rural areas – watched pirated films. The specific conditions and socio-political implications of pirated VCDs challenged the hegemony and rules of dominant national and transnational media networks. The cursive practices of film mediation evaded censorship and circumvented the lack of choice in films which were available through national mainstream channels. They moreover resisted the West's global economic domination and power by subverting legal sales and copyrights. However, the VCD circuit as an alternative site for film distribution and consumption did not weaken the position and influence of Indonesian elites. As before they had corrupted the networks of layar tancep now, elites appropriated the circulation of VCDs to profit from piracy through the production, distribution, and sales of illegal films, or by having their share in 'security' levies. *Beth* and *film independen, Jelangkung* and Cinema 21, as well as post-Soeharto film festivals and (pirated) VCDs illustrate how alternative film cultures and the powers that be opposed and also used each other in the post-Soeharto mediascape.

PART 2

Film discourse practices

3

Histories, heroes, and monumental frameworks

FILM HISTORY: NEW ORDER PATRONAGE OF FILM PERJUANGAN
AND FILM PEMBANGUNAN

Historiography is as much about contemporaneous imaginations of society as it is about the past. In this section I discuss representations of Indonesian film history of the New Order and the film genres which represented its ideologies and discourses about the past. Historians and scholars in literary criticism have reflected on the structures of representation and interpretation in historical discourses. Historian Hayden White (1999) in his article '*Literary theory and historical writing*' considered the way in which the techniques of historiography and literature overlap each other. White argues that historical discourse is by definition an interpretation of past events by means of narration. In the process of narration facts are only part of what constitutes the understanding of a historical event. The way in which the facts are cast in communicating or explaining an event also affects the meaning of facts. Or, in the words of literary theory scholar Linda Hutcheon (1988:89): 'the meaning and shape are not *in the events*, but *in the systems* which make those past "events" into present historical "facts"'. I have chosen to focus on two specific time-bound genres, which typified New Order rule and historiography: *film perjuangan* (struggle [for Independence] film), which was actually created under the Old Order of President Soekarno, and *film pembangunan* (development films).

Film-maker, writer, and academic Trinh Minh-ha (1993:190) has argued that the colour red symbolizes different things in different cultures (for instance: joy, anger, warmth, or impurity): 'To say red, to show red, is already to open up vistas of disagreement. Not only because red conveys different meanings in different contexts, but also because red comes in many hues, saturations and brightnesses, and no two reds are alike'. Picking up on this theme, I study the context of such dominant modes of engagement as the use of heroes and authority figures in *perjuangan* and *pembangunan* films. In addition, I analyse the creation of particular connotations of these aspects both in national and transnational political discourses.

The first *film perjuangan*, fictional films with plots revolving around the struggle to gain Indonesian Independence from Dutch colonial rule, were produced around 1954. The majority of these films recounted stories of Indonesian heroes fighting against the Dutch colonizers throughout the whole of the colonial period. Between 1958 and 1965 in particular, films extolling the struggle for Independence were produced in large numbers. This production ran parallel to and supported Soekarno's national political rhetoric. In 1958 his call for a 'Return to the Rails of the Revolution', a slogan that involved the assertion that the 'right to wield governmental power [...] lay with those who led the Revolution', and the consequent availability of funding for films about the struggle for Independence strongly stimulated their production (Feith 1962:554, as quoted in Sen 1994:36).

Quite apart from the president's rhetoric, the broader political setting also exerted an enormous influence on film production and other aspects of the world of cinema. In the early 1960s, Indonesian cinema was caught up in the national polemics comprehensively dividing Indonesia starkly into 'left' and 'right'. The thought behind this division can be traced to Soekarno's increasingly radical national politics. In 1957, relying on the support of the army, he overthrew the multiparty democracy that had been established in Indonesia after 1949, replacing it with what he called 'Guided Democracy'.[1] In the following years, the government grew more authoritarian, more nationalistic, and more anti-Western. In a very intricate juggling act Soekarno tried to balance power between the Indonesian army, which had made enormous political and economic gains in the early years of Guided Democracy, and the Partai Komunis Indonesia (PKI, Indonesian Communist Party), which could be counted on to provide a considerable portion of Soekarno's mass support base. By 1959, PKI was 'the most energetic and militant supporter' of Soekarno's radical nationalist politics, which championed anti-imperialism and anti-feudalism' (Mortimer 1974:79, as quoted in Sen 1994:28).

The nation was polarized into left and right. The left was connected to the Communist Party, which displayed a growing tendency to align itself with the president. The right was associated with a number of army, liberal, and Islamic parties, which were

1   For a discussion on Soekarno's rule, see Legge 1972.

enjoying growing support from the governments of Western capitalist nations, particularly the United States and Great Britain. Mirroring the politics of the time, film-makers were also divided into left and right. Leftist film-makers and members of cultural organizations affiliated with PKI especially tended to be actively engaged in linking film to national and nationalist politics. They saw their role as trying to articulate a cultural critique and model for a film culture of opposition to Hollywood cinema. Leftist film organizations and film-makers also vociferously supported the periodic bans that were imposed on films from Hollywood and Britain, as part of Soekarno's policies of Confrontation against what he perceived as the encroachment of Anglo-American power in Asia.[2]

Krishna Sen has shown that in this setting, films about the revolution made by film-makers on either side of the divide articulated differences in constructing post-Independence imaginations of Indonesian society. She points out that the two most prominent film-makers of the time, Usmar Ismail and Bachtiar Siagian, produced different narratives about the revolution. In historical films set in the context of the revolutionary war, Usmar Ismail, who received his film education in the United States and could be associated with the right, focused on the private psychological world of his characters, who were without exception heroic fighters. In each of his films Ismail used a standard pattern in which the 'hero-villain' represented a 'good- evil' juxtaposition of the *pejuang* (revolutionary) versus the *penjajah* (the colonial rulers) (Sen 1994:45-6). Alternatively, leftist film-maker Bachtiar Siagian chose to explore the historical and social situation of his characters. His stories deviated from the common nationalist narrative formula in not representing 'us', the Indonesian nation, against 'them', the Dutch, but in focusing on a social revolution in which the struggle against foreigners included an attempt to identify and challenge the structure of repression within Indonesian society itself (Sen 1994:45).

President Soeharto and his New Order regime came to power after the coup of 30 September 1965. During that night six senior generals and, by mistake, one lower-ranking officer were killed. The New Order blamed PKI for staging the coup and with the coming to power of this regime, leftist film texts were erased. In the aftermath of the coup, films produced by leftist film-makers were banned or destroyed, and many alleged communist film-makers were killed or imprisoned. Simultaneously a total reversal of anti-imperialistic film policy was set in motion, and the ban on films from Hollywood

2   Sen 2003:149-50. See Sen 1994:29-35 for more details on these organizations and protests against American films and Soekarno's anti-imperialistic film policy.

and Britain was lifted. In New Order national film history, nationalist cinema and the *film perjuangan* films, which contained stereotypical juxtapositions, were assiduously cultivated. Usmar Ismail was transformed into a *tokoh* (prominent figure) in Indonesian cinema, and the films about the revolution that he had produced were held up as examples of what the basis of national cinema should be. Other kinds of film texts, such as those of Bachtiar Siagian and other 'leftist' film-makers, were consigned to oblivion.

Under the New Order, Usmar Ismail and his films about the revolution came to represent the basis of national cinema in Indonesian film history.[3] After 1965 he was hailed as the father of Indonesian cinema. Furthermore, the day on which the shooting of his film *Darah dan doa* (released as *The long march* in English) commenced, 30 March 1950, was marked as Hari Film Nasional (Day of National Film).[4] Usmar Ismail was appointed the father of Indonesian cinema for two reasons: on account of the subject matter of his films and because of his anti-leftist pro-Western position in the politics of the film industry in the 1960s. Usmar's political stance was particularly apparent in an article he wrote in 1970, called 'The dark era of national film history'. In this article, he placed the forces led by the Lembaga Kebudayaan Rakyat (LEKRA, Institute of People's Culture, the key cultural mass organization affiliated to PKI) and PKI in opposition to the forces of democracy in the film world.[5] Sen (1994:35) mentions that the spirit and words of the title of that article have since been reproduced in almost every account of Indonesian film history under the New Order.

Under this regime the revolution films produced by Usmar Ismail received many plaudits, and there were many imitators creating the same type of *film perjuangan*. With a few exceptions, the New Order *perjuangan* films either consisted of narratives about heroes of (New Order) Indonesian history, or were based on folk stories about such fictitious heroes as Si Pitung and Jaka Sembung. Films of the latter type tended to feature stereotypical images of aggressive, bearded, red-headed, swearing Dutchmen. A phrase very often used by colonial rulers in these films was '*Gotvedomseg*' (Dutch for 'Goddamnit', pronounced in an Indonesian way). As

---

3 For more about characteristic traits and narratives of Usmar Ismail's films, see Sen 1994:21-2, 38-41.
4 There were some dissenting voices, most notably that of R.M Soetarto, who was representing the Indonesian government when the Japanese studio Nippon Eiga Sha was handed over to the Republic of Indonesia on 6 October 1945. This was the day that he wished to see commemorated.
5 Ismail 1983. The article, entitled 'Sejarah hitam perfilman nasional' in Indonesian, was published on 6 October 1970 in the newspaper *Sinar Harapan* under the pseudonym S.M. Ameh.

the background to the films about the fictitious heroes was also the struggle for Independence, many schoolchildren and Indonesians in general accepted these fictional tales as real historical accounts (Eddy 1993). The basic ingredient of all *perjuangan* films, whether those which survived the coup of 1965 or those produced under New Order rule, was that their themes revolved around heroes and heroism, as were those in the films by Usmar Ismail.

Whereas the foundation of Indonesian film history was represented by the production of *film perjuangan*, the New Order was represented by the genre of *film pembangunan* (development films). Films in this genre epitomized the political strategy and vision of the New Order government, which was based on the encouragement of economic development and modernization. Particularly during Ali Murtopo's term of office as Minister of Information (1978-1983), the Dewan Film Nasional (DFN, National Film Council) stimulated the idea that films should portray 'the struggle of scientists, technocrats, and others to improve the prestige of the nation' (Sen 1994:120). Once again in the New Order *pembangunan* films the focal characters were heroes; but now the protagonists were heroes of development who came to the village to teach the local, traditional people how to become modern, to trust the national government, and to distrust the villain, usually represented by local, traditional, spiritual leaders or shamans (Sen 1994:120-2). These propagandist *pembangunan* films were generally screened by mobile cinemas travelling from one village to another.

Both in their content and in the practice of their distribution, films in this genre ran parallel with the course adopted in the promotion of films and development policies of the United States Information Agency (USIA) in the early 1950s. In 1953 the agency was assigned the task of producing and distributing a massive number of political and 'pedagogical' films to so-called Third World countries. Set in the rivalry of the Cold War between the United States and the Soviet Union, the distribution of these films was part of the official development policy of the US government. Linked to the Point 4 Development Programme launched by President Truman in 1949, this policy was implemented to 'win the hearts and minds of the non-Communist world' (Naficy 2003:192). In August 1953, Truman initiated USIA policy contrived to

> [t]ell people throughout the world the truth about official aims and acts of the US, to expose and counter hostile efforts to distort those aims and acts to present a broad and accurate *picture* of the life and culture of American people (Naficy 1984:190).

As a consequence, specific countries in the Third World, primarily those thought to be susceptible to communist ideology, were subjected to an enhanced marketing campaign, which included the distribution of American films and documentaries (Naficy 2003:192). Iranian film-maker Hamid Naficy wrote that in Iran this meant that American-made films were shown to schoolchildren and rural populations using mobile film vans, as well as being presented to the general public in commercial cinemas.

The USIA films that Naficy had to watch and review when he was a schoolboy show a remarkable resemblance to New Order development films. Naficy (2003:193) states that USIA films used a certain formula: 'The world of the village is shown to be disturbed by a disease, such as tuberculosis or dysentery, but soon stability and calm is restored thanks to an external agent.' Naficy (2003:193) continues: 'The diegesis of these films was peopled with a central character (usually a young boy such as Said who suffers from tuberculosis), and a central authority figure (such as Doctor Khoshqadam) who treats him.' Both the restoration of order and the central role of an (external) authority figure are identical to the New Order development films. In this context Sen (1994:121) has remarked that 'In serious films dealing with social issues [...] the solution to rural anarchy comes from outsiders who are professionals.' Under the New Order, the restoration of order was a fundamental part of development and other films. As Sen argues, almost every film produced during the New Order followed the same pattern. It depicted a situation in which order was overturned, requiring the combat of disorder, followed by a restoration of order at the end of the film (Sen 1994:159; Sen and Hill 2000:146). In short, these films were cast in the same mold as the USIA films. In films such as *Desa di kaki bukit* (Village at the foot of the hill, Asrul Sani, 1972), *Dr. Siti Pertiwi kembali ke desa* (Dr Siti Pertiwi returns to the village, Ami Prijono, 1979), and *Joe turun ke desa* (Joe comes back to the village, Chaerul Umam, 1989) such external authority figures as doctors and engineers safeguard village life from harm.[6]

Parallel to the political discourse and stance of the United States' government in the promotion of USIA policy films in the early 1950s, the modes of engagement of *film pembangunan* of the post-1965 New Order government can be linked to the then political discourses and policies which were dominated by anti-commu-

---

6 For a detailed description of *Dr. Siti Pertiwi kembali ke desa*, a New Order propaganda film promoting the government's rural health scheme, its education programme by sending out urban volunteer workers as set out in the Second Five Year plan, and the transmigration programme, see Sen 1994:121-4.

3 Histories, heroes, and monumental frameworks

nism and pro-development ideologies. It is very likely that USIA policy was also implemented in Indonesia in the 1950s. Presumably the production and distribution of *gelora pembangunan* films, those films, mostly documentaries and newsreels, about successes in development screened in cinemas and shown in villages by mobile cinema units under the auspices of the Perusahaan Film Negara (PFN, State Film Corporation), were stimulated by USIA policy. The financial aid and assistance granted by America in the 1950s to help establish the Indonesian film industry was conceivably also part of USIA strategies. Krishna Sen mentions that under the Technical Cooperation Administration (TCA) programme, in 1950 the PFN received US$ 500,000 from the American government for new film equipment. In addition, the US government paid for ten experts to be stationed in Indonesia for six years to oversee the implementation of the scheme. Moreover, a number of Indonesians working in cinema were sent to the US to train in various aspects of film-making under the Colombo Plan and TCA (Sen 1994:25).

Besides Usmar Ismail, such other film professionals as Asrul Sani (poet, intellectual and film director), Jayakusuma (academic and expert on traditional theatre), Nya Abbas Acup and Wahyu Sihombing (both film directors), and Soemardjono (highly respected senior film editor), who had all received their education in American academic and professional institutions too and were also committed to anti-leftist pro-Western film politics, held some of the key positions in film schools and professional cinematic bodies after 1965 (Sen 1994:38). However, I was not able to find any data that explicitly mention USIA involvement in supporting the Indonesian film industry, the training of film-makers, or the production and distribution of propaganda development films. Still, if the same kind of film texts were produced by the USIA, inspired by the same kind of political discourses and policies, it would seem fair to draw the conclusion that *film pembangunan* must have been produced for similar reasons.

Naficy (2003:193) argues that the US policy of technological transfer and development aid was based on the perception of 'underdevelopment' as a threat to the homogenization of the world, in order to create global markets founded on Western consumerist ideology. Naficy described how the majority of the chief authorities in the USIA films dispensing well-being and prosperity were Point 4 development agents and physicians. He argues that '[these] figures invoked and legitimized by proxy the power, knowledge, competence, authority, and, indeed, the right of both the Iranian government (by whom they were employed) and the entire Western economic and industrial apparatus (which trained and sponsored them) to solve indigenous local problems' (Naficy 2003:194). The heroes of *film perjuangan*, and particularly the authority figures in *film pembangunan* of the New Order, were used in the same way and endorsed the same ideology. They legitimized and supported New Order rule and its development policies, driven by the desire to become part of the modern globalized (capitalist) consumerist world.

FILM AND HISTORIOGRAPHY: PROMOTION AND REPRESENTATIONS
OF NEW ORDER HISTORY

As well as promoting its development policy through film, the regime used propaganda films to present its version of national history. Both the production and distribution of films which featured propaganda messages had been part of the mediascape ever since the medium of film entered Indonesia. First under Dutch colonial rule (1900-1942) and later under the Japanese occupation (1942-1945), various propaganda films were produced for the edification of national and transnational audiences. After Indonesian Independence in the 1950s, the PFN began producing short propaganda films. These films were generally designated *film gelora pembangunan* ('zeal for development' films), and were intended to arouse enthusiasm for modernization among the Indonesian rural masses.[7] These films, and later under the New Order other films produced by different government institutions, tended to be crammed with messages about the benefits of development. They also included instructional films showing how the development policies of the different government departments should be implemented (Prakosa 1997:185).

Gelora pembangunan films and instructional films that encouraged development were shown either at mobile cinema screenings or in cinemas before the feature film was screened. In the 1980s, the films also began to be broadcast on the state television channel TVRI. Most of these films were labelled documentaries. As

---

7 Prakosa 1997:184. I think the production and distribution of these *gelora pembangunan* films in the 1950s was instigated by USIA policy. Writing about USIA films in Iran, Naficy says that these encompassed films from the United States dubbed in Persian/Farsi, as well as newsreels created specifically for the Iranian market. These newsreels dealt with the US Point 4 Programme, military and development programmes, activities of the royal family, earthquakes, a variety of human interest stories from the US, as well as programmes about improving primitive health, nutrition, and agricultural methods (Naficy 2003:192).

they overtly promoted government doctrines, the genre of documentaries was equated with propaganda (Prakosa 1997:190, 198). The films were all much of a muchness. Nearly all documentaries opened with the image of an aeroplane, followed by a map that set out the compass bearings, the plane landing in some remote area, and the image of native people doing their local dance to welcome the plane and the visitors it had brought.[8] The aim of the documentary was to depict the success of a particular development project, or the exoticism of the preferably remote area, or a combination of both. All was accompanied by a voice-over, using a particular documentary pitch, with some 'cheery' music typically associated with this type of film playing in the background. Gotot Prakosa claims few viewers were charmed by the New Order documentaries. They were simply too predictable and therefore boring. Consequently, as this unpalatable fact became apparent, a more sophisticated approach was embarked on and propaganda messages were wrapped up in drama fiction narratives. In 1983 the majority of development instruction and propaganda films used drama to get their messages across (Prakosa 1997:194).

Around the same time at which drama documentaries (docudrama) or fiction films were being used to spread New Order propaganda, there was a heightened interest in producing films about Indonesian history. In 1978 Brigadier General Dwipayana, the chief presidential image-builder, was installed as head of the Pusat Produksi Film Negara (PPFN, Centre for State Film Production, the former PFN). After 1965, PPFN had produced only a limited number of newsreels and documentaries. It had been reduced to operating mainly as a film-processing studio. Resurrected under Dwipayana's supervision, the state-run production company was given new tasks and resources (Sen 1994:66). Obsessed by ideas about the need to educate the young in their national history because of an imminent shift of generations, Dwipayana was committed to the production of big-budget feature films about New Order history and the heroic role of the head of state. In 1979 the production of films that represented key narratives of New Order history commenced.

Krishna Sen and David Hill (2000:11) have noted that 'Explicitly in film and television the New Order defined the media as vehicles for the creation of a 'national culture' that would allow uncontested implementation of its development policies and more generally its authoritarian rule'. Next to this creation of a 'national culture', film was also an instrument to portray and strengthen the

---

8 Garin Nugroho, personal communication December 2003 in Yogyakarta.

'national fiction' (Anderson 1983) of the regime. The New Order based its legitimacy to rule on certain key narratives rooted in a constructed past. These key narratives developed into a 'national fiction' that shaped the depiction and imaginations of the nation. The most insistent of these narratives were based on three historical events. Under the New Order, these events were referred to as though they were film titles themselves: the Serangan Umum ('General Attack'; the six-hour penetration of Yogyakarta by the Indonesian forces on 1 March 1949 led by Soeharto); the Peristiwa G30S/ PKI ('The Incident of the 30 September Movement/Indonesian Communist Party'); and Supersemar, the acronym for Surat Perintah Sebelas Maret (11 March Instruction), which placed the mandate to rule Indonesia firmly in Soeharto's hands in 1966.[9]

A film was made featuring each of these three 'highlights' of history. These were intended to represent, pass on, and sanction the New Order version of the said historical events. The General Attack was actually represented twice. The first film about this event was produced in 1979. *Janur kuning* (Yellow coconut frond, Alam Surawijaya) focuses on Soeharto as the historical and narrative hero. The second film was produced in 1982. *Serangan fajar* (The dawn attack, Arifin C. Noer) is also about the General Attack, but not only about Soeharto. The film has three interlinked stories –'the aristocratic family, 'the poor family', and the 'war of Independence' – and depicts Soeharto in a more symbolic role.[10] Both films were big-budget productions. The first was funded by revenues from the president himself and, even though this was not acknowledged officially, from the state oil company Pertamina. The second film was produced by PPFN (Sen 1994:90, 97), which also produced the film *Djakarta 1966* (Arifin C. Noer, 1982), about the signing of the instruction of 11 March 1966. *Djakarta 1966* concentrated on the chronological structure of this event (Kristanto 2005:227). However, soon after its premiere the film was taken out of circulation and during the New Order it was archived to be irretrievable in the Pusat Perfilman Haji Usmar Ismail (PPHUI, Haji Usmar Ismail Film Centre) in Jakarta. Presumably the reasons for its vanishing act were some very positive reviews of the film praising the representation of President Soekarno, its storyline focusing on the lives of two fictitious students and not on particular *tokoh*, and the nuanced depiction of good and bad (Arifin 1989; Anirun 1989).

---

9   Birgit Meyer drew my attention to the fact that references to historical events in Indonesia were presented as if they were the titles of films.
10 For a detailed description of the films, see Sen 1994:90, 97.

The most important historical narrative and film of the New Order regime was about the coup of 1965. The film *Penumpasan pengkhianatan G30S/PKI* (Eradication of the treason of the 30 September Movement/Indonesian Communist Party, Arifin C Noer, 1982), 271 minutes long, is a docudrama that followed the exact details of the official New Order history of the events surrounding the coup (Kristanto 2005:231). The account of the 1965 coup was extremely relevant to the way in which the country was ruled under Soeharto. In her book *History in uniform*, which discusses the central role of the Indonesian military in the production of official history, Katharine McGregor (2007:109) has argued that 'The official version of the coup attempt was used to define Indonesian core values, including a commitment to religion and morality'. The New Order version stated that PKI and PKI alone was the mastermind behind the coup and was therefore totally culpable. New Order official history, as it was printed in history books and taught in schools, suggested that after the Madiun Affair in 1948, in which PKI rebelled against the central government, the Communist Party had insidiously built up its strength. Over the years, the party infiltrated and indoctrinated leftist and communist members of the military forces and directed the latter to rebel against the legitimate authority.[11] Plans were made to oust the government of President Soekarno and install PKI in power. On the night of 30 September 1965 a group of young army officers under the leadership of Colonel Untung, aided and abetted by members of PKI, abducted six senior generals and one lower-ranking officer, and brutally slaughtered them. Chaos followed, but order was restored when troops under the control of Major General Soeharto captured Untung and crushed the communist leadership (Mackie and MacIntyre 1994:10).

The urgent need for the restoration of 'peace and order' in the wake of events of 1965-1966 was the imperative factor cited to validate the repressive rule of the Soeharto regime. Passed over in silence in New Order history, but providing the very basis of its rule, was the purging and subsequent mass slaughter of presumed communists and leftist-orientated individuals that was unleashed by the coup of 1965. The post-G30S terror campaign of 1965-1966 is estimated to have led to the massacre of between 500,000 and one million people. Another half a million people were imprisoned without trial, many for more than a decade. The New Order diligently fuelled the fear of a possible recurrence of the chaos that had proved so destructive in the aftermath of the coup. PKI was

---

11 Sulistiyo 1997:55-6. There were at least five versions of who was behind the coup. For more details, see Sulistiyo 1997:55-69.

accused of being a seething source of evil, opposed to the state ideology Pancasila, and the party was subsequently demonized in the mass media.[12] Accusations of being a communist had repercussions on whole families, a contagion passing on from one generation to the next. To the very end of Soeharto's rule, Indonesian people were repeatedly warned about the persistent 'latent danger of communism'. When forces opposed the New Order government they were invariably accused of espousing communist ideologies. The fear of a recurrence of the events of 1965-1966 and of the harsh repercussions which befell anyone accused of being a communist, was a powerful tool wielded to achieve the precious order so desired by the New Order.[13]

The film *Penumpasan pengkhianatan G30S PKI* was produced by PPFN. Its production commenced in 1982 and it was finished two years later. The film, with the revealing initial title *Sejarah Orde Baru* (SOB, History of the New Order), was based on the work of the military historian Nugroho Notosusanto. In 1981, when plans were made for the production of the film, Dwipayana, the head of PPFN, believed such a film could only be made under close government supervision (Sen 1994:82). *G30S/PKI* was produced to present the 'historical facts' behind the coup. In a speech that President Soeharto delivered to the parliament of the Fourth Development government in 1984 before the compulsory screening of the film, he stated that the purpose behind the making of *G30S/PKI* was to inform the people, particularly the younger generation, about the dark side of Indonesian history, urging them to exercise vigilance so as to ensure that such an incident would never happen again (Atmowiloto 1986:6). Dwipayana supported the president's standpoint and argued that now that the older echelon of army officers and bureaucrats had been replaced by a younger generation, it was essential that those who were infants at the time of the coup in 1965 be informed of the 'facts' about 'the viciousness of PKI'. He believed that by watching the film they would not side with and be seduced by communist ideologies (Atmowiloto 1986:5).

---

12 The Pancasila refers to the five-principle Indonesian state ideology implemented after Indonesian independence. The five principles are: 1. Belief in the One Almighty God (*Ketuhanan Maha Esa*), 2. Just and Civilized Humanity (*Kemanusiaan yang adil dan beradab*), 3. The Unity of Indonesia (*Persatuan Indonesia*), 4. Democracy guided by the consensus of deliberations amongst representatives (*Kerakyatan yang dipimpin oleh hikmat kebijaksanaan dalam permusyawaratan/perwakilan*), 5. Social justice for all Indonesian people (*Keadilan social bagi seluruh rakyat Indonesia*).
13 For more on New Order historiography and the implication of the military in its construction of the past, see McGregor 2007.

Dwipayana was not alone in his idea. Within a few months of the film's release, many government officials and bureaucrats began the task of organizing mandatory screenings for members of the Angkatan Bersenjata Republik Indonesia (ABRI, Armed Forces of the Republic of Indonesia), government officials and bureaucrats, and schoolchildren. The New Order government never actually initiated these first screenings formally. However, it was not very long before the film was being used officially as a vehicle to transmit the New Order's representation of the past. In 1984, G30S/PKI was made part of a compulsory screening programme in schools and government departments on 30 September. Moreover, it was also made part of the curriculum of the Pendidikan Sejarah Perjuangan Bangsa (PSPB, Education in the History of the Struggle of the Nation) for history classes in schools. In this guise it was screened in 'P4 Pancasila' classes, state ideology indoctrination courses which were also obligatory for university students and civil servants.[14] To date, the film is the single most screened, and presumably most-watched of all Indonesian films (Kristanto 2005:231; Sen and Hill 2000:148). A crucial aspect of the distribution and exhibition of *G30S/PKI* was the government's ceaseless propaganda that the film depicted historical facts, and showed the one and only true version of the events surrounding the 1965 coup.

Under New Order rule, no other films dealing directly with the 1965 coup were produced. As the film *G30S/PKI* was already there to represent the historical facts of the coup, all other films, which might have presented other versions of the subject, were precluded. There were only three other films that were set in the context of the struggle against communism. The first of these, *Operasi X* (Operation X), was produced in 1968 by the 'devoutly Islamic and anti-communist' film-maker Misbach Yusa Biran (Kristanto 2005:73; Sen 1994:81). The second, *Penumpasan sisa-sisa PKI Blitar Selatan (Operasi Trisula)* (Extermination of the remnants of PKI of South Blitar (Operation Trisula), BZ Kadaryono), was produced by PPFN in 1986. It dealt with the capture of communists in East Java in 1965-1966 and was presented in the form of a docudrama. As the plot of the film was so startlingly black and white, completely devoid of any nuances, it was perceived as being pure, unadulterated propaganda.[15] The

---

14 From 1980 under the New Order students and civil servants had been compelled to follow a mandatory state-sponsored indoctrination course in the state ideology Pancasila. These sessions were known as P4, short for Pedoman Penghayatan dan Pengamalan Pancasila (Directives for Instilling and Implementing Pancasila).
15 Kristanto 2005:290. The closing scene of the film addresses the idea of propaganda for development so blatantly that it borders on the farcical. By employing the same 'cheery' music score that was generally used in propaganda documentaries and the inescapable voice-over, this scene rips the film out of its historical context and places it in the rhetoric of the New Order present.

third film, produced for television with the title *Terjebak* (Trapped), directed by Dedi Setiadi, was produced in 1996. The soap's production was initiated by the 1996 Committee of the 'Day of Commemoration of the Sacred Pancasila', which also supplied the outline of the screenplay. Its theme was the riots that flared up after state troops attacked the office of the political opposition party Partai Demokrasi Indonesia (PDI, Indonesian Democratic Party) on 27 July 1996 and it unashamedly represented the members of this party as part of 'current communist activities'.[16]

Above I mentioned the important role of heroes and authority figures in *film perjuangan* and *film pembangunan*. Furthermore, I alluded to the emphasis on the restoration of order as an inevitable ingredient in all New Order films. New Order history films shared both these traits. Obviously, in films about the highlights of New Order history the hero was Soeharto. The head of state was represented as both the hero of the struggle for Independence and of the 1965 coup. Importantly, the films emphasized that after the coming to power of the New Order after 1965, order was restored in the nation. Another recurrent feature in New Order films dealing with history was the juxtaposition of sources of 'evil' versus 'good', whereby 'good' sources were associated with Islam. In many films set in the past, both those dealing with New Order historiography as well as fictional historical tales, the protagonists were pious men or women. To give an example, both *G30S/PKI* and *Operasi Trisula* contain a scene in which brutal men (communists) violently storm into a Mosque and the house of pious Muslims respectively. There they attack innocent people who are praying, and trample on the Quran. These antagonists are depicted clearly showing contempt for Islam.

In other scenes in both films there is no doubt that the good are religious. In *Operasi Trisula* all protagonists are adherents of Islam as indeed they are in the film *G30S/PKI*. However, the latter is more subtle in that it also highlights the Christian background of General Pandjaitan. In the scenes in the film that feature Pandjaitan and his family at home, Western classical music (which many Indonesians may assume to be 'Church music') is played. The camera also captures crosses on the wall. Likewise, in New Order films set in the past and based on fictional heroes, Islam was depicted as the nurturing source of the good which defeats all evil. For example, the films about Betawi (native Jakarta) folk legend Si Pitung and comic book character Jaka Sembung, which

---

16 'Sinetron "Terjebak" akan ditayangkan memperingati Hari Kesaktian Pancasila', *Harian Pelita*, 26-9-1996; Iwan 1996. For more about the production of *Terjebak*, see Wardhana 2001a:363-70.

were produced in the 1980s, refer to Islam as an aid to overcoming problems.[17]

The opposition between evil communism and good Islam in the historical films was part of the political discourses of the regime. Communists were accused of not believing in God, and generally speaking atheism was equated with communism. In *History in uniform* McGregor suggests that the manner in which the bodies of army generals and lieutenant were dumped in the well at Lubang Buaya (Crocodile Pit) was particularly offensive to followers of Islam. She moreover mentions that in the first published army version of the coup attempt it was noted that the coup had failed first and foremost because of 'the hands of God' (McGregor 2007:69-70). However, McGregor also points out that particularly in New Order historiography of the late 1970s and early 1980s, Islam, mainly in its radical form, was represented as a threat to the Pancasila and national stability. Only by the late 1980s concessions were made to support the promotion and practice of Islam as a religion, as opposed to political Islam. At that time President Soeharto had re-evaluated the Muslim vote after the implementation of the 'sole foundation' (*asas tunggal*) legislation – which required all organizations to make Pancasila their sole basis – and had made a move towards embracing Islam personally (Liddle 1996:614). Accordingly, in New Order representations in film, but also in museums and textbooks, followers of such 'extremist' and political Islamic groups as Darul Islam (House of Islam), who strove for an Islamic state after Independence, were presented as 'crazed bandits devoid of religious feelings' (Heider 1991:105) rather than as Muslims who used the religious teachings properly.[18]

The use of religion (mostly Islam) as the source of good in films was also part of a new code of ethics for film-making, which was launched by the Film Council in 1981. One of the instructions in this Ethical Code was that 'Dialogue, scenes, visualization, and conflicts between the protagonist and antagonist in the story have to focus on devotion to and the glorification of the One and Only God.' [19] New Order historical films represented the past with modes of engagement which emphasized heroism and contrasted the sources of evil with religion. Hence, it may come as no surprise

---

17 See for example the description of the films *Jaka Sembung sang penakluk* (Jaka Sembung the conqueror, Sisworo Gautama, 1981) and *Si Pitung beraksi kembali* (Pitung strikes again, Lie Soen Bok, 1981) in Kristanto 2005:217, 224.
18 McGregor 2007:187, 191-2. For more on the political background and representations of the threat of extreme Islam and Islamic terrorism, see McGregor 2007:176-93.
19 'Dialog, adegan, visualisasi, dan konflik-konflik antara protagonis dan antagonis dalam alur cerita seharusnya menuju ke arah ketakwaan dan pengagungan terhadap Tuhan YME.'

that, as mentioned in the first section, some believed that films about the fictional characters Pitung and Jaka Sembung, which applied similar narrative devices, represented real-life national heroes. In Part Three I shall examine ideas and representations of heroes, reality and religion in film in more detail.

'FILM IN THE FRAMEWORK OF': G30S/PKI AND HAPSAK

The ways in which audiences read films do not necessarily coincide with the intention of film-makers.[20] Presumably to safeguard and drive home one particular reading of (propaganda) films as much as possible, under the New Order these films were subjected to the practice of 'framing'. The films were screened in the 'framework' (*dalam rangka*) of a particular event or (special) occasion. In 1997 the writer and scholar Umar Kayam launched the notion 'art in the framework of' (*kesenian dalam rangka*). In his article Kayam pointed out the practices of neo-feudalism, which were rooted in such different fields of Indonesian society as politics, business, bureaucracy, education, and the arts. Referring to the latter, Kayam argued: 'In the field of the arts, these are constructed with reference to the supremacy of the authority in power and within a colossal presentation of 'art in the framework of' the ritualization of the nation'.[21] Kayam's phrase 'art in the framework of' can be easily transferred to the convention of screening 'films in the framework of': the practice of positioning and framing films in a specific context among other things to influence their assessment by their audience. New Order history films in particular lent themselves to screening in specific frameworks connected to national celebrations and commemorations of historical events. On national holidays, or on other particular occasions of collective remembrance, these films

---

20 See for example theories about the practice of 'reading against the grain', which emerged in the 1970s feminist, gay and lesbian readings of Hollywood cinema. In these readings the Hollywood films, which were made from a heterosexual perspective, were decoded from the perspective of different sexualities. Since then a great deal of research has been done on the discrepancies in ideas between those who produce films and those who consume them. For example, Umberto Eco put forward the theory that the audiences possess a power of selectivity to exposure, perception, and interpretation to reshape texts to fit the audience needs (Eco 1989). For other research on alternative or oppositional readings and freedom of audience perceptions of texts, see Ang 1991, 1996; Lang and Lang 1983; Jhally and Lewis 1992; Liebes and Katz 1990; Livingstone 1991; Real 1982. For theories about the encoding and decoding of texts, see Hall 1980; Morley 1980; Radway 1984.
21 Kayam 1997. 'Di bidang kesenian, kesenian dibina dalam acuab [sic] kejayaan sistem kekuasaan dan dalam pementasan kolosal "kesenian dalam rangka" ritualisasi negara.'

3 Histories, heroes, and monumental frameworks

featured on television, in cinemas, and at mobile cinema screenings. This linking of films to the commemorations or celebrations of historical events was one element in a strategy to furnish and empower the New Order's 'invention' of the past (Hobsbawm and Ranger 1983).

In this section, I analyse the 'frames' and practice of 'framing' films connected to the concept of 'film in the framework of'. My analysis covers the most extreme example of the practice of framing a film under the New Order: the role of the film *G30S/PKI* as part of the annual celebration – and media event – of the Hari Peringatan Kesaktian Pancasila (Day of Commemoration of the Sacred Pancasila, henceforth Hapsak). I use the term 'media event' as it was coined by Dayan and Katz (1992). However, in contrast to Dayan and Katz (1992:22), who discussed live events in democratic nations, the media events of the New Order had a totalitarian background. Therefore some traits in the media events as postulated by Dayan and Katz will be alien to Hapsak.[22]

The production of films to promote key narratives of the history of the New Order alone was not enough. To reach the goal of consolidating the New Order version of history, the films about the 1949 General Attack on Yogyakarta and the Incident of G30S/PKI were also assimilated into celebrations of collective remembrance. One exception was the film about the 11 March Instruction, which was denied the same treatment and status as the other films. As mentioned earlier, soon after production the film *Djakarta 1966* somehow disappeared. The first special screening of the film *Janur kuning* was held on 1 March 1980, in the context of the commemoration of the General Attack. Ten days later, on 11 March, the film was presented to the public as part of the celebration of the 11 March Instruction. Until the mid-1980s, every 1 March *Janur kuning* was shown on television to commemorate and pass on New Order images of national history. Thereafter the more successful film *Serangan fajar* replaced *Janur kuning*. Because of the more modest role of Soeharto, audiences perceived *Serangan fajar* to be less blatant propaganda. *Pengkhianatan G30S/PKI* was also connected to the commemoration of a historical event: the coup of 1965. Every year from the mid-1980s until 1997 the film was broadcast simul-

---

22   For example, the concept that media events and their narration are in *competition* [my italics] with the writing of history in defining the contents of collective memory should, in the case of Hapsak, be read as being *in conjunction* with the writing of (New Order) history enacted in the event (Dayan and Katz 1992:211). I use the term to connect the screening of the film *G30S/PKI* to a 'preplanned' mediatized event which highlights 'some central value or some aspect of collective memory', and 'is broadcast live on television' (Dayan and Katz 1992: ix, 5-9).

taneously on all national television channels on the evening of 30 September as part of the annual commemoration and celebration of Hapsak on 1 October.

G30S/PKI was screened for the first time on the Indonesian state television channel TVRI in the framework of Hapsak on 30 September 1985. After the advent of private television stations in 1993, all commercial broadcasters participated without exception. The simultaneous screenings became part of the ritual of Hapsak which formed a national holiday of the New Order. From 1967 onwards, every year early in the morning on 1 October a military ceremony was held at the Monumen Pancasila Sakti (Sacred Pancasila Monument). The ceremony was broadcast live on television, and rerun a couple of times during the day.[23] The Pancasila monument was built in Jakarta in 1973 near Lubang Buaya, the dry well in which the bodies of the murdered generals were found. A marble column was constructed around the well-head, and at some distance from the well stands the Pancasila monument. It consists of a huge stone shrine with a bronze relief representing the New Order version of events as they took place on the night of 30 September 1965. Embellishing the top of the shrine are statues of the murdered generals and officer in a defiant stance, with the national symbol of the mythical eagle-like bird Garuda bearing a plaque with the five symbols of Pancasila on its chest in the background. There is another plaque, which reads: 'We the generals perished to defend the honour of the sacred Pancasila.' Furthermore, an old wooden school building, the place where according to New Order history the abducted generals were tortured and mutilated by members of PKI, has been made into a museum with a diorama. On display are human-size puppets of the abducted generals, tied to chairs and 'bleeding' as they are tortured by male and female 'communists'. In the background an audiocassette plays sound fragments of the film *G30S/PKI.*

---

23   Until 2001 the Hapsak ceremony was broadcast live on television. Under the presidency of Abdurrahman Wahid (1999-2001), and particularly under the presidency of Megawati Soekarnoputri (2001-2004), the commemoration was downplayed. In 2000 the government changed the name Sacred Pancasila Day to Commemorative Day for the Betrayal of Pancasila (*Peringatan Hari Pengkhianatan (terhadap) Pancasila*). In that same year Megawati, who as vice-president served as inspector of the ceremony due to the president's absence, did not carry out the second part of the ceremony during which President Soeharto customarily visited the diorama, the preserved well and the Pancasila monument. Since then it was only inserted in small segments in the daily news programmes. When Megawati was president herself in 2002 and 2003, she did not attend the ceremony; nevertheless, it continued to be held. Since the installation of Susilo Bambang Yudoyono as president in 2004, the Hapsak ceremony has been restored. At least until October 2008, the president presided over the ceremony as usual.

Every 1 October the field around Lubang Buaya would be filled with representatives of the military and groups of schoolchildren, lined up in regimented fashion. At the back of the ranks of the military and schoolchildren, enormous placards bearing the images of the murdered generals would be erected. Under the trees near the old school building, an orchestra consisting of around 200 children, selected from both primary and high schools, would play the national anthem and other songs extolling bravery and urging remembrance. Among the guests invited to attend the ceremony would be the president, military officials, members of parliament, foreign diplomats, and relatives of the murdered generals. The broadcast of Hapsak invariably followed the same pattern. Before the ceremony commenced, either a studio discussion was held or such old archive material as newsreel footage was shown, while a voice-over recounted the New Order account of the events; sometimes there was a combination of both. Every time this account began by enumerating particular events leading up to the 1965 coup, before focusing on the coup itself and the heroic deeds of Major General Soeharto. It always ended with a warning about the ever-present latent danger of those who sympathized with communist ideologies. Thereupon the studio would switch over to Lubang Buaya to show the arrival of the president and vice-president and their wives.

Each year the composition of the ceremony consisted of two parts, beginning with a solemn service of observance and ending with a livelier commemorative component. The former commenced with the arrival of the president, who would advance to a podium where, once he had taken up his position, a colonel would ask for his permission to begin the service. After that, the national anthem would be played and the president, as master of ceremonies, would authorize the beginning of the observance by ordering the participants to bow their heads. Following a minute's silence the national anthem would be played again, after which another component of the service would begin. During this part of the ceremony, four documents – the text of the Pancasila, the first lines of the National Constitution of 1945, the Ikrar (pledge or charter, to honour and defend the Pancasila), and a prayer – were read by parliamentary ministers. The Ikrar document would be signed as proof that the ceremony had taken place that year. The documents would be handed over by high-school students, two boys and two girls, dressed in uniforms resembling those worn by the navy; they would march to the officials, hand over the documents, and then march back to their places in military fashion. The service would be closed by order of the president and concluded by the playing of the national anthem.

In the second part of Hapsak the president and vice-president and their wives, followed by foreign diplomats, would pay a visit to the well, the monument, and the old school building-cum-museum. This completed, the president would shake the hands of the wives and relatives of the murdered generals. Finally, at the end of the ceremony he would listen to the orchestra of school children. Often the president would shake the hand of the conductor and pat the soloist (a small boy either singing or playing violin) who had just performed the touching melody 'Gugur bunga di taman bakti' (Fallen flowers in the garden of devotion, composed by Ismail Marzuki) on the shoulder. As the president left Lubang Buaya the orchestra wcould play an upbeat song paying tribute to bravery. In this second part of the ceremony every year the television commentator could be heard to repeat the same 'mantras' as the president and his company were filmed walking from one site to another. These mantras began by mentioning various treacheries perpetrated by communists, starting with the rebellion against the central government in Madiun in 1948, up to the coup of 1965. Then he or she would sum up the content of the pledge, which stated that those who attended the ceremony (and watched the television programme) were aware of the coup perpetrated against the legitimate government attempted by PKI and its 30 September Movement, which had ushered in 'a national tragedy culminating in the vicious and inhumane death of the heroes of the Revolution'.[24] This national tragedy had been allowed to occur as the result of a lack of caution about the actions of PKI, which had deliberately deceived a part of the Indonesian people in its attempts to eradicate Pancasila and its denial of the oneness of the Indonesian nation. In conclusion, the commentator would warn that the Indonesian people should remain vigilant to the latent danger of communism. In the meantime, as a background to the voice of the commentator, the orchestra of schoolchildren could be heard playing national songs of remembrance and bravery.

Both the outline and gist of the media event Hapsak and the screening of the film *G30S/PKI* as part of the commemoration of the 1965 coup were components in a conscious effort to refurbish collective memories.[25] Dayan and Katz (1992:211-2) argued that

---

24 The phrases '*kejam dan keji*' (brutal and vicious) and '*di luar batas-batas peri kemanusiaan*' (beyond the bounds of human dignity) were repeatedly used when referring to communists.
25 For more on collective memory and monuments, see Lasswell 1979; Mosse 1980; Nora 1984.

3 Histories, heroes, and monumental frameworks

media events can be perceived as electronic monuments, and this label can also be applied to the film *G30S/PKI*. As an annual rite commemorating the 1965 coup it served to buttress the power bases of the New Order regime. The four elements forming the nucleus of the Hapsak media event were: the frequent screening of the same newsreel images before the Hapsak commemoration would begin; the standard use of specific nationalist songs; the repeated citation of certain 'mantras' and the commentator's seemingly endless reiteration that the account consisted of historical 'facts'; and the emphasis on the 'latent danger of communists'. The event was to ensure that history would be remembered in a particular way, thereby propagating and fertilizing New Order representations of Indonesian history. However, these elements were also responsive to contemporaneous political needs. In an article about the basis for and changing context of the Hapsak commemoration, McGregor points out the subtle changes of the meaning of the day during the course of the New Order. She shows how over time the day became an occasion on which such new enemies of the regime as extremist Islam and other possible political threats to the regime, labelled 'atheists', were defined in response to changing political circumstances.[26]

The film *G30S/PKI* as an electronic or audio-visual monument to the New Order was produced to create and bolster collective memories. Initially it was used to serve as a 'medium of memory' which transferred 'sets of images' of a social understanding of events, represented as memory (Watson 1994:8); later it was transformed into a monument. It can be accepted as a monument of the New Order not least because of the status it achieved and the position it assumed as part of official discourses and strategies advocating a certain version of history. This bestowed on it an enormously influential position in Indonesian collective memory. In 2001, senior journalist and founder of Tempo magazine Goenawan Mohamad quoted a survey that showed that more than 80 per cent of the respondents believed that the film presented a factual account of the event.[27] The film was made widely known

---

26 McGregor 2002. McGregor demonstrates that Hapsak initially served just as a means to reaffirm the army's claim to have led the nation in a righteous victory over communism. In the early 1980s, the meaning of the day expanded to include threats to Pancasila from Islam as well as communism. Over time, the commemoration became a means to redefine the label 'communist' and apply it to any opposition. Finally, in the 1990s, Hapsak acquired an increasingly religious nature. By then the day had become a celebration of opposition to atheism rather than an affirmation of Pancasila (McGregor 2002:66).
27 Mohamad 2001:131. '[K]ejadian-kejadian yang digambarkan dalam film tersebut adalah benar-benar terjadi'.

through the mechanisms of its distribution and exhibition as an essential part of Hapsak, as well as through the extensive compulsory screening programmes mentioned earlier. In contrast to the Pancasila monument, which was physically confined to Lubang Buaya, Hapsak and the film *G30S/PKI* were not bound to a place, but were mobile. Hapsak, and the screening of *G30S/PKI* on the eve of Hapsak, travelled to its audiences; if the television happened to be turned on, the event would enter the space of Indonesian households through its simultaneous broadcast on all national television channels.

But, in contradistinction to Hapsak, the film *G30S/PKI* was not restricted to television alone. Every 30 September it was and could be attended in Indonesian cinemas across the country, where the film was screened as part of the history curriculum, making it obligatory viewing for schoolchildren. *G30S/PKI* even travelled abroad, where it was screened at Indonesian embassies as part of the state-constructed P4 Pancasila training course for Indonesian students and bureaucrats.[28] The films *Janur kuning* and *Serangan fajar* can also be interpreted as mobile audio-visual cultural monuments of the New Order. Both films represented historical key narratives of the regime and were accorded a treatment comparable to the film *G30S/PKI*. They were screened on 1 March in the framework of the commemoration of the General Attack, or at other celebrations or occasions connected to Indonesian Independence. In the case of *Janur kuning* (1979) and *Serangan fajar* (1982), the audio-visual monuments were produced even before physical version of the historical incident was constructed: the monument dedicated to the General Attack, the Monumen Yogya Kembali ('Return of Yogyakarta' Monument), was built as late as 1985. However, because the films were never made compulsory as *G30S/PKI* was, they never achieved the monumentality accorded that film.

The linking of New Order films about history to events commemorating the past is an example of the use of film 'in the framework of'. In its connection to Hapsak the film *G30S/PKI* offers an extreme example of this practice. Besides the New Order history films, there were other films also screened in particular frameworks. These frameworks were not necessarily connected to national holidays or celebrations of the past or of the

---

28 Buana-R 1985; *Pengkhianatan* 1985; '"G30S" diedarkan diluar negeri', *Pos Film*, 20-10-1985.

3 Histories, heroes, and monumental frameworks

state, even though they were often used in this fashion.[29] In the case of the New Order history films, the rhetoric of framing was fashioned to provide a two- pronged thrust: to give a form and context for the way the films were intended to be read, and to make the watching of these films a rite of commemoration.

CONCLUSION

Certain genres emerge in certain times and reflect contemporaneous socio-political inclinations. This phenomenon can be found in the production of particular film genres and the traits they exhibit, the discourses about these genres and their meanings, and the position they are assigned in discourses and in national film history. In early discussions about the new genre of independent film in

---

29 To give a few examples of films that were made for certain events, or certain events of which the screening of films was an important part, between 1993 and 1997: In 1993 the films *Janur kuning*, *Detik-detik Proklamasi* (Seconds of the Proclamation [original title *Detik-detik Revolusi*, Seconds of the Revolution], 1959, Alam Surawidjaja]), *Lebak membara* (Blazing battle 1982, Imam Tantowi), *Operasi Trisula* and *Kereta api terakhir* (The last train, 1981, Mochtar Soemodimedjo) featured 'in the framework of' the Day of Heroes (Hari Pahlawan) on 10 November, and in 1994 on National Film Day (Hari Film Nasional) (*Jambore film* 1993). In 1994 the film *Saur sepuh (Satria Madangkara)* (What the ancestors say (knight of Madangkara) 1988, Imam Tantowi) was screened 'in the framework of' providing the public with information about transmigration, and to stress the importance of 'unity and integrity' ('Penyuluhan transmigrasi dengan film', *Berita Yudha*, 18-7-1994). Also in 1994, to counter the film *Death of a nation* by John Pilger, which is an account of human rights violations by the Indonesian state in East Timor, the Indonesian version presenting the 'true historical facts' about East Timor was produced (*Pemerintah akan buat film* 1994). It was planned to screen this 'counter-propaganda' film in July 1995 'in the framework' of the Day of the Integration of East Timor (Hari Integrasi Daerah TimTim), and again in August 'in the framework of' the Commemoration of 50 Years of Indonesian Independence (Peringatan 50 Tahun Indonesia Merdeka) (*Kalangan DPRD* 1995). Elsewhere during the commemoration of the golden jubilee of Indonesian Independence various films were screened, amongst them *Janur kuning*, *Serangan fajar*, *Soerabaia 45* (Surabaya 45, 1990, Imam Tantowi), *Perawan di sektor selatan* (Maiden in the south sector, 1971, Alam Surawidjaja), and *Enam jam di Yogya* (Six hours in Yogya, 1951, Usmar Ismail) ('Mendikbud Wardiman hadiri pemutaran film perjuangan untuk pelajar', *Jayakarta*, 18-8-1995). In 1996 a 'personal audio-visual monument' to 'Ibu Tien' (Mother Tien), the then recently deceased wife of President Soeharto, entered production with the title *Kasih ibu selamanya* (Mother's enduring love) (Handiman 1996; *Ibu Tien* 1996). Furthermore, in 1996 the television soap *Pedang keadilan* (Sword of justice) was produced and screened in the framework of the golden jubilee of the Indonesian police force. The soap featured six police officers and 'horrific killing scenes' in an effort to teach offenders against the law a lesson (*Enam anggota Polri* 1996). Finally, between 1996-1997 the film *Fatahillah* (1997, Imam Tantowi and Chaerul Umam), recounting the founding of Jakarta, was produced as part of a project of the Governor of Jakarta; the film was to be screened on 22 June 1997 in the framework of the 470th birthday of the capital ('Pemda DKI Jakarta gaet GPBSI memproduksi film Fatahillah', *Jayakarta*, 9-8-1996).

the autumn of 1998, confusion arose about how to understand this Reformasi genre. Because of its name, it was sometimes thought that the themes of *film independen* were drawn from the struggle for Indonesian independence, just as were the familiar *film perjuangan*. *Film perjuangan*, *film pembangunan*, and docudrama/propaganda documentaries were important film genres of the New Order. These genres reflected its rule and rhetoric, and were linked from the perspective of film history to New Order discursive practices. The genres acquired a meaning idiosyncratic to the way in which they were used during the Soeharto regime.

An analysis of the conventions in text production and consumption of New Order history and development films exposes the socio-political climate of the time. These genres contained parallel modes of engagement of the New Order version of the past and of its concomitant ideologies. History and development films invariably contained the same kind of characters (heroes, authority figures), and themes (restoration of order, 'good' Islam combatting its selected source of evil (often communism), and claims to represent factual reality). These features mirrored the dominant discourses on how to characterize society under New Order rule. I hasten to stress that the dominant narratives and generic conventions of heroes and authority figures, claims to factual reality, and the restoration of order are not restricted to either Indonesia as a nation or the New Order alone. On average, worldwide film texts feature heroes, the victory of good over evil, and a restoration of order. In performing this function, documentaries and films present truth claims in many different contexts. However, as Trinh Minh-ha (1993:195) has argued, the colour red and its symbols do not have an absolute and universal signification. The value it is attributed varies between one culture and another and also proliferates within the confines of each culture.

Likewise, the film genres and films that were representative of New Order historiography and its ideologies delineated the dominant socio-political discourses of the regime. In this account, an important element was found in the socio-political context of New Order rule and its resemblance to the political climate in Iran in the 1950s. Both countries adopted an anti-communist stance and exhibited virtually identical films promoted by USIA film policies.[30] The logical corollary is that the production of film texts and the

---

30 McGregor (2007:220) has pointed to similar anti-communist discourses in the politicized militaries of Brazil and Burma. Moreover, she argues that in such communist states as the People's Republic of China and the former USSR, overtly political educational content also upheld the deeds of heroes and strongly emphasized martial patriotic themes (McGregor 2007:37).

3 Histories, heroes, and monumental frameworks |

promotion of certain genres can be seen as part of a political discourse, outlook, and policy which involved, but simultaneously transcended, Indonesian boundaries. Another element addressing the context of New Order politics was the unrelenting promotion and advocacy of the head of state (mainly in the film *G30S/PKI*) as a hero and an authority figure, who restored order after the 1965 coup, protected Indonesia against communism, and was therefore entitled to rule the nation. Examining discourse practices at the intersection of text production and consumption, the account of the convention of screening films in the framework of a particular event or occasion also opened a window to New Order political affairs. The examples of New Order historical films, and particularly the connection of *G30S/PKI* to the media event Hapsak, leave no doubt about the way the films, and indeed the past, should be read and remembered.[31] To screen the films as part of rites of commemoration was to assign a uniform shade of red to historiography.

---

31 On dissident readings and the way in which *G30S/PKI* was interpreted by critical audiences during the New Order, see Sen and Hill 2000:148-50. For comments on *G30S/PKI* after about ten years of reform, see for example the online discussion at http://www.indowebster.web.id/archive/index.php?t-19475.html (accessed 19-12-2011).

4

Post-colonial histories, common people, and commercial frameworks

The New Order can be construed as a neo-imperialist or neo-colonialist regime (Anderson 1990; Sen 2003). Particularly in the period immediately after the resignation of President Soeharto, discussions began to emerge in the world of film which addressed concepts of post-colonialism in cinema. This chapter examines a variety of post-colonial discourses and discourse practices in film after the eclipse of the New Order. The guiding theme is Fairclough's premise (1995:52) that all ongoing changes in society and culture are expressed in the media's diverse and conflicting shifts in discursive practices. I analyse the way in which, after the stepping down of President Soeharto, new post-colonial discourses and imaginations of society were reflected in film discourse practices. I explore the emergence of alternative genres and try to pinpoint the continuations in particular modes of engagement, the dominant representations of topics which are part of the central discourses in a society, and the practice of framing films, which continued to survive during Reformasi. As argued by Fairclough (1995:65), the discursive practices of an unsettled society are on average variable and unstable, while the discursive practices of a conservative and established society are unitary and conventional. Using this argument, I will examine variations and continuities in representations of Indonesian history and society during the traumatic yet exciting times of Reform.

COUNTER-HISTORY: CHANGES AND CONTINUITIES IN POST-SOEHARTO
MODES OF ENGAGEMENT

In the euphoric atmosphere of Reform that prevailed after the resignation of President Soeharto, attempts were enthusiastically made in all kinds of fields to adapt to changes in the socio-political conditions of the Indonesian nation or to set them in motion. Some debates addressed the problem of New Order historiography and the need to 'set history straight' (*meluruskan sejarah*).¹ Hence dominant representations of New Order film history also came under fire. In addition to questioning the highlights in film history, several debates concentrated on New Order propaganda historical films. The contents and compulsory screening of the film *Penumpasan pengkhianatan G30S/PKI* in particular were targeted.

The excitement of Reform and the concomitant sudden freedom of expression generated new developments in discursive practices which inevitably involved the contents and mediation of films. Different film-makers, both professional and amateur, began to produce films in order to present new versions of history and society. In a short time, there was a rise in the production of documentaries. A large number of the new documentaries told alternative or counter-histories to those which unfolded under the New Order. Generally speaking, these documentaries tended to focus on the victims of Soeharto rule. Those who had suffered were given a platform to tell their stories about the atrocities committed under the New Order. Several non-governmental organizations, both foreign and domestic, aided in producing and funding these documentaries. The film *Kameng gampoeng nyang keunong geulawa* (Aryo Danusiri, 1999), for example, was supported by the Indonesian Institute for the Study of Human Rights and Advocacy Elsham, and his film *Penyair negeri Linge* (The poet of Linge homeland, 2000) by the Ford Foundation. The film *Perempuan di wilayah konflik* (Women in conflict zones, Gadis Arivia, 2002) was produced by the Yayasan Jurnal Perempuan (Women's Journal Foundation); *Lahir di Aceh* (Born in Aceh, Ariani Djalal, 2003) was produced by the Tifa Foundation and Offstream Production; *Pena pena patah* (Broken pens, Sarjev Faozan, 2002) was produced by the Coalition of NGO's on Human Rights in Aceh; and *Kado buat rakyat Indonesia* (A present for the Indonesian people, Daniel Indra Kusuma, 2003) was supported by the Centre for Democracy and Social Justice and the Indonesian Centre for Reform and Social Emancipation.

Besides documentaries, a few fiction films based on true stories of human rights violations were also produced. For example, the docu-drama *Puisi tak terkuburkan* (English title: *A Poet*, Garin

---

1   For more on the debates on the need to 'straighten history', see Schulte Nordholt 2004:11-2. Another comprehensive study on coming to grips with New Order historiography during reform is Zurbuchen 2005.

Nugroho, 1999) was about Ibrahim Kadir, a traditional poet from the village of Takengon in Aceh, who in 1965 was accused of being a communist activist. He was imprisoned for twenty-two days and witnessed a variety of cruel executions. *Marsinah* (Slamet Rahardjo, 2002) was about the murder of a woman factory worker by the authorities in East Java in May 1993. *Kutunggu di sudut Semanggi* (I'll be waiting at the corner of Semanggi, Lukmantoro, 2004) was based on the Semanggi tragedy of November 1998. Many counter-history film and documentary productions circulated at independent-film screenings and film festivals, both in Indonesia and abroad. Some even reached Indonesian cinemas, but hardly any of these films were ever screened on Indonesian television, enabling them to attract the same attention and reach enjoyed by the New Order history films in the past.

The new documentaries and their screening at film festivals and other venues gradually set in motion a shift in the meaning of the genre. From being a propaganda instrument under the New Order, documentary was transformed into a genre which, in the words of documentary film-maker Lexy Rambadeta, gave a 'voice to the voiceless'. Nevertheless, the notion that the documentary genre almost invariably contained propaganda lingered on for quite some time. The legacy of the New Order associated with this genre was apparent in the film-makers's choice to produce either a documentary or a fiction film after the collapse of the New Order regime. If their objective was to make a claim that the contents of the film represented facts based on reality, some film-makers would, in fact, prefer to make a fiction film rather than a documentary. To cite one example, in 2000 the Universitas Muhammadiyah Malang (UMM, Muhammadiyah University in Malang) wanted to produce a film which would give an account of the propagation of Islam in Indonesia. This film was to be based on authentic historical evidence obtained from sources collected by the Muhammadiyah. The principal of the university, Mahadjir Effendi, said they had decided to make a fiction film instead of a documentary 'to avoid the practices of manipulation, as had been done in the historical documentary G30S/PKI'. In his opinion a fiction film was not only easier to digest, it was also more 'objective'.[2]

Although there was a discernible rise in documentaries which countered New Order propaganda and historiography, particularly in the first years of Reform many new productions employed structures, styles, and formulas which did not deviate greatly from New Order propaganda and history films. This practice will be

---

2   'UMM buat film penyebaran Islam di Indonesia', *Media Indonesia*, 18-7-2000.

explored in the next section. Bill Nichols postulates that the use of certain styles and modes of production in documentaries defines concepts of historical representation. He argues that such modes of documentary production as 'expository', 'observational', 'interactive', and 'reflexive' function in the same fashion as genres, in that they are ways of characterizing films by their likeness to rather than their differences from one another. But instead of co-existing as different types of imaginary worlds (science fiction, westerns, melodrama), modes represent different concepts of historical representation. Nichols claims that different modes may co-exist at any moment in time and can be transposed across different periods and national cinemas. The creation of a new mode is the result of challenge and contestation elicited by a previous mode (Nichols 1991:22-3). As Nichols links modes of documentary production to different concepts of historical representation, this presupposes that the appearance of new modes also challenges previous models of historical representation. Nichols' argument about modes of production applies equally to modes of engagement. However, in early post-Soeharto documentaries specific New Order modes of engagement were repeated, even though the purpose of the films was to edit and re-edit collective memory. In the following section I will analyse this process, bearing in mind that the reproduction of New Order audio-visual styles, structures, and narratives in post-Soeharto documentary productions may also simply relate to the widespread practice of *jiplak-menjiplak* (the replication, imitation, or blatant copying) of film formulas.

The post-Soeharto documentary *Mass grave* (2001, Lexy Rambadeta) addresses an aspect of Indonesian history which was passed over in silence under New Order rule. The film is about the exhumation in Central Java in 2001 of a mass grave. The grave contained the remains of alleged PKI members who were massacred in the mountains of Wonosobo, sometime in 1965-1966. In its opening scenes, *Mass grave* instantly recalls the visualization of New Order documentaries and the film *Penumpasan pengkhianatan G30S/PKI*. The similarities are particularly striking, though, in the composition of the last fifteen minutes of the film. The closing scenes of *G30S/PKI* are devoted to the retrieval of the bodies of the slain generals from the dry well of Lubang Buaya. Soon after the start of the scene, the image of the tops of the trees clustered around the well are shown, shot from a low angle. Then from a top angle the camera zooms in on the well from which the decomposing bodies of the generals are taken out one by one. Thereupon, the camera moves back filming the bystanders. The position of the bystanders, among them the actor playing the role of Major General Soeharto,

4 Post-colonial histories, common people, and commercial frameworks

was a detailed reconstruction from the historical archive material of the event. On screen a text appears alerting the audience that the voice which they are about to hear is the authentic recorded live speech of Soeharto obtained from archive material. At the same time the speech begins to be broadcast in the background, the soundtrack of 'Gugur bunga di taman bakti' (which was composed during the presidency of Soekarno to pay respect to national heroes who had fallen in the struggle for Independence) begins to play. At that point, the original colour image of *G30S/PKI* is replaced by black-and-white archive material. In the minutes that follow the film continues by cross-cutting shots of the re-enacted drama, copying the archive material of the incident in detail, with real footage of the occasion in black and white.

The film ends by showing archive material of the state funeral of the generals and the authentic live speech delivered by General Nasution in 1965, in which he recalls the sacred tasks of the Armed Forces as defenders of freedom, the people, and the highest authorities of the nation. He asserts his belief that the slain generals are national heroes who paid the ultimate price and that the living members of the Armed Forces should continue to uphold these values. In both the dramatized version, which is filmed in colour, and in the historical black-and-white footage, some shots of photo and film cameras are included in order to emphasize that these cameras captured and recorded the event to which the viewers bear witness.[3] By comprehensive use of the cross-cutting of fictional film with historical audio and visual archive material in the last fifteen minutes of the documentary, *G30S/PKI* emphasized it was not merely a representation of the past, but a representation of the facts: 'the true story'.

The documentary *Mass grave* reproduced the structure and some of the visual aspects of Hapsak and the last fifteen minutes of *G30S/PKI*. However, the human remains exhumed could not have been more different: not those of the generals at Lubang Buaya, but those of the people killed in massacres in 1965 in Central Java. Just as in the film *G30S/PKI*, after its opening scene, which shows a map of the location, *Mass grave* begins with the depiction of the tops of the trees encircling the mass grave in Wonosobo. Then the camera zooms in on the exhumation of the skulls and bones of people who perished in the bloody aftermath of the 1965 coup. After this opening sequence, the documentary introduces black-and-white archive material. This time it is not the set-up of the scene itself, but the

---

3 I would like to thank Patricia Spyer and P.M. Laksono, who brought this use of cameras in the film to my attention.

insertion of old stock footage and newsreel images which remind the viewer of New Order documentaries. The same material was televised each year under the New Order before the Hapsak ceremony commenced to illustrate the story of the historical events which occurred in 1965. The visual structure and style of the opening scenes of *Mass grave* revived and repeated images which easily could have been part of the collective memories of Indonesians who lived through the New Order. I am thinking especially of the image of the retrieval of the decomposing bodies of the murdered generals from a dry well at the end of *G30S/PKI*. This image was now replaced by the dry bones of the victims from the mass grave in Wonosobo, brought to the surface one by one. Importantly, in *Mass grave* old stock footage and newsreel images, familiar to many, were used again, but this time provided with a new narration exposing the atrocities committed at the founding of the New Order.

The second example of a post-Soeharto documentary which reproduces particular emblems of the film *G30S/PKI* and the Hapsak ceremony is Tino Saroengallo's 1998 documentary *Student movement in Indonesia*. It depicts demonstrations and rallies and the ensuing violent clashes between student activists and the Indonesian army in Jakarta in 1998. The documentary recounts the incidents at the Trisakti University and at the Semanggi flyover in which students were shot dead by Indonesian military. In this documentary an important audio motif of *G30S/PKI* and the Hapsak ceremony, the song 'Gugur bunga di taman bakti', appears and is commented on. In *G30S/PKI*, 'Gugur bunga' is used as a theme song at the end of the film. In the last fifteen minutes the soundtrack of the song is heard as though from a great distance as the bodies of the generals are retrieved. The song can be heard more loudly in the background to the live speeches of Soeharto and Nasution. 'Gugur bunga' was a leitmotif during the Hapsak ceremony, in which it featured over and over again. Often the song was played exactly at the moment when the president either headed for the children's orchestra or when he was standing in front of it. The song also often featured in the background to the newsreel and stock footage broadcast before the Hapsak ceremony commenced. In *Student movement*, students sang the song to commemorate the Trisakti incident. In the documentary, a voice-over comments that the students and the army were singing the same songs of bravery and nationalism.

The reproduction of certain audio and visual structures or emblems from the film *G30S/PKI* and the Hapsak ceremony can be seen as quotations of important New Order electronic monuments which tell new histories. Ella Shohat and Robert Stam (1994:353) suggest that 'The same filmic images and sounds provoke distinct reverberations in different communities'. To paraphrase them, in post-Soeharto Indonesian communities, some filmic images and sounds evoked specific reverberations. Quotations of audio and visual aspects of the film *G30S/PKI* and the Hapsak media event might have acted as an instant trigger to the subtexts of these themes, which relate to conceptions of heroism and nationalism. Although this was not necessarily the intention of the directors of the films, the examples demonstrate a juxtaposition of old images and new narrations, and new images and old narrations.[4] The altered use of emblems which were part of memory sites of the New Order now abstracted from their source functioned as a device which re-structured national history and public memory. At screenings of *Mass grave* in Jakarta in 2002 and 2003, audiences commented that the film instantly brought to mind images of the decomposing bodies of the generals in the epic *G30S/PKI*. In their theory of media events, Dayan and Katz (1992:211) postulate that the collective memory in a society is edited and re-edited by quoting from earlier events. These Indonesian documentaries, in which specific monumental images and sounds were used in a different context, are examples of such a process. In the case of *Mass grave*, the same mode of visual representation was employed to reverse the authorized story and tell quite another tale: that of the victims of the New Order.[5] In the documentary *Student movement*, the melody 'Gugur bunga di taman bakti' was quoted to usher in new national heroes: the Trisakti students who were killed by the Indonesian army.

The emphasis on victims and newly created heroes in two very disparate documentaries can be used to illustrate preoccupations with certain modes of representation in a majority of documentaries which were produced after the end of Soeharto rule. In the first few years of Reform, many new and 'counter-propaganda' films and documentaries were used to provide a forum for victims and shape new heroes to displace the old, hackneyed ones. Apart from the documentary *Student movement*, which used the song 'Gugur bunga'

4 In April 2007, when I asked Lexy Rambadeta whether he had *G30S/PKI* in mind when producing *Mass Grave*, he answered that the film had not crossed his mind for a minute. He had looked at more 'universal' modes of documentary production, like those used by the Australian television network ABC. The editor of *Mass grave*, Laurensius 'Goeng' Wijayanto, whom I met in December 2005, however, remarked that the film *G30S/PKI* was in his thoughts all the time while he was working on *Mass grave*. This could not have directly influenced the content or style of the film, though, since Goeng had simply followed Lexy's script and instructions.
5 Besides digging up the dead of New Order rule, *Mass grave* contested the narratives of evil communists versus good Islam. The documentary shows a group of angry Muslim men who violently try to prevent the reburial of victims of 1965 in the village's graveyard.

to define the heroes of the Reformasi, the reproduction of the conventional narrative trait of heroism in New Order propaganda and historical films was significant. In December 2003, the organizing committee of the Indonesian Documentary Film Festival (FFD) in Yogyakarta allowed me to watch all fifty or so films which were to participate in the FFD competition that year. Watching these films, it struck me that a substantial part of the documentaries followed a New Order or *gelora pembangunan*-dictated style. As mentioned in Chapter 3, this kind of documentary begins with a map and a voice-over which, assuming a particular documentary narration pitch, gives precise information about the setting or location of the film. In the meantime, some sort of unrelated entertaining 'cheery' music score can be heard playing in the background. Most of the films I saw which began in this fashion could be fast-forwarded to just a few minutes before the end. There indisputably the hero of the story would emerge. Depending on the subject of the documentary, all the main characters – the housewife, the person collecting the garbage, or the man cutting trees for a living – were positioned as heroes, fulfilling the ordinary day-to-day 'heroic' deeds of common people. The overt *gelora pembangunan* type of documentaries stood no chance of selection in the competition. Instead, the festival committee chose films which were either shot in a 'Discovery' or 'National Geographic' channel style, or entries which exhibited more creative modes of documentary production. In 2004 and 2005, most documentaries entering the FFD competition had discarded the styles and contents of the New Order. By this time they were not much different to those featuring in international documentary film festivals worldwide.[6]

The fact that post-Soeharto documentaries continued to depict heroes has to be seen as a legacy of the New Order, in the sense that this narrative trait conveyed a partial extension of its textual conventions. It put forward a particular understanding of the modes used in the representation of documentaries which were formed under Soeharto rule.[7] The parallel trend in the new documentary

---

6   For a database of contemporary Indonesian documentaries, see http://www.in-docs.com/index.cfm. In-docs was founded in 2002 by Yayasan Masyarakat Mandiri Film Indonesia (YMMFI, Society of Indonesian Films), the founder and organizer of the Jakarta International Film Festival. Through In-docs, YMMFI promotes and encourages the production and development of documentary films by Indonesians. In-docs organizes a series of such programmes as discussions about documentaries, film screenings, and workshops for documentary production. In-docs is supported by the Ford Foundation, Hivos, and the Open Society Institute. For more on FFD, see their website: http://www.festivalfilmdokumenter.org (accessed 23-1-2012).

7   For more on the structure of documentaries in relation to (generic) text conventions and parallels with other texts, as well as the use of certain styles in relation to institutional discourse, see Nichols 1991:18-23.

4 Post-colonial histories, common people, and commercial frameworks

productions, which now highlighted the victims of the regime, was part of the same discourse; only the point of view was turned around 180 degrees.[8] Nevertheless, there was also an important innovation in both the post-Soeharto documentaries on victims of New Order rule and those featuring new heroes. Their chosen focus was the common people: victims, students, housewives, or people collecting garbage. These documentaries revealed a shift from the 'voice of authority' to the 'voice of the voiceless' and they substituted *tokoh* for ordinary people. The emphasis on victims and newly found heroism in the early post-Soeharto documentaries initially showed that dominant discourses and narrative structures of New Order historiography were being reproduced.[9]

POST-COLONIAL HISTORIES AND IDENTITIES: FILM ISLAMI

Representations of Islam in Indonesian audio-visual media and Muslim participation in the Indonesian mediascape both increased significantly after the resignation of President Soeharto. The rise of Islamic film production companies and the empowerment of Islamic film communities required that new practices of Islamic self-representation be found. One group of young Islamic filmmakers in particular shaped new discourses on the position and representations of Islam in Indonesian and transnational audio-visual media. This new film movement explicitly referred to the post-colonial discourses deriving from Third Cinema theories. Moreover, their discourses indicated affiliations with communities worldwide.

Film and Islam were not easily united. Under the New Order, *ulama* (Muslim religious scholars) discussed the issue of film officially for the first time in 1983. In the same year, the film *Sunan*

---

8 For more about the emphasis on victims in audio-visual and other media after the resignation of Soeharto, see Wiwik Sushartami's research on the victimization of women in post-Soeharto Indonesian media (forthcoming).

9 A different narration and representation of heroes and history was depicted in the film *Gie* (Riri Riza, 2005). *Gie* is based on the life and diaries of the Chinese-Indonesian student activist Soe Hok Gie, who opposed the rule of President Soekarno in the 1960s. Gie gradually turned into a cult figure following his death mountain climbing in 1969. His diaries were banned during New Order rule, but they were read and popular among dissidents. Scholar of Indonesian cinema Intan Paramaditha, in her article 'Contesting Indonesian nationalism and masculinity in cinema', shows the way in which in Riza's production, Soe Hok Gie is portrayed as an unconventional hero. She compares representations of nationalism and gender in the films *Penumpasan pengkhianatan G30S/PKI* and *Gie* and analyses the ways in which *Gie* redefines established, New Order imaginations and conceptions of nationhood and gender relations (Paramaditha 2007).

Kalijaga (Sofyan Sharna) was produced. The film was based on the legend of Sunan Kalijaga, the first of the nine holy men who are believed to have disseminated the teachings of Islam in Java. In conjunction with the production of *Sunan Kalijaga*, a dialogue about film was organized between *ulama* from the Majelis Ulama Indonesia (MUI, Indonesian Council of Muslim Scholars) and film journalists. In newspapers it was said that most *ulama* believed it was unfitting to watch a film in a cinema, which was associated with indecent films and such improper behaviour as secretly kissing in the dark on a date (Bintang 1983; Jasin 1985). The aim of the dialogue was to explore to what extent film could be used as a form of Islamic preaching or *dakwah* (Islamic religious intensification activities),[10] and to find a way to combine the traditional mediation of oral preaching with the visual aspects of film. As some subjects may not be visualized in Islam, questions were raised about how religious teachings should be presented, and in what way certain specific religious principles could be represented in filmic symbols. However, most of the discussion concentrated on the film *Titian serambut dibelah tujuh* (English title: *The narrow bridge*, Chaerul Umam 1982), which was screened before the discussion in order to give the *ulama* an idea of what an Islamic film could be like.[11]

Approximately a year and a half after the initial formal discussion the first 'official' Indonesian Islamic mission film was produced. The fiction film with the title *Sembilan wali* (Nine saints, Djun Saptohadi, 1985) was based on various legends and folk-tales about the *wali sanga* which circulated in Indonesia. Following closely in the footsteps of *Sembilan wali* came another 'nine-saints film'. Once again this film, which bore the title *Sunan Kalijaga & Syeh Sitijenar* (Sofyan Sharna, 1985), was about Sunan Kalijaga and his dealings with a renegade. The premiere of this film was watched by 250 *ulama*, who had gathered in Jakarta to attend the third national MUI meeting from 20 to 23 July 1985. Although in the past many *ulama* had believed that watching films was *haram* (proscribed), this time those who were interviewed were generally approving. Nevertheless, they did not miss the opportunity to stress that particularly films which contained any slightly sexual scenes, such as nudity or unmarried men and women socializing together, were still prohibited. Perhaps because of the lack of titillating scenes, the film *Sunan Kalijaga & Syeh Sitijenar* proved not to be particularly enthralling: many *ulama* fell asleep while watching it. When their opinion about

---

10 On the rise and context of *dakwah* in Indonesia, see Schulte Nordholt 2008:165-76.
11 'Ulama dan pers diskusikan kemampuan film sebagai medium syi'ar Islam', *Berita Minggu & Film*, 14/20-8-1983.

the film was asked, most of them could not comment because they had missed part or nearly all of it (Jasin 1985).

From 1989, discussions about the connection between film and Islam began to find their way into newspapers and magazines. The link between the two was also the subject of a number of conferences and gatherings. In these discussions various questions were addressed, such as: How should the production of 'entertaining' *dakwah* films be tackled? How could these be made to function as an alternative to oral preaching traditions? Was it possible to find a formula for a film with religious themes which would be acceptable to all parties? What role could be assumed by *ulama* or other religious authority figures in the production of films? There was a tacit agreement that the involvement of religious authorities was essential to pre-empt errors which could easily ignite the spark of protest. Should they merely act as consultants with the task of ensuring that everything to do with religion in that particular film was represented 'the right way'? Or should their involvement be more extensive? Should *ulama* also invent or propose ideas for films, indeed even become actors themselves, in order to attract an Islamic audience?[12] Apart from these questions, most of which addressed the content of Islamic films, the bulk of the discussions about film and Islam was motivated by the perceived need for the production of Islamic films in modern Indonesia.[13]

Between 1994 and 1996, Islamic intellectuals stressed that in the present era of information and globalization it was extremely important to set up some resistance to the influx of films from overseas. They were convinced these films promoted nothing but secularism, sex, and violence (Arief 1996). If the Indonesian community were to produce Islamic films, Indonesians, of whom the majority were adherents of Islam, would be offered a lifeline by which to hold onto their own culture. Indonesian films did not escape criticism. Quite apart from 'hot' film productions, various films which the general public called 'Islamic mission films' were also frowned upon. Islamic scholars were concerned that broader audiences might become confused and believe that Indonesian horror and mystery films were actually *dakwah* films. Viewers indeed thought these types of film contained elements of religious

---

12 'KH Abdurrahman Arroisi; Agar dapat dijadikan sarana dakwah sulit mencari kriteria film bertema keagamaan', *Harian Terbit*, 1-9-1990; 'Sinetron atau film berthema agama hendaknya libatkan pakar agama', *Angkatan Bersenjata*, 20-11-1993; Cahyono 1989; Mahmud, Nashir and Agus Suryanto 1990.
13 'Pesantren jangan jauhi dunia kesenian dan film', *Angkatan Bersenjata*, 14-7-1993; Mahmud, Nashir and Agus Suryanto 1990.

propagation because of the frequent *deus ex machina* role accorded Islamic figures. These were generally religious teachers or other Islamic symbols, which were introduced to restore order at the end of such films. In addition to horror films, other films which *ulama* considered to depict controversial scenes were also perceived by its audiences as Islamic mission films. Among them were several films which featured the famous actor and *dangdut* (popular music) star Rhoma Irama. General audiences were quick to interpret these as promoting Islam, because both in and outside the film world Rhoma Irama presented himself as a pious Muslim who brought faith to the people. The Islamic scholars thought otherwise, saying that Irama's films tended to feature too many 'hot scenes' to deserve the epithet of *dakwah* films.[14]

Alongside discussions about the need for more Islamic films there was a call for the establishment of Islamic film production companies. In 1996, Islamic organizations such as the mass organization Muhammadiyah took steps to found production houses furnished with all the equipment needed for film production.[15] The zeal to establish Muslim film production companies was due to the victory of religious organizations in a political argument with the government. In May 1996, the government had issued a draft for new legislation on broadcasting which, among other regulations, prohibited the founding of private broadcasting organizations based on religious principles. After a vigorous discussion, fierce protests, and tough negotiations, the religious organizations won their case. On 18 June 1996, the incumbent Minister of Information, Hartono, announced that religious groups would be allowed to found their own broadcasting organizations. This victory gave a strong incentive to go ahead with the setting up of Islamic film production companies.[16]

As well as the plans and efforts to found production companies, strenuous attempts were made to empower young Muslims in audio-visual media. In 1993, at a seminar in Cirebon about the role

14 For example, the film *Satria bergitar* (The knight with a guitar, Nurhadie Irawan, 1983) shows scantily dressed females. There is also a scene set in the bedroom featuring the antagonist and his spouse. Even though the couple just talks, it was deemed inappropriate to have a scene set in a bedroom.
15 'Film bernuansa Islam tidak mendidik', *Media Indonesia*, 13-7-1996.
16 'Lima organisasi agama menolak pasal 9 RUU siaran', *Harian Ekonomi Neraca*, 22-5-1996; 'Kelompok keagamaan boleh bersiaran', *Harian Terbit*, 19-6-1996; 'Menpen; Kelompok keagamaan boleh dirikan lembaga penyiaran', *Angkatan Bersenjata*, 18-6-1996; Haryanto, Wijanta, and Tjiauw 1996; 'Lima lembaga keagamaan beri masukan RUU penyiaran', *Angkatan Bersenjata*, 22-5-1996; 'Menpen; Kelompok keagamaan boleh dirikan lembaga penyiaran', *Kompas*, 18-6-1996.

of *pesantren* (Islamic boarding schools) in the era of industrialization, film-maker Erros Djarot stated that *pesantren* possessed great potential in helping to shape an Islamic art and film industry. He argued that *santri* (Islamic scholars) should not keep themselves aloof from the world of art and cinema. Instead of feeling downhearted watching non-Islamic films, *santri* should produce films themselves.[17] In 1997, generated by the fear of a tidal wave of films from overseas and the annoyance aroused by incorrect, stereotypical representations of Islam in Indonesian films, workshops and discussions were organized in Islamic schools, universities, and organizations. These were set up to convince principals of Islamic schools and universities and heads of Islamic organizations that their students and members should become involved in film production and train to become skilled at it.[18]

After the resignation of President Soeharto, the developments of the past few years in conjunction with the climate of Reform led to a significant rise in activities which combined film with Islam. The number of professional production houses for Islamic films grew, and some Islamic organizations supported film production training courses for Muslims. Taking the bit between their teeth, different Islamic organizations participated in the organization of Islamic film screenings and discussions about audio-visual media. In addition to the cinema clubs of mainly Muhammadiyah universities, many newly established Islamic film communities embraced these activities enthusiastically. Among the new communities were M-Screen Indonesia (Muslim Screen Indonesia), Muslim Movie Education (MME), Fu:n Community (based on the Arabic word *al funnuun*, which means art), and the Salman Film-maker Club a film community connected to the Salman Mosque, which is part of the Technical University of Bandung. Such communities were composed mostly of young amateur and professional film-makers, Islamic students, and members of youth branches of established Islamic communities and organizations. A number, such as the Fu:n Community, also involved artists from the Jakarta Art Institute, Teater Kanvas, and Teater Bening, members of the non-governmental organization Mer-C, and Forum Lingkar Pena (FLP, Pen Circle Forum). The film crew affiliated to the Muhammadiyah production house PT Media Cipta Utama and some activists of other

17 'Pesantren jangan jauhi dunia kesenian dan film', *Angkatan Bersenjata*, 14-7-1993.
18 'Umat Islam harus ambil bagian ciptakan cerita sinetron', *Angkatan Bersenjata*, 24-9-1997; 'Seniman Muslim mesti kuasai audio visual', *Republika*, 12-7-1997. Cinema clubs at Muhammadiyah universities, for example, provided video cameras and other material to train students in film production (personal comunication with Chaerul Umam, in Jakarta October 2003).

organizations also participated.[19] The communities, led by young Muslim students and film-makers, showed a marked tendency to discuss motivations for the production of Islamic films and shape the rules and regulations required to govern this undertaking. Discussions waxed on subjects such as the way in which women should be depicted in Islamic films; the need to take breaks for prayer during the shooting of films; and whether or not Islamic films could be consumed by men and women in the same space at the same time.

To strengthen the Islamic film movement, a national association of Islamic film communities was founded in July 2003. The Morality Audio Visual Network (MAV-Net) consisted of representatives from six film communities and institutions: the Fu:n Community, M-Screen, Kammi, Rohis Mimazah, IKJ, MQTV Bandung, and a representative from the Pesantren Darunnajah.[20] At the basis of this network lay the debates mentioned earlier about the need to resist the hegemony of foreign films and to strengthen the position of Islam in mainstream Indonesian audio-visual media. In the opinion of MAV-Net members, domestic 'Islamic' films and soaps, which after the fall of Soeharto were mainly screened on television during the Islamic fasting month of Ramadan, had nothing to do with Islam. They argued that access to 'real' Islamic films in Indonesia was restricted to pirated VCDs. These VCDs consisted of feature films, documentaries, and television series from Cairo, the United Kingdom, and Australia; but they also included films about Taliban training camps or Czech warfare, which were on sale and were considered Islamic films.[21] In a manifesto MAV-Net underlined that it was extremely important to fight the film and television industry by producing films which were based on Islamic 'visual ethics'.[22]

19 Teater Kanvas is an Islamic theatre group founded by Zack Sorga, a graduate of the Jakarta Art Institute. The theatre group consists only of men. Teater Bening is a theatre group which consists of women only. Mer-C is an Islamic non-governmental organization which offers humanitarian aid. It was founded by Jose Rizal while he studied at the University of Indonesia. Forum Lingkar Pena is a group of predominantly young Islamic writers.
20 Also the Islamic boarding school Daarut Tauhid, AA Gym's Manejemen Qolbu Television and Manejemen Qolbu Cooperation, the Islamic women's magazine UMMI, Islamic youth from the Sunda Kelapa Mosque, and the magazine *Aku Anak Saleh* (I am a pious child) were mentioned as having joined the MAV-Net. Moreover, the MAV-Net worked together with such professionals in the field of audio-visual media as film directors Riri Riza, Chaerul Umam, Marissa Haque, Syaeful Wathon, Slamet Rahardjo Djarot, and Islamic artists such as Igo Ilham, Syamsudin Noor Moenadi, Rizal Basri, Moh. Ariansyah, Effendy Doyta, Zack Sorga, and others.
21 'Dakwah era baru dengan VCD', *Majalah Suara Hidayatullah*, January 2002, http://hidayatullah.com/2002/01/muamalat.shtml (accessed 25-9-2002).
22 When I spoke to Agres Setiawan, co-founder of MAV-net, in March 2007, he said that his opinion had changed and that his view about the need to counter commercialism and transnationalism had become less radical.

4 Post-colonial histories, common people, and commercial frameworks

While the exact delineation of these Islamic visual ethics was still being debated, some main principles were set out in a pamphlet written by Ustaz (term of address for an Islamic teacher) Ahmed Sarwat from Pusat Konsultasi Syariah (Centre of Syariah (Islamic Law) Consultation). In this pamphlet, Ahmed writes that a film is only truly Islamic if Islam is the guideline in all the film mediation practices. He gives examples of the use of Islamic principles, from the production of an Islamic film (the producer, actors, and crew all have to be (devout) Muslims), to distribution (sponsors must produce halal goods), up to exhibition and consumption (the screening time should not be during hours of prayer, and cinemas should provide for a division between male and female audiences) (Sarwat 2003).

In the MAV-Net manifesto, the need for the production of films based on Islamic visual ethics was linked to an early theory of Third Cinema put forward by Teshome Gabriel. In 1985, Gabriel (1985:355-69) created a model which distinguished three phases of development in Third World national cinemas: the first phase of national cinemas in the Third World was characterized by the mimicry of Hollywood film productions; the second phase encompassed appropriations from traditional cultural products in both form and content (films about exotic traditional cultures); the third marked the engagement in a critical reassessment of traditional cultures, and the use of Third World filmmakers' own film languages, consisting of their original images, representations, and imaginations of society. This third phase often featured guerrilla sentiments and the deconstructions of conventional Eurocentric film themes and representations of First and Third Worlds.[23] While Gabriel's model did not cover the huge amount of Indonesian films which combined elements of Hong Kong action films, Indian, and Latin American melodrama, plus all types of B-films from the US and elsewhere, the MAV-Net manifesto still used it to account for the need for Islamic films based on Islamic visual ethics. Islamic film was to constitute an authentic Indonesian and oppositional cinema, which would counter both the flow of films from the West and the allegedly corrupted commercial mainstream Indonesian cinema.

23 Sen argues that in Indonesian cinema under the presidency of Soekarno, Gabriel's third phase was represented by leftist film-makers who were opposed to imperialist Hollywood films. She states that when the New Order came to power, the third phase of cinema in Indonesia was erased (Sen 1994:46-7). Hence, the only movies surviving under the New Order were Gabriel's first-phase copies of Hollywood films, and second-phase films which showed exotic images of traditional Indonesian cultures.

| *Contemporary Indonesian film*

The founding of this oppositional cinema was not exclusively influenced by ideas about the position of Muslims in Indonesian domestic media and society. By 1999, discourses had emerged which extended ideas about the representation and position of Muslims to transnational media and world politics. Some Islamic scholars and television reviewers even argued that the distribution and exhibition of films and television series from the US and other imported entertainment in Indonesia was a carefully planned mission by the West to destroy Islamic religious principles.[24] They believed that this mission was part of a strategy launched by Zionist Jews to control representations of the world. In these discourses, it was claimed that in the US, Jews controlled 80% of the Hollywood film industry and consequently strove to control and misrepresent the facts of world history, seizing the opportunity to undermine Islamic religious principles.[25]

Influenced by the same kinds of ideas, the communities affiliated to the MAV-Net network announced they were committed to countering the 'colonization of mainstream media by Zionists, imperialists, capitalists, and communists'. They saw themselves as part of an Islamic *umat* (religious community) which transcended the borders of Indonesia. Therefore, besides presenting an alternative cinema and defying the misleading representations of Islam on a national level, the goal of the *film Islami* movement was also to contribute to and increase the number of truthful representations of Islam worldwide. In forming a network which supported transnational Islamic film mediation practices, they strove to gradually convert the position of Western culture and ideologies, and their representations of history, in mainstream film mediation channels worldwide.

FILM IN THE FRAMEWORK OF RAMADAN

In the early years of Reform, the mechanism of screening films in a certain framework or relating them to a particular context persisted, in spite of the flow of discourses on reformation, and changes in conventional film mediation practices. The perception that there was a need to screen films as part of a specific occasion was highly

---

24 For a broader discussion of the emergence of these discourses in Indonesian society, see Schulte Nordholt 2008:170-1.
25 'Ali Sahab; Serial film TV meracuni generasi muda; ulama lebih mirip selebritis', *Harian Terbit*, 30-6-1999. For example, the series *Melrose Place* and *Beverly Hills 90210* by 'Jewish producer' Aaron Spelling were seen to promote free sex and profoundly non-Islamic lifestyles.

4 Post-colonial histories, common people, and commercial frameworks

conspicuous in post-Soeharto debates about the commemoration of Hapsak. Although discussions raged about the discontinuation of the propaganda film *G30S/PKI* as part of the media event, the screening of a film on 30 September was not questioned.[26] There was also no controversy about the convention of relaying a film simultaneously on all television channels.[27] In this section I will return briefly to the framework of Hapsak, after which I will further investigate the practice of screening films in the framework of another event during Reformasi. As the focal point of my argument, I will concentrate on 'Islamic' television programmes shown as part of the Islamic fasting month of Ramadan. I choose to link the Islamic fasting month with the practice of screening films in particular frameworks, both to stay within the 'frame' of the set up of Chapter 3, as well as in order to relate to Aulia Muhammad's analysis of the framing of Islam during Ramadan, which will be discussed in detail below. Special programming on television during Ramadan is not uniquely Indonesian. Also in, among other countries, Egypt, Malaysia, Syria, Turkey, and several other countries in the Middle East, television stations broadcast special programmes during Ramadan.[28]

On 1 October 1998, the commemoration of Hapsak was carried out in the conventional manner; the only omission was the screening of *G30S/PKI* as part of it. The official reason given for not screening the film was that it was damaged. However, it was also said that the screening of *G30S/PKI* was discontinued because after twelve consecutive years of screening, television viewers must be bored watching it over and over again.[29] There were also some who suggested that *G30S/PKI* was not consonant with the new era of Reform because the film was inclined to 'make a cult of a certain person' (*pengkultusan seseorang*), and to take the shape of a 'certain individ-

---

26 The continuation of the ceremony and the commemoration of Hapsak were also not questioned. However, in 2000 historian Taufik Abdullah criticized the sacredness of the Pancasila and its national day, because in the aftermath of the day being commemorated many people were killed and imprisoned and Pancasila was used to rule out all other ideologies, principles or beliefs (McGregor 2007:107).
27 Pengganti film G30-S/PKI mulai digarap', *Merdeka*, 4-9-1998; 'Bukan Sekedar Kenangan ditayangkan serentak 30 September 1998', *Republika*, 22-9-1998; 'TVRI tidak lagi tayangkan film G-30-S/PKI', *Media Indonesia*, 24-9-1998.
28 For a study of changes in television programming during Ramadan in Syria, see Christmann 1996 and Salamandra 1998. For an analysis of Ramadan programmes in Egypt, see Abu-Lughod 2002; Armbrust 2006.
29 'TVRI tak akan tayangkan film Pengkhianatan G 30 S/PKI', *Pos Kota*, 25-8-1998; 'Selamat tinggal Pengkhianatan G30 S PKI', *Sinar Pagi*, 25-8-1998; 'Film G-30 S/PKI dicabut; penggantinya tak singgung peran Soeharto', *Merdeka*, 26-8-1998.

ual's personal monument' (*monumen pribadi seseorang*).[30] There was a general feeling that the viewers needed something new instead. Hence, on 29 and 30 September 1998, *G30S/PKI* was replaced by a television drama with the title *Bukan sekadar kenangan* (BSK, Not just a memory). It was emphasized that unlike *G30S/PKI*, *BSK* did not represent any personal monument, but was about common people.

In a new guise – above all, a love story – the intention of *BSK* was still to convey the traditional message: warning of the latent danger of communism. Moreover, *BSK*, just as *G30S/PKI*, was screened simultaneously on all television channels. Diverging from the former practice, however, it was agreed that *G30S/PKI* would not be replaced by one single film; a new film would be produced each year.[31] This idea, however, never materialized. In subsequent years, and particularly under the presidency of Megawati Soekarnoputri (2001-2004), the Hapsak ceremony lost much of its credence. The Soekarno family had never accepted the official New Order version about the end of Soekarno's presidency, which paved the way for the legitimate succession of Soeharto, the version celebrated in the Hapsak ceremony. Since Megawati's presidency, the ceremony has not been broadcast on television in its entirety, but only in fragments inserted in daily news programmes.

As well as the initial endeavour to screen a film as part of the Hapsak media event, there was also an attempt to create new commemorative and other, more general events and relate these to specific film screenings. Either films were specifically produced and screened for certain events, or efforts were made to fit a film into an event. An example of the latter practice was apparent in the frequent changes of the title of the documentary *Student movement* to fit different film screenings. Under its original title, *The army forced them to be violent*, the documentary had been shown on campuses in Indonesia and at different film festivals abroad since 1998. However, at the instigation of LSF, its title was changed before it was certified to enter Indonesian cinemas.[32] Notwithstanding Reformasi, it was still unacceptable to be too critical of the Indonesian army in films. Consequently, the title was changed to the neutral *The student movement in Indonesia*, by which name it was screened in the top-end cinemas of the 21 Group in August 2002. In November

---

30 'Film G-30-S/PKI diganti bukan sekadar kenangan', *Harian Ekonomi Neraca*, 24-9-1998; 'TVRI tidak lagi tayangkan film G-30-S/PKI', *Media Indonesia*, 24-9-1998.
31 'Film G-30 S/PKI dicabut; penggantinya tak singgung peran Soeharto', *Merdeka*, 26-8-1998; 'Pengganti Pengkhianatan G30 S PKI sepenuhnya fiktif, tanpa tokoh yang dikultuskan', *Sinar Pagi*, 27-9-1998; '"Bukan Sekadar Kenangan" gantikan film "G-30-S/PKI"', *Media Indonesia*, 30-9-1998.
32 In 1992 the Badan Sensor Film had changed its name into Lembaga Sensor Film.

4 Post-colonial histories, common people, and commercial frameworks

of that year the documentary could again be seen in Indonesian cinemas. It was deemed perfectly suitable for the commemoration of the 'first Semanggi tragedy' (*Tragedi Semanggi I*), which had occurred on 13 November 1998. On that day, demonstrating students and a hapless bystander died after being fired upon by the Indonesian military near the Semanggi flyover in Jakarta; approximately 239 people were injured. On 13 November 2002, exactly four years after the incident, the documentary *Student movement* was screened in eight cinemas belonging to the 21 Group to commemorate the incident (Ati 2002). To suit the occasion of its re-release the title was first changed to *Empat tahun Tragedi Semanggi I* (Four years [after the] first Semanggi tragedy).[33]

The showing of films as part of a specific event or occasion is comparable to the broadcasting of 'Islamic' programmes on television during Ramadan. During the Islamic fasting month in Indonesia, the normal broadcasting schedule on television is interrupted. Television stations are suddenly flooded with Islamic programmes, and regular programmes which contain elements of violence, sex, and mysticism are rescheduled. As soon as Ramadan is over all programmes which may be construed to have ill effects on people return, and their Islamic counterparts disappear again.[34] While the celebration of Ramadan on television during the New Order tended to be a rather modest affair, in post-Soeharto Indonesia it turned into booming business. In an interview, film director Ali Sahab in 2003 commented that during the launch of private television ten years earlier, Ramadan had not yet been commercialized. At that time Christmas was an even greater show than Ramadan. Sahab claimed that in due course the religious atmosphere disappeared from Ramadan television programmes. He commented that the fasting month had been turned into a spectacle in which only entertainment counted.[35]

Signs of the development which was to transform Islam into a lucrative television business first began to emerge in 1999. Private television stations began to compete for a share of the advertisements in Ramadan programming, which increased by approximately 15% during the Islamic fasting month.[36] The number of advertisements rose as some special products, among them *sarung*,

---

33 'Student movement in Indonesia', http://kafegaul.com/resensi/article/index.php?nomor_film=450 (accessed 6-1-2003); Ati 2002.
34 'Ulama Jatim protes tayangan sadisme di TV', *Republika*, 4-3-1996.
35 'Ali Sahab; Tayangan Ramadan menjadi komoditas hura-hura', *Cek & Ricek* 270, 17/23-11-2003.
36 'Iklan naik, sinetron unggul', *Harian Terbit*, 11-1-1999; 'Berebut kue iklan di bulan Ramadhan', *Republika*, 22-11-2000.

halal food products, and soap, were advertised only during Ramadan. In 2001 there was a particularly marked rise in the business and profits of Ramadan programming on television. In that year, several newspaper articles referred to the fierce competition between private television stations to grab a share of the advertisements, for which there were significant price increases in the Islamic fasting month.[37] Although competition between the television stations increased, at that juncture there was hardly any change in the formulas of Ramadan programmes, either compared to what had been broadcast during the fasting month in previous years or to regular programming.

Implementing the laws of the market place and making a conscious attempt to copy tried and tested formulas, various television programmes were rerun during Ramadan. The questions in conventional quiz shows concentrated on matters of religion, and several soaps which revolved around the psychological or practical problems of people and the way in which religion could help to solve them, were launched. Nevertheless, despite a change in outward appearances (protagonists were dressed in Islamic clothes) and a change in prime time (to one hour before sunrise (*sahur*) and the breaking of the fast at sunset (*maghrib*)) quiz shows still focused on entertainment and soaps sold melodrama. Apart from these kinds of shows, Ramadan programmes were produced which were in line with the worldwide television trend of recent years. This trend had been marked by a mushrooming of infotainment and gossip programmes about the lives of artists and the 'rich and famous', clustered under the heading 'celebrities'. The only difference in the domestic infotainment shows produced during Ramadan was that female artists and presenters covered their heads and that some religious messages were inserted in the intervals. Often these Ramadan messages were delivered by an Islamic authority figure, for example a *kyai* or an *ustaz*, who had been invited for the occasion to be a guest star.[38]

In 2002, this propensity to include a religious authority figure began to be a feature in all types of Ramadan programmes. Standing out among them was the *kyai* and businessman Abdullah Gymnastiar, commonly known as AA Gym, who turned up almost everywhere. He featured in no less than nine television shows, which were divided

---

37 See, for example, 'Karena produsen berlomba2 pasang iklan; Ramadhan bawa berkah bagi TV swasta', *Pos Kota*, 4-11-2001; '"Perang" program TV menjelang sahur', *Warta Kota*, 10-11-2001; 'Program Ramadhan di televisi', *Warta Kota*, 10-11-2001; 'Ramai2 gaet pemirsa; Televisi bersaing tayangan Ramadhan', *Warta Kota*, 2001; 'Acara lama mendominasi program Ramadhan di TV', *Kompas*, 11-11-2001; 'Program TV Ramadhan mencari berkah dan rupiah', *Media Indonesia*, 18-11-2001.
38 'Kuis dan ceramah hiasi TV selama Ramadhan', *Warta Kota*, 22-10-2002.

4 Post-colonial histories, common people, and commercial frameworks

over five private television stations.[39] AA Gym owned the television production company Manejemen Qolbu Televisi (MQTV, Management of the Heart Television) and produced and sold his own programmes. Other popular Islamic authority figures who appeared on national television that year were *dai sejuta umat* (Islamic preacher for the masses (lit. 'millions')) Zainuddin; Lutfiah Sungkar, a popular *Betawi* (native Jakartan) *kyai*, who had the gift of being a spellbinding speaker and who was also the leader of the political party Partai Bintang Reformasi (PBR, Star of the Reformation Party); and famous actor and *dangdut* singer Rhoma Irama.[40] In 2003 the number of Ramadan programmes increased yet again. In their bid to compete with one another, the programmes varied from (sequels to) Islamic soaps, quiz shows to Ramadan programmes which were interspersed with elements of comedy, music, or *wayang* (literally 'shadow', traditional theatre with leather or wooden puppets). There were also live broadcasts of the preaching of Islamic leaders from mosques in different cities. In pride of place though was the increasing trend of featuring popular Islamic leaders in television programmes. AA Gym was by far the most popular. Advertisers of special Ramadan products fought with each other to fill the advertising slots around his programme,[41] but other such prominent Islamic leaders and personalities as Quraish Sihab and Arifin Ilham also appeared on various shows.

AA Gym's appearance on almost every television channel during Ramadan can be attributed to his credibility as an Islamic expert at that time, but the widespread media trend which focused on artists, the rich and famous, and popular people (the celebrity circuit) cannot be discounted either in seeking a reason for his success.[42] Just as regular programming, which featured popular

39 On television station RCTI, AA Gym featured in *Manajemen qulbu spesial Ramadhan*; on SCTV in *Membuka pintu langit, Gema Ramadhan, Sambut Ramadhan,* and *Gema takdir*; on Indosiar in *Kisah2 teladan* (a children's programme); on Trans TV in *Ceramah Ramadhan AA Gym*, and on TPI, in *Sentuhan qolbu Ramadhan*. See 'Ramadhan di TV, AA Gym laris manis', *Warta Kota*, 1-11-2002; 'Serba AA Gym', *Rakyat Merdeka*, 5-11-2002.
40 'Ramadhan di layar televisi', *Warta Kota*, 9-11-2002.
41 'Bersaing program Ramadhan', *Bisnis Indonesia*, 26-10-2003; 'AA Gym di televisi; Dari subuh ketemu subuh', *Cek & Ricek* 270, 3/9-11-2003.
42 In 2006 AA Gym's popularity severely dropped following the news that he had taken a second wife. His popularity with women in particular, who formed the largest part of his fan base, decreased. The problem was not polygamy per se. Even though many Indonesian Islamic women do not support it, they acknowledge that the Islamic creed permits polygamy. However, the fact that AA Gym took a young and beautiful ex-Miss Indonesia model divorcee as his second wife, and not, for example, a hideous old widow, made people question his principles. In public opinion Gym's second marriage was merely based on lust. Despite the consent of his first wife and the validity in Islam to marry again, he was considered to have betrayed his first wife and family. This public view thoroughly damaged his credibility and image as a reputable person. As a result television contracts were pulled and the success of his business ventures declined with approximately 80%.

artists, comedians, and other celebrities, famous *kyai* were used to woo advertisers and attract as many viewers as possible. In 2003, an article in the newspaper *Bisnis Indonesia* mentioned that the fashion for featuring Islamic leaders on television during Ramadan had led to the birth of the category of '*kyai* artists'. The article suggested that the 'camera face' of *kyai* artists was very important in reaching the masses, and not necessarily for the sake of *dakwah*; such personalities were also attractive to advertisers in the lucrative business of Ramadan programming.[43]

Others were less enthusiastic about the direction which was being taken. Several Islamic leaders and some television reviewers criticized what they regarded as the commercialization of Islam. In 2004, the Indonesian Ulama Council, which had tried to steer the contents of Ramadan programmes since 2001 by handing out a yearly award for 'Best National Ramadan Television Programme', remonstrated about what it saw as the trend in which Islamic television during Ramadan was being 'degraded to mere entertainment'.[44] Noted television reviewers, among them Akhmod Seku and Indra Tranggono, joined the chorus of disapproval of the use of Islam in the Ramadan programmes, castigating these programmes as nothing more than a 'formality'. Their criticism was based on the argument that these programmes were devoid of any real substance and for that very reason could be seen as examples of Umar Kayam's notion of performing arts 'in the framework of'.[45] Aulia Muhammad wrote that he experienced a sense of vacuity as he watched television during Ramadan. In his article, he connected this sense of emptiness to Henry Lefebvre's analysis of meaninglessness which he had read about in Dick Hebdige's book (1979:117) *Subculture; The meaning of style*. Aulia criticized the Ramadan programmes for their blatant focus on the outward appearance of famous artists and the depiction of 'seasonal repentance', or, as he expressed it, 'the selling of tears'. Each year during Ramadan celebrities donned a recognizably Muslim costume and, in an orgy of self-abasement, burst into tears on entertainment shows, begging forgiveness for the scandals in which they had been involved. Aulia's objections were based on Baudrillard's conception (1998:110, 193) of the loss of the intrinsic meaning of seasonal changes and differentiations in 'consumer society' – a

43 'Camera face perlu jadi pertimbangan', *Bisnis Indonesia*, 26-10-2003.
44 Tayangan program Ramadan, diamati ketat', *Kedaulatan Rakyat*, 4-11-2004.
45 See also interviews with Veven Wardhana in Kusumaputra 2002, and remarks by film director Ali Sahab in 'Ali Sahab; Tayangan Ramadan menjadi komoditas hura-hura', *Cek & Ricek* 270, 17/23-11-2003.

society in which consumption forms the total be-all and end-all of everyday life. In other words: the celebrities during Ramadan merely '[spoke] with their clothes'. The clothes reflected the seasonally dictated life- styles and temporary identity assumed during the fasting month. In Aulia's opinion, celebrities dressed up and acted the roles required by the sentiment evoked by Ramadan because they believed that the television audiences expected it of them. Aulia argued that the annual circus surrounding Ramadan reflected 'the real post-modern face of television as a sea of illusion, an imaginary world, and hyper-reality, which should not be believed' (Muhammad 2004). In this context, the previous use of a framework during the New Order to direct the reading of a film was discarded, at least in part. Rather than directing the meaning or reading of a film, the framework itself had now become the focal point.

CONCLUSION

After the stepping down of President Soeharto, new post-colonial discourses and imaginations of society were reflected in both the discourse practices of text production and in the conventions of framing films at the level of text consumption. The new-found freedom of expression offered by the socio-political situation of Reform induced several tentative, incomplete, and contradictory changes in the shifting discursive practices of the media (Fairclough 1995:52).

The first tentative and incomplete changes and some continuity could be discerned in the modes of engagement in post-Soeharto documentaries. Such documentaries as *Mass grave* and *Student movement* substituted new narrations for old images, and new images for old narrations. Nevertheless, as well as most of the documentaries produced in the first few years after the fall of Soeharto, they used the same modes of engagement of New Order representations of history and society in film. In their narratives, most documentaries followed either the New Order/USAI development film formulas, or what may be designated the Usmar Ismail mode of heroism. The difference in the post-Soeharto documentaries was that the viewpoint was anti-New Order. A majority of the documentaries focused on newly created heroes or on victims of Soeharto's rule, but there was also a change in the discourse. The heroes of the post-Soeharto documentaries were not authority figures, but victims and common people.

The changes in discourse practices relating to the continuation of the convention to screen films in the framework of a certain event were contradictory. In the context of the screening of 'Islamic' television films and programmes during Ramadan, these contradictions were to some extent related to discourses of the *film Islami* movement founded in 2003. Paradoxically, at the same time when an association of *film Islami* groups was founded to promote Islamic visual ethics for film, Indonesian commercial television turned the screening of soaps and programmes containing features of Islam into a booming business. A survey of the discourses about media representations of Islam during Ramadan shows that in contrast to the idea of Islamic visual ethics, which inserted Islam into all aspects of film mediation practices, the television shows during Ramadan mostly availed themselves of their outer shell.

The commercialization of Ramadan programmes is part of a broader trend of commodification of religion in the sphere of entertainment, in Indonesia and elsewhere in the world.[46] Not only Islam is affected by this trend of commercialization; other religions, too, are progressively turned into marketable products in mass media and as part of lifestyle markers.[47] The commodification of religion is seen as constituting part of a trend of neo-liberal capitalism. In Indonesia, commercial Islam started with the rise of affluent middle classes following the economic growth during the New Order in the 1990s. Ariel Heryanto has described the way in which the formation of a new middle-class identity and the analogous establishment of a capitalist domination gave a boost to the advance of new Muslim elites. In his analysis of the 'new' Muslims, Heryanto shows the development of an increasing amalgamation of religion and politics with consumptive lifestyles.[48] Various scholars have argued that in the past decade, Islam in Indonesia has turned into a commodity.[49] Islam sells well in lifestyle products, such as clothes, food, health services, travel and tourism, as well as across a broad range of media, such as books, magazines, music, radio and television talk

---

46   For example, Lila Abu-Lughod and Walter Armbrust have described similar developments in Egypt. Abu-Lughod (2002:127) analysed the rise in production and popularity of big-budget religious and religious-historical series on Egyptian television during Ramadan at the end of the 1990s; also in the context of Ramadan on television, Armbrust (2006) researched the blurring of boundaries between religious observances and entertainment.

47   For examples of the commodification of Christianity in the sphere of entertainment in the United States, see Moore 1994; Forbes and Mahan 2000; for examples from Ghana, see Meyer 2004, 2007.

48   Heryanto 1999:164, 173-6. In his study on Islamic consumption in Malaysia, Fischer (2009) shows that the promotion of Islamic consumption by the state has produced an alternative form of Islamic neo-liberal capitalism.

49   Fealy 2008; Hasan 2009; Hoesterey 2008; Nef-Saluz 2007.

4 Post-colonial histories, common people, and commercial frameworks

shows, soaps, religious text messages on mobile phones, and films. Some see the 'consumption of Islam' as a positive development, in that it brings new religious meaning into the lives of Muslims, and further supports a society based on religious principles (Fealy 2008:16). To others, however, the commercialization of Islam has meant an erosion of its religious essence. As Islamic scholar Ahmad Syafii Maarif argues, to many people it seems to be more about '*looking* Islamic than *being* Islamic' (Fealy 2008:35-7, italics in original). In Islamic discourses, proponents of the latter argument, such as Aulia Muhammad and the *film Islami* groups, perceived the programming of Islamic soaps and other series in the framework of Ramadan as nothing more than a commodity at the disposal of the television industry. In this context the spirit of the Ramadan soaps and programmes was stifled by the framework in which they were screened.

Also on other occasions, the use of frameworks can be connected to commercial motives. Films were often screened in the framework of certain events as a ploy to sell more tickets. Conceivably, the change of the title of Tino Saroengallo's documentary *Student movement* to fit the commemoration of the 'first Semanggi tragedy' was based on commercial premises too. By re-releasing the documentary under another title, it was anticipated it would attract more viewers. In the previous chapter I have argued that as an instrument employed by the New Order, one important function of a framework was to direct the reading of film and television productions. In the post-Soeharto mediascape, however, frameworks should rather be seen as tools to make these productions more saleable.

The shallowness, the temporal identities, and the 'hyper' reality of the Ramadan programmes and soaps were all decidedly antithetical to discourses which urged the need for truthful self-representations and Islamic visual ethics. The lack of authenticity spawned by this backdoor commercialism was also in contrast to the emphasis on 'getting history straight', and the stated bid for 'true' and 'real' representations of history and society. Moreover, when the Ramadan programmes and the post-Soeharto documentaries are compared, the emphasis on the allure of celebrities in the former stands out starkly in contrast to the focus on common people in the majority of post-Soeharto documentaries.

The focus on both reality and common people as well as celebrities – both secular and religious – is not limited to Indonesia; this too is a phenomenon that can be observed in global media trends. In the case of reality and the common people, in post-Soeharto Indonesia there were two readily identifiable shifts: from an emphasis on the voice of authority to the 'voice of the voiceless' and to ordinary people in the production of post-Soeharto documentaries; and a marked tendency on television to broadcast programmes featuring the man in the street. The emphasis on factual reality and common people began as part of the discourses which questioned New Order historiography and its imposition on society. In the first few years of Reform, numerous talk-shows on television addressed these issues, and over time, people tired of these shows. Corresponding to transnational trends in television, the initially overriding truth and reality in these rather serious talk-shows was replaced by the production of all types of light-entertainment reality shows featuring common people. In the same vein, the focus on celebrities in Ramadan programmes was part of a worldwide trend on television, which showed popular infotainment and gossip programmes about the rich and famous. Hence, while television was crammed with reality shows featuring ordinary people, it was also flooded with celebrities. The emphasis on celebrities in programmes broadcast during the fasting month even resulted in the birth of celebrity *kyai*. This invention of the celebrity *kyai* corresponds with another global television trend: a new religious format evolving around charismatic media personalities.[50]

In 2004, 'Islamic' soaps and series managed to escape the framework of Ramadan, and were subsequently screened outside the confines of the fasting month. However, they were still made for commercial reasons and they still contained prefabricated televised representations of Islam. The focal point of these soaps was that they were based on true stories, spiced up with elements of mystery – such as supernatural occurrences – and scenes in which people indulged in paroxysms of tearful repentance. An important component was the major role assigned to heroes in the guise of Islamic authority figures, *kyai* celebrities, or sometimes personalities who combined these two traits. In Part Three I will look more closely at reality shows, true stories, and representations of Islam outside of the framework of Ramadan.

---

50 For similar developments in Egypt, see Bayat 2002; in Ghana, see De Witte 2003; in Israel, see Lehman and Siebzehner 2006; in Mali, see Schulz 2006; in Turkey, see Öncü 2006.

PART 3

Film discourse practices

5

The *kyai* and hyperreal ghosts
Narrative practices of horror, commerce, and censorship

In recent years there have been several publications about horror films and the connotations of horror in different societies which argue that horror serves as a field for the dramatization of cultural and universal nightmares.[1] Scholars have written about horror film being an outlet which exposes social taboos, or a channel for political critique. Sometimes in their discussions they have related the use of horror to theories about the role of carnival in certain societies.[2] It is not my intention here to discuss the Indonesian horror genre from any of these perspectives. The prime focus of this discussion will be on horror as a form of imagining and as a technical means of 're-presenting' elements of what constitutes the nation (Anderson 1983).

I examine the position of forms of imagination in the context of film narrative practices and debates on what kind of representations of society are acceptable in Indonesian audio-visual media. On one level, I consider horror from the perspective of film genres, discussing certain formats or formulas within such genres. On this level, horror is a forum for identity formation. Benedict Anderson (1983:30) turned to the basic structure of two forms of imagining, namely the novel and the newspaper, which 'provided the technical means for "re-presenting" the *kind* of imagined community that is the nation'. Building on this idea, I investigate discourses about Indonesian films which identify and imagine certain communities through the horror genre. In what way are audiences, communi-

---

1 An earlier version of this chapter was published in *Inter-Asia Cultural Studies* (Van Heeren 2007).
2 See, for example, Carroll 1990; Coates 1991; Schneider 2003. Gladwin (2003) discusses horror film in Indonesia in relation to politics. On the subject of carnival and film as deconstruction of political and aesthetic representations, see Shohat and Stam 1994:274; on the subject of carnival in film as a form of anti-canonical resistance, see Shohat and Stam 1994:302-6. For horror films related to Bakhtin's theory of the carnivalesque, see Creed 1995.

ties, and classes identified and constructed around horror film? How is the character of horror film and its audiences determined by particular film formats (film versus television) or formulas? How have these identifications changed after the fall of President Soeharto in May 1998?

On another level, the chapter moves beyond the concept of imaginations and the labeling of small-scale communities and genres. In this part, I reflect on discourses about film formulas within the horror genre which are indicative of developments and problems in the search for a representative image of what constitutes the modern Indonesian nation. I explore discourses about tolerable modes of representation of the supernatural in film and television and as part of modern Indonesian society. The principal concern is the relationship between discourses about the genre and modes of representation weighed against socio-political strategies and commercial interests.

HORROR FILMS UNDER THE NEW ORDER: COMEDY, SEX, AND RELIGION

The horror genre has a long history in Indonesian media culture and it is found in writing, in radio and television programmes, as well as in cinema. The first horror film in Indonesia was produced by The Teng Cun in 1934 and had the title *Doea siloeman oeler poeti en item* (The two transmogrifications of the black and white snake).[3] Since this pioneering effort, Indonesian horror films have been screened in cinemas, mobile cinemas, and on television in varying numbers. During the 1950s and 1960s horror films were pushed into the background as, at the time, there was a great interest in producing films which featured the Indonesian Revolution and the struggle to wrest Independence from Dutch colonial rule (1945-1949). It was only at the beginning of the 1970s that horror films were starting to be produced again (Kristanto 1995).

Since the film *Ratu ular* (Snake queen, 1972), the number of horror films screened in Indonesian cinemas increased. In fact horror films were about the only kind of films still produced after 1993, when the Indonesian cinema collapsed. But it was not before May 1998 that a revival of horror film production truly began. After 1993,

---

3 A *siluman* (present-day Indonesian spelling) is a human being who has assumed a theriomorphic guise for nefarious purposes.

most top-end cinemas screened mainly imported US films, while home-produced Indonesian films that tended to feature the erotic and horror genres were shown in lower-class cinemas throughout the country. Newspaper articles in 1993 and 1994 claimed that horror films were representative of the Indonesian film industry, and indeed associated the Indonesian film industry with horror films. This stereotype is similar to the way that the US has westerns, China has kung fu films, Japan has films about ninjas and samurais, and India has love stories featuring a liberal dose of singing and dancing.[4] Indonesian cultural commentators have tried to explain the appeal of horror films by stating that the genre is closely related to the psyche of Indonesian people and is generally inherent to Eastern culture, which they assume to be synonymous with mysticism and the occurrence of supernatural beings and events. These explanations were based on the assumption that every region and ethnic group in Indonesia had its own superstitious beliefs and mystery tales recounting supernatural events. Some film producers even thought that horror stories formed a characteristic cultural asset of Indonesian culture. They were convinced that this feature should be exploited in films for both the Indonesian and the foreign market.[5]

The Indonesian horror film as a genre has its own format and peculiarities. Horror films are also labelled *film mistik* (mystical films) or *film klenik* (superstitious films). Generally speaking, anything can happen in these films, and the story does not necessarily have to make sense. Apart from these generalizations, some main features can be detected.[6] Karl Heider (1991) noted that horror films were the most common type of film in Indonesia at the beginning of the 1990s. He delineated the productions of Indonesian horror as films set in the present but resembling the 'Indonesian legend' film genre, which dramatized traditional legends or folktales. It is true that, just as the 'Indonesian legend' genre, horror films often draw their inspiration from traditional Indonesian folk beliefs, above all those about supernatural powers. Heider also points out the use of 'horribly humorous' scenes as a distinctive aspect of Indonesian horror films. As an example, he remarks upon the recurring scenes in which supernatural mon-

---

4 'Tema mistik dan horor bisa menutupi tekor', *Pos Film*, 24-1-1993; Joko 1994.
5 'Tema mistik dan horor bisa menutupi tekor', *Pos Film*, 24-1-1993; 'Film mistik Indonesia mencoba menembus pasar luar negeri', *Suara Pembaruan*, 20-11-1993; Joko 1994. This point was also made by Hasim 1997; Suyono and Arjanto 2003.
6 Both Indonesian and foreign critics of Indonesian horror films have commented that the storylines are often hard to understand. See for example www.iluminatedlantern.com, and www.dvdmaniacs.net in relation to remarks about Indonesian horror films abroad.

sters attack their victims. In his viewing experience, this raised uproars of laughter from the audiences (Heider 1991:44). Indeed, the element of humour or comedy is a frequent component of the horror genre in Indonesia. Another example of a frequently used comic scene is when someone mistakes a ghost for a real person and vice versa (Suyono and Arjanto 2003). A prototypical Indonesian horror film from the 1970s is usually set in a village and revolves around the quest for *ilmu* (spiritual knowledge) or *ilmu gaib* (supernatural powers). An inherent part of such supernatural powers or black magic is that such forces always have some inherent weakness (*pantangan* or 'taboo'), a prohibited action or certain spell by which the powers can be undone. The best way to break the spell cast by magical powers is by reciting a verse from the Quran, but other, more peculiar *pantangan*, such as eating more than three portions of sate (Suyono and Arjanto 2003:71) or encountering a monkey (Kristanto 1995:145) have also been used in horror films.

Besides supernatural powers and humour, there are two other distinct features of Indonesian horror films, namely their use of sex and the appearance of religious symbols or of religious leaders as protagonists.[7] The use of sex emerged in the 1970s and was used to titillate the audience. By the 1980s and 1990s, the extravagant use of erotic elements, which debased them to the level of smut and kitsch, had become the main ingredient of such films. The central themes of these 'horror-sex' films were men having an affair, *tante girang* (in English: 'merry aunt', a pushy woman of loose morals), rape, and promiscuity. The use of sex was not confined to horror but was part of a wider trend of Indonesian films from the 1970s, capitalizing on its selling power.[8] However, particularly in horror films, sex was made fairly explicit. The second classic feature of horror films, the use of religious symbols and a *deus ex machina* in the form of a religious leader, who is able to overcome all evil at the end of the film, emerged in the 1980s (Suyono and Arjanto 2003:72). The protagonist in horror films since the 1980s has mainly been a *kyai* or some other religious figure with Islamic connections. There is, however, also at least one instance in which a Roman Catholic Priest is the religious protagonist; he conquers a Dutch ghost which is haunting an old

---

7 Heider (1991:67-9) does not specify these features in relation to Indonesian, though he does mention the use of sex in Indonesian films in relation to narrative conventions under the heading of 'sexuality'.
8 Heider remarks that sex in Indonesian cinema was either downplayed or presented as sadism. He observed that in Indonesian films, sex is often represented as rape (Heider 1991:66).

colonial house in the film *Ranjang Setan* (Satan's bed, 1986, Tjut Djalil). In the 1981 movie *Mistik (punahnya rahasia ilmu Iblis leak)* (Mystic (the vanishing of the secret devilish knowledge of the evil spirit), 1981, Tjut Djalil), for which Bali is the setting, the hero is a Hindu priest who defeats evil.

The central role of a religious figure in horror films is a perceptible effect of the Ethical Code of Film Production in Indonesia, which was drawn up in 1981 by the National Film Council (henceforth Film Council) under the Minister of Information, General Ali Murtopo (1978-1983). The Ethical Code was based on censorship guidelines drafted by the Film Censor Board (BSF), as laid down in a ministerial decree in 1977. In 1980, the BSF drew up its own further guidelines for censorship in the Kode Etik Badan Sensor Film (BSF Ethical Code). These guidelines were elaborated in the Kode Etik Produksi Film Nasional (Film Council's Code of Ethics) and issued in 1981 (Sen 1994:69). The Code of Ethics of the Film Council was drafted by eight commissions, including the commission for 'film and national morality' (*film dan moral bangsa*), the commission of 'film and the awareness of national discipline' (*film dan kesadaran disiplin nasional*), and the commission for 'film in its relation to devotion towards the One and Only God' (*film dalam hubungannya ketakwaan terhadap Tuhan Yang Maha Esa*). The last-mentioned commission recommended that all filmic aspects had to lead to devotion and the praise of God. It also demanded that '[t]he storyline ought to be composed in such a way that it gives the audience the impression that what is bad will definitely be made to endure the consequences of its actions and suffer; that what is good will surely receive a reward and happiness'.[9] Consequently, most films made under the New Order in the 1980s and 1990s followed a predictable pattern of good versus bad in which the good always triumphed.[10]

Even though there was never an official prescription that a religious figure had to be the hero of horror films, many producers of such films today have the impression that during the New Order, a *kyai* had to be part of horror movies. Ali Tien, former producer of production company Cancer Mas, suggests that by 1981, BSF had sanctioned horror films, stipulating that they should fulfil a reli-

---

9 'Jalan cerita disusun sedemikian rupa sehingga menimbulkan kesan kepada penonton bahwa yang jahat itu pasti akan menerima/menanggung akibatnya dan menderita, dan yang baik itu pasti menerima ganjaran dan kebahagiaan.'
10 Suyono and Arjanto 2003:72. Another pattern of New Order films was that a film evolved from a depiction of a situation of order, followed by the descent into disorder, with order being restored at the film's conclusion (Heider 1991:34-8; Sen and Hill 2000:138, 143-6).

gious mission. Likewise, in the experience of Ferry Angriawan of Virgo Putra Film, a horror film in the 1980s which did not feature a *kyai* at the end of the story would be banned from being screened. Hence, in his opinion, a *kyai* would often appear where his sudden intrusion did not make any sense in the story. According to producer Budiati Abiyoga, who used to be on the jury of the Indonesian Film Festival under the New Order, the outline of the Code of Ethics led to a tendency to use religion for religion's sake. As an example, she recalls the depiction of a Quranic verse with the added phrase: 'This is not approved of by the Quran,' straight after a sex scene (Suyono and Arjanto 2003:72).

In his catalogue of Indonesian films produced between 1926 and 1995, Kristanto (1995) shows that horror films had already begun to use religious symbols as early as the 1970s and many *kyai* regularly turned up in horror films from 1978 onwards. The use of religious heroes in horror films before the 1980s led Krishna Sen (1994:53) to describe the guidelines of the Code of Ethics as representing 'no more than a setting out of practices already in operation in the censorship system'. The fact that directors today believe it was a prerequisite to feature a *kyai* in horror films may indeed offer a clue to the way film censorship under the New Order worked. As Sen suggests, there were relatively few cases of film censorship under the New Order in which BSF intervened directly by excising sections of a film or banning films altogether. Prescriptions issued by such other film institutions as production companies, professional film organizations, film schools, and festivals shaped the kind of films which would be produced and as such worked as a system of self-censorship (Sen 1994:50-1).

The detailed censorship regulations which had been made public by 1980 contributed to an increase in self-censorship in the film industry (Sen 1994:70). Possibly because the use of a *kyai* in horror films was a successful formula resorted to in order to prevent a film from being banned, many film-makers did not take recourse to other formulas with no proven success. Although films which used *kyai* prevailed, not all horror films since the 1980s in the film catalogue mention the role of religious figures. Other formulas were also possible. For example, some horror films were based on traditional legends or placed in a mystical setting and did not feature a religious figure.[11]

11   For example, *Bangunnya Nyai Roro Kidul* (The awakening of Nyai Roro Kidul, 1985, Sisworo Gautama), *Putri Kunti'anak* (The witch's daughter, 1988, Atok Suharto), *Pembalasan Ratu Laut Selatan* (Revenge of the Queen of the South Sea, 1988, Tjut Djalil), *Kisah cinta Nyi Blorong* (The love story of Nyi Blorong, 1989, Norman Benny).

Be that as it may, after the implementation of the Code of Ethics in 1981, many horror films did use religious leaders and symbols because of the perceived need to include them. Such an inclusion was well worthwhile, for these films were sure to pass the Board of Censors even though they might show all that God had forbidden. Under the influence of the combined commercial interests of the film producers and government film regulations, under the New Order a bizarre situation developed whereby the horror film genre was simultaneously equated with sex and with religious propagation (*dakwah*), the latter represented through the use of Islamic symbols and Islamic religious leaders.

HORROR FILMS FOR TELEVISION: NEW NARRATIVES AND DEBATES
ON THEIR BOUNDS

Besides on the silver screen, horror and mystical films during the New Order could also be watched on television. At the beginning of the 1990s, when there was a sudden rise in the number of commercial television stations, many film directors who used to produce films for the cinemas crossed over into television production. Even before the production of mystical television films began around 1995, many old horror films were aired on television. Both domestic and imported US horror films were usually shown on Thursday night, referred to in Indonesia as 'Friday eve' (*malam Jumat*). Friday is a religious day for Muslims and at noon Muslim men are supposed to perform communal prayers in the mosque. The significance of this day will be discussed later.

In 1995-1996, the private television station RCTI began to produce and screen the *sinetron misteri* (mystery series) *Si Manis Jembatan Ancol* (The sweetie of Ancol bridge). Later this was followed by the *sinetron komedi misteri* (comedy-mystery television series) *Jin dan Jun* (Jin and Jun). Because of the success of these programmes, other television stations soon followed suit, though during a very short time, the number of comedy-mystery series was limited. This probably had to do with the fact that then Minister of Information Harmoko 'recommended' reducing the screening of Indonesian mystery series in 1996 – a recommendation which, strikingly, did not seem to apply to foreign products of the same genre.[12] Despite Harmoko's recommendation, a year later, in July 1997, every private television station had its own Indonesian mystery series. RCTI

---

12 'Sinetron misteri kian diperbanyak', *Harian Terbit*, 2-9-1996.

added two series similar to *Si Manis Jembatan Ancol* and *Jin dan Jun* to their programme: *Kembalinya Si Manis Jembatan Ancol* (The return of the sweetie of Ancol bridge) and *Tuyul dan Mbak Yul* (Tuyul and Miss Yul), and a mystery series based on a Javanese folk legend, *Misteri sinden* (The singer mystery). Other private television stations didn't drag their heels and quickly produced their own mystery series: *Hantu sok usil* (The fidgety ghost) and *Janda kembang* (The virgin widow), both of the folk-legend type on SCTV, *Dua dunia* (Two worlds) on Indosiar, and *Misteri* (Mystery), recounting people's stories of encountering the supernatural, on Anteve (Pudjiastuti and Redana 1997).

Unlike the screening of Indonesian horror films in cinemas, which passed virtually unnoticed apart from some protests decrying erotic film posters, there were fierce debates about televised horror films and the mystery television series. These debates began in 1994, when the Head of the First Commission of Parliament (*Ketua Komisi I DPR*) Aisyah Amini criticized the Department of Information for permitting television stations to screen horror films as a matter of routine on *malam Jumat*. Her argument was that broadcasting these productions at that specific time of the week 'gives that evening a bad image' (*membuat image jelek tentang malam itu*). She was worried that it would cause people to regard that evening as one full of fear, whereas it should actually be a very virtuous point of time in the week [for Muslims].[13] The debate about the screening of mystical films on *malam Jumat* and the possible harm to the 'image' of Friday continued until 1995 and was the probable motivation behind the edict issued by Minister of Information Harmoko's appeal to reduce the screening of horror and mystery films on television in 1996.[14] Another discussion, in 1994, revolved around the need to re-censor horror films, primarily those which were produced for the cinema, before these were screened on television. In the words of Harmoko, this was essential 'because the characteristics of television viewers are different from [those who attend] cinemas' (*[s]ebab, karakteristik penonton televisi lain dengan bioskop*).[15]

Yet another debate, launched in 1995 but only becoming an issue in 1996/1997, revolved around the prevailing idea that mystical films would lead Indonesian people astray from reality and set them apart from modern life. The anti-campaign was run largely by the government, aided and abetted by individuals and Islamic groups who saw mystical films as an obstacle to Indonesia becom-

---

13 'Film horor di TV dikritik anggota DPR', *Jayakarta*, 5-2-1994.
14 'Ali Sahab; Film horor TV rusak citra malam Jumat', *Republika*, 12-6-1995.
15 'Film horor di TV dikritik anggota DPR', *Jayakarta*, 5-2-1994.

5 The kyai and hyperreal ghosts

ing a modern, pious nation. They declared that mystery films were devoid of any educational value, and therefore might harm the mental and spiritual development of the people. Generally speaking, the popularity of mystery films was inversely related to the dominant discourse of the New Order, with its constant reiterations about the 'development' of Indonesia into a modern nation. It was feared that mystery films would fuel superstition and the belief of Indonesian people in the supernatural; this would thwart development. Moreover, some Muslim groups and authorities had great difficulty coming to terms with the idea that these series would show concepts contrary to religious teachings. The complaints raised were that these series depicted a realm outside reality, were far from rational, and were devoid of any educational value.[16]

Interestingly, in the debates about mystery films on television it transpired that the main problem was not the mystical itself. Several articles made the point that this was an enduring part of Indonesian culture, and the existence of mystics and belief in supernatural powers in Indonesian society was not denied. All kinds of shamanism, superstition, mystical objects, ghosts, and a seemingly endless number of other supernatural creatures were cited as an undeniable part of the beliefs and culture of the Indonesian people.[17] To a great extent Indonesian horror films built on that foundation, and even those who protested against horror films often professed a belief in ghosts, *jin* (genies), *tuyul* (a spirit which obtains wealth for its human master), and other supernatural beings. Yet, there was a particular narrative allotted to the supernatural in which it was supposed to operate. In horror films set during the New Order, which was ruled by policies of development, there was no space for the supernatural. In legends of the past, or under the guidance of a religious authority, who would step in and restore order at the end of the film, however, the supernatural was tolerated. Similarly, newspaper articles which voiced complaints about mystery films did not pay much attention to films of the legendary or folk-story type. Their objections to mystery films and television series applied to those films and series which diverged from the sanctioned modes of addressing the issue, or which were felt to be out of kilter with leading state and Muslim discourses. Hence, heated debates about

---

16 'Film mistik bisa jadi "narkotik psikologis"', *Angkatan Bersenjata*, 14-2-1995; 'Sinetron misteri kian diperbanyak', *Harian Terbit*, 2-9-1996; 'Ubah jam tayang sinetron misteri', *Republika*, 9-10-1997; 'Menpen minta; LSF tidak loloskan film tentang jin dan setan', *Angkatan Bersenjata*, 25-2-1998; Gus 1997; Suryapati 1997.
17 'Dari diskusi "Pengaruh siaran radio dan TV terhadap anak" tayangan mistik sudah dianggap berlebihan', *Media Indonesia*, 7-10-1997; Hasim 1997; Gus 1997; Nurudin 1997; Pudjiastuti and Redana 1997; Suryati 1996.

mystery films in newspaper articles from February 1995 to April 1998 were about defining 'authorized' narrative practices for the supernatural or mystical.

Most debates in articles from September 1996 to April 1998 were about the mystery television series, which had adopted a new formula. This required a new definition and demarcation of the supernatural and the rational. The mystery series *Si Manis Jembatan Ancol* was based on an urban legend of Jakarta about a female ghost and set in the present. The series *Jin dan Jun* was about a girl called Jun, who finds a *jin* in a bottle who becomes her friend. *Tuyul dan Mbak Yul* was about a girl who befriends a *tuyul*; it bore a very strong resemblance to *Jin dan Jun*. None of these three series depicted the familiar horror legend type, nor did they feature a *kyai* as rescuer. In *Si Manis Jembatan Ancol* a ghost, Mariam, settles the scores with evil. She helps murder victims to take revenge, haunt, and kill their murderer in retribution. The series of the *jin* and *tuyul* type, which had a mystery-comedy format, solved problems with humour.[18] Initially the majority of those with objections to these new series were Islamic groups and persons with Muslim backgrounds. Later their ranks were joined by government ministers, psychologists, and others who can loosely be styled 'authorities'. *Si Manis Jembatan Ancol* and, in particular, the series about *jin* and *tuyul* were considered problematic as they were thought to pose an indirect challenge to religious (Islamic) and state discourses on the sanctioned forms of imagining the supernatural and reality.

Among those with Muslim backgrounds the difficulty lay not so much in the fact that the series did not feature a *kyai* to step in and clarify and resolve the plot. On the contrary, on various occasions Muslims protested against a perceived misuse of Quranic verses in mystery films: verses were used simply as a spell to exorcise ghosts, rather than as an intrinsic part of a code of belief. Some Muslims were also greatly upset by the unrealistic depiction of *kyai* in horror films, which accorded the religious teachers supernatural powers and had them tossing around balls of fire. It was a problem of negotiating and demarcating representations of the fictitious and the real, on the basis of 'facts' emanating from competing worldviews.

The debate about narrative practices and the bounds of representing the supernatural and the rational in mystery television series was launched in 1996, when the chairman of the Majelis Ulama Indonesia (MUI, Indonesian Council of Muslim Scholars), Hasan Basri, stated that *Jin dan Jun* and *Si Manis Jembatan Ancol* indi-

---

18 I thank Dimas Jayasrana for providing me with useful information and comments about these series.

rectly disputed religious teachings.[19] While Basri did not divulge his objections to mystery series, Imam Tantowi, film director and screenplay writer, did. Tantowi stated he did not object to mystery films, as long as the content or message of these films did not contravene religious teachings or mislead the viewers. It was on these grounds that Tantowi did not approve of *Si Manis Jembatan Ancol*: the series was about a female ghost and, in Islam, there are no such things as ghosts. However, Tantowi, who held a minority viewpoint amongst those protesting against new horror formulas, did not have a problem with *Jin dan Jun*. Even though he had seen it only once, he did not think its content strayed too far from Islamic teachings, in which the existence of *jin* is acknowledged.[20] He said that he assumed the film-makers had consulted a Muslim *jin* first.[21]

His opinion was one of a few voiced and it was only gradually that the *jin* and *tuyul* series specifically emerged as the subject of a heated debate.[22] In an article in the newspaper *Pikiran Rakyat*, critic Abdul Hasim wrote about the return to Indonesian television of the mystical in a new format. Hasim (1997) states that, unlike earlier in horror films, in this new format, the *jin* and *tuyul* were no longer presented as frightening creatures, but were 'kind, friendly, and often very close to human beings and their everyday lives'. This atypical representation of *jin* and *tuyul* was perceived as problematic. Besides the fear that such series would reinforce people's belief in *jin* and *tuyul* (Gus 1997),[23] the greatest objection expressed in most articles was that mystery series were either not in accordance with people's general perception of *jin*,[24] or not in harmony with Islamic teachings.[25] Hence, in some articles it was denied that the appearance of *jin* and *tuyul* in mystery television series was part of Indonesian culture, and allegations were made that they had been

---

19 'Ketua MUI; Jin dan Jun tak ada gunanya', *Pos Film*, 22-9-1996.
20 In Islam, the existence of *jin* (Ar. *jinn*) is completely accepted. Muslims believe that jinn are ethereal or fiery bodies, intelligent, imperceptible, with the capacity to assume different forms and capable of performing heavy labour. Their relationship to Iblis or Shaitans (the Devil or devils) in general is obscure. In Sura xviii.50, Iblis is said to be of the jinn; Sura ii.34 however, implies that he was one of the angels. As a consequence great confusion followed, with many legends and hypotheses being spawned (Gibb and Kramers 1974).
21 Suryati 1996. Literally, he said: 'So, it seems it has not strayed too far from religious teachings because possibly they talked to a Muslim jin first' ('Jadi, rasanya, tidak terlalu menyimpang jauh dari kaidah agama, karena mungkin mereka telah berdialog terlebih dahulu dengan jin muslim'). This also relates to the point about people raising objections to mystery films and at the same time emphasizing their belief in supernatural issues.
22 Many viewers of the series, probably the majority, apparently had no objections.
23 'HSBI prihatinkan sinetron mistik', *Harian Terbit*, 14-4-1997.
24 'Ubah jam tayang sinetron misteri', *Republika*, 9-10-1997.
25 'HSBI prihatinkan sinetron mistik', *Harian Terbit*, 14-4-1997.

borrowed from Indian fairy tales[26] or were attempts to imitate films from Hong Kong (Suryati 1998). Refuting the allegations that the mystery series were based on Indian fairy tales Raam Punjabi, owner of the very successful production house Multivision Plus, which produced some of the most popular programmes on Indonesian television, including *Tuyul dan Mbak Yul*, stated that the *tuyul* in his series was closely modelled on descriptions of *tuyul* in old Indonesian folk tales.[27] Punjabi, who is of Indian descent, has often been criticized for his background; critics claim that his soaps do not represent Indonesian culture and are only the purveyors of dreams.

In February 1998, Minister of Information Hartono instructed LSF to ban films and television series with *jin* or *tuyul* as a theme. His stated reason was that these were not didactic. Hartono felt that if a story in a television series presented the goodness or kindness of a *jin*, this did not accord with reality/the truth: 'Honestly, I've never seen a *jin*. So how can we tell if there are good *jin*. Please do not cause a rift in our nation by purveying items which are at odds with religion. Do not teach the people to see something that does not exist'.[28] The former Director General of Radio, Television and Film, Alex Leo Zulkarnaen, was also disturbed by false representations of *jin* in television series. In an interview in which his opinion was asked on the increase in number of the members of LSF to specifically censor mystery films, he made the remark: 'Can you imagine producing television series with a *jin* as the main character, going so far as to have the *jin* called Uncle Jin or Aunty Jin. They [all parties involved in the production and screening of television series] go overboard selling dreams.'[29] Despite the ban on the *jin*-type mystery comedies in February, the series were still being screened in March 1998, with *Jin dan Jun* the most popular. When asked about the actions taken by the Department of Information to end the screening of such series, the Guidance Council of Film and Video answered that a letter had been sent to all private television stations requesting them to obey broadcasting regulations and reduce the number of films with superstitious themes.[30] How-

26 'HSBI prihatinkan sinetron mistik', *Harian Terbit*, 14-4-1997.
27 'Setelah dikritik MUI "Tuyul dan Mbak Yul" akan berubah cerita', *Berita Yudha*, 7-11-1997.
28 'Terus terang, saya tidak pernah melihat jin. Lalu bagaimana kita bisa bercerita bahwa jin ada yang baik. Tolong bangsa kita jangan diasah dengan hal-hal yang bertentangan dengan agama. Jangan mendidik masyarakat untuk melihat sesuatu yang tidak ada.' ('Menpen minta; LSF tidak loloskan film tentang jin dan setan', *Angkatan Bersenjata*, 25-2-1998.)
29 'Masak bikin sinetron yang tokohnya jin, sampai jin-jinnya dipanggil Om Jin atau Tante Jin. Mereka itu menjual mimpi terlalu berlebihan.' See 'Mantan Dirjen RTF Leo Zulkarnaen; 'masak bikin sinetron yang tokohnya jin", *Sinar Pagi*, 7-3-1998.
30 'Seputar tayangan takhayul; TV swasta dapat peringatan', *Harian Terbit*, 16-3-1998.

ever, before the regulations could be enforced, Reformasi, the bid for change in every possible field after thirty years of New Order rule, culminated in the stepping down of President Soeharto in May 1998.

HORROR FILMS FOR CINEMA AND TELEVISION: DEVELOPMENTS OF REFORMASI

During and after Reformasi the world of film was overwhelmed by a host of new developments. Under the presidency of B.J. Habibie (1998-1999), a process of democratization of the media was set in motion. During the presidency of Abdurrahman Wahid (1999-2001), the Ministry of Information was officially abolished, but LSF continued to exert its function, even though its position was called into question. As discussed in chapters 2 and 4, the euphoria and disorder accompanying Reformasi gave rise to new film genres and also redefined the use and substance of film discourse and narrative practices. The spirit of Reform also had an impact on the genres of horror films and mystery television series. Two distinct changes were introduced for horror films: newly released horror films often ignored the old formula of the film genre, and from 2001 onwards they were being screened in top-end cinemas.

The first horror film produced for the cinemas after the fall of Soeharto, *Jelangkung*, represented both these changes. In October 2001 this film, which was shot on digital video camera and directed by the young film-maker Rizal Mantovani, was shown in major cinemas in Jakarta. As discussed in Chapter 2 the story, based on urban legends in Jakarta, was totally different from that of New Order horror films. Shot in music-video style and with a soundtrack of popular music, the film tells the story of a group of teenagers who set out on an adventure to look for ghosts in haunted places in and around Jakarta. On a camping trip to a little village, Angker Batu in the hills of West Java, one of them conjures up a ghost by using a *jelangkung*, as a result of which the whole group is haunted. Nowhere in the film does a *kyai* appear, nor are any other religious symbols apparent. Moreover, the film does not have a mystical setting and, even though it is about legends, these are filmed as part of reality and the lives and beliefs of teenagers in present-day Jakarta. After its success in Jakarta, *Jelangkung* was screened in cinemas throughout the country; it was the box office hit of 2001, reaching 1.3 million viewers. Following *Jelangkung*, more horror films, the bulk of them produced by young film-makers, were released and screened in top-end cinemas: *Titik hitam* (Black point, November 2002, Sentot Sahid), *Satu nyawa dalam denting lonceng kecil* (One soul in a little tinkling bell, November 2002, Abiprasidi), *Peti mati (The coffin)* (February 2003, Mardali Syarief), *Jelangkung*'s sequel *Tusuk jelangkung* (Demon's spike, March 2003, Dimas Djayadiningrat), and *The soul* (November 2003, Nayato Fio Nuala). None of these films made any pretence about inserting religious elements and, apart from *Peti mati,* which was set in the 1960s, the films were situated in the present.

This seems to provide evidence that during Reformasi, the Code of Ethics for film production was abandoned. Horror films for cinemas were being produced in a new style and their formulas were more varied. The appearance of a *kyai* was no longer perceived as obligatory. Moreover, most films which reached the top-end cinemas depicted the mysterious in the present, as part of modern life. Did this signify the end for the *kyai* then? It did not. In cinemas, the *kyai* was still found where he had always been since the 1980s: in the lower-class theatres, primarily those located in the outskirts and kampung areas of the city and in rural areas. Even though most contemporary Indonesian horror films used new styles and formats, a horror film released in November 2002 still adhered to the old New Order format of horror films. *Kafir (Satanic)* (Infidel (Satanic), Mardali Syarief), was inspired by a true story which occurred among the people of Cigugur in West Java during the fight for Independence in 1945. Through flashbacks, it tells the story of a shaman who is obsessed by the idea of becoming a *wali* after he has gone in search of spiritual knowledge (*ilmu*) and has become an apprentice to a mysterious, allegedly immortal man on a mountain. Moving to a small village with his wife and son, he sets up a practice as a healer there. But as the story advances, he becomes involved in practices of black magic, and after he has been killed, the earth refuses to receive his body.[31] In *Kafir (Satanic)*, as in the old New Order horror films, an Islamic authority figure comes to the rescue by restoring peace and order. Film critic Joko Anwar (2002b) writes: 'Watching the latest release of locally made horror flick *Kafir* (Unbeliever), the joy of watching such campy horror movies in the '80s would certainly come back to the audience's

---

31 In 2003, the producer and director of the film had to defend their statement that they had based the film on a true story from Cigugur before the National Commission of Human Rights. The people of Cigugur were of the opinion that the film insulted their ancestors and presented a false representation of history, misrepresenting the teachings of the religious figure Pangeran Madrais, whom they believed was referred to in the film ('Komnas HAM panggil sutradara "Kafir"', *Sinar Harapan*, 16-4-2003; 'Film Kafir diprotes', *Kompas*, 17-4-2003; 'Produser film Kafir datangi Komnas HAM', *Bisnis Indonesia*, 19-4-2003).

mind'. He mentions that *Kafir* was made by an 'old-time film director', while other recently released horror films had been the work of new talents (Anwar 2002c). In contrast to *Jelangkung* and other films made by young film-makers, *Kafir (Satanic)* was released in lower-class cinemas. Its producer, Chand Parwez, claims the film was very popular, especially in rural areas (Anugerah 2003).

Apart from the *kyai*'s enduring presence and popularity in old-style horror movies mostly found in rural areas, this figure also appears in a new mystery television format after the fall of Soeharto. Due to the momentum of Reformasi, the February 1998 decree, which enforced the reduction of the screening of *jin* and *tuyul* series, never came into force. A year later, in March 1999, when questions were asked about the continuation of mystery series on television, it was said that people needed entertainment and that it would be better not to ban these series until there was more political stability.[32] By 2001, the screening of horror films and mystery series on television had increased considerably. Initially, reruns of old horror films and mystery television series were screened, but gradually the production of new series and television films ensued.[33] By the end of 2001, a new formula of mystery series for television had emerged. At the root of this new formula lay the re-instatement of religious authorities in the form of *kyai*, *ulama*, or simply people with authority speaking on behalf of Islam. When a new television series, *Kismis* (an abbreviation of *kisah misteri*, mystery tales), was screened by private television station RCTI in 2001, it launched a new formula in the mystery genre called *infotainmen horor* (horror infotainment), which would eventually lead to the return of the religious figure. Inspired by the huge success of *Jelangkung*, *Kismis* was based on the reconstruction of existing legends and stories about ghosts and haunted sites in Indonesia.[34]

Kismis follows a formula where the programme host, a model (Caroline Zachri), interviews people who have had a blood-curdling experience (*peristiwa seram*). After the interview, the stories of the informants are visualized in a semi-documentary-style reconstruction. For example, a couple of young men happened to be walking home late at night after having played cards. Along the way, they see a beautiful woman to whom they are attracted, but as they come closer, her face suddenly transforms into a hideous apparition. Rumours abounded that the well they had just passed was haunted. In the first year of the series, the programme was

---

32 'Sinetron mistik terlibas politik', *Harian Terbit*, 15-3-1999.
33 'Klenik dan tayangan misteri yang tetap digemari', *Kompas*, 5-8-2001.
34 'Acara horor di TV dan radio; Iiih ngeriii... tetapi, bikin penasaran lho', *Kompas*, 13-1-2002.

24 minutes long and included three separate accounts by three sets of informants. Screened on Thursday evenings at ten o'clock, its slot was filled with commercials and it proved popular with television viewers (the first couple of episodes had a rating of about 7% to 9% according to the AC Nielsen survey).[35]

In the wake of *Kismis'* success, similar programmes soon followed suit. In 2002 there were three: *Percaya nggak percaya* (Believe it or not) and *O seraam* (O scaary!), which were screened by Anteve, and *Dunia lain* (The other world), which was broadcast on Thursday evening by Trans TV. The series *Percaya nggak percaya* greatly resembled *Kismis* in that it was also about true ghost stories and legends, and was presented by a model (Arzeti Bilbina). Some episodes of *Kismis* and *Percaya nggak percaya* dealt with the same subject, such as the story of a haunted house in Pondok Indah, South Jakarta, but in *Percaya nggak percaya*, the presenter did not interview informants herself but just introduced excerpts of mystery stories. These mystery stories were told to a reporter who went on location accompanied by an informant and an eyewitness. As proof of the authenticity of the story in *Percaya nggak percaya*, the reporter was accompanied by a supernatural expert/practitioner (*praktisi supernatural*). This person would relate what he 'saw' at the haunted site, and at times transmit (that is 'speak on behalf of') the wishes of the ghosts or other creatures at a certain location. The inclusion of strange occurrences in a part of the programme was a standard part of the series. A foggy image or shadow would appear on the television screen, or perhaps some eerie sounds would be heard, and a narrator (either a voice-over or the reporter on location) would then say: 'That is not simulated, but is actually happening' (*itu bukan rekayasa, tetapi kejadian sesungguhnya*).[36]

Taking a slightly different tack to *Kismis* and *Percaya nggak percaya*, Anteve's second series *O seraam* recounted various ghost stories based on people's own experiences. This horror infotainment programme was interactive and people could phone in and recount the uncanny events they had personally experienced. This programme also included a quiz about a ghost story.[37] The third new horror infotainment programme, *Dunia lain*, had a host (Harry Pantja) who challenged people to stay overnight at haunted

---

35 'Acara horor di TV dan radio; Iiih ngeriii... tetapi, bikin penasaran lho', *Kompas*, 13-1-2002; Anugerah 2002.
36 '"Infotainmen horror" di televisi hasratnya mencekam, wudjudnya menggelikan', *Kompas*, 22-9-2002.
37 '"Infotainmen horror" di televisi hasratnya mencekam, wudjudnya menggelikan', *Kompas*, 22-9-2002.

locations. They were then asked to narrate their experiences the next day. One episode entitled 'Hantu kuburan Cina' (Ghost of the Chinese graveyard, broadcast on 19 September 2002) begins with a man narrating how he regularly desecrates Chinese graves when digging up the riches rumoured to be buried inside. Once when he was engaged in this nefarious pursuit, a ghost suddenly appeared. In the next segment of the programme, someone was dared to stay overnight at the grave where the ghost had been seen. The camera then filmed that person remaining at the grave all night long, and recorded all movements. After sunrise, the reporter returned and asked the person about his experiences.[38] As in *Percaya nggak percaya*, during the recording eerie sounds could be heard and images, which were said to be authentic, appeared on screen.

Even though they still greatly resembled one another, the various horror infotainment programmes made strenuous efforts to find diverse forms to transmit authentic experiences of the supernatural as facts and part and parcel of the daily lived reality of Indonesian people. The key word reiterated in the depiction of the supernatural in the horror infotainment series was 'real'.[39] All series were based on true stories (*kisah nyata*), and what was recorded or reconstructed was claimed to be authentic and not fabricated (*bukan rekayasa*). Although in 2002 for the authentication of the supernatural experiences the stories of eyewitnesses and the help of a paranormal or supernatural expert was deemed sufficient, by 2003 religious authority, through the participation of a *kyai* or an *ulama*, was once again favoured as an essential part of horror infotainment programmes. It was in this year that the number of horror infotainment series markedly increased. Besides the above-mentioned programmes on RCTI, Anteve, and Trans TV, other television stations now also broadcast their own horror infotainment series. To compete with this, in January 2003 *Kismis* came up with a new segment of thirteen half-hour episodes called *Kismis; Arwah penasaran* (Mystery tales; Lost souls). Again the series was about true stories, but this time the focus was restricted to the category of ghost stories about the wandering souls of people who had died by suicide or had been murdered, consequently leaving behind their unresolved problems on earth. The director of the new series, CC Febriono, claimed that *Kismis; Arwah penasaran* was different from the other mystery series which had recently swamped the television stations.

38 '"Infotainmen horror" di televisi hasratnya mencekam, wudjudnya menggelikan', *Kompas*, 22-9-2002.
39 On post-Reformasi television programmes focusing on the depiction of what is 'real' and on 'facts', 'truth', and 'authenticity', see Arps and Van Heeren 2006.

Its scope extended far beyond exploiting the scare factor of the stories of lost souls, as the programmes of other television stations did; *Kismis; Arwah penasaran* would also find a solution at the end of the story. Publicity contained such sentences as: 'For example, to help the lost soul enter the Hereafter in peace the mediation of a *kyai* is required', and: 'And indeed a good solution is still to ask Allah for help.'[40] An example of *Kismis; Arwah penasaran* screened on 5 January 2003 was the story of Eriya, a girl from Kampung Asem, Cililitan, East Jakarta, who was murdered when she was six months pregnant. She was found with her throat slit open, her head nearly severed from her trunk. Her soul wandered through the area in search of the person who had killed her and people from the village often encountered her ghost. All was well after an *ustaz* had prayed for her. She was then able to return to her world (*kembali ke alamnya*) in peace (Anugerah 2003). By June 2003, the producer of *Percaya nggak percaya* felt that his programme also required the prestigious assistance of a religious co-star. Initially the series had consisted of several parts, but now it was thought best just to maintain the *cerita misteri* section about people who had experienced a supernatural event. As a new development, the programme would no longer merely give a 'news coverage of mysteries' (*liputan berita seputar misteri*), but would also involve the participation of an Islamic paranormal medium, who would lead prayers and beseech permission and guidance from Allah before location shooting commenced. The participation of a paranormal medium on location as well as a break at sunset to observe the sunset prayer (*sholat Maghrib*) would be a hard and fast rule. It was felt that this would ensure that the production of the series would not encounter any hindrance from the spirits which it may have disturbed.[41]

The most extreme example of a marriage between horror realities and symbols of Islamic authorization was the horror reality show *Pemburu hantu* (Ghosthunters), which hit the screens in early 2004. In this programme ghosts were caught 'live' on screen. The concept of *Pemburu hantu* was based on the Hollywood blockbuster *Ghostbusters* (Ivan Reitman, 1984), a film about a team of men hunting down and catching ghosts. In *Pemburu hantu* this theme was applied in real life. People at home could call the television programme to report ghostly apparitions or some haunted place. The

---

40 'Misalnya untuk mengembalikan arwah penasaran ke alam baka dengan tenang membutuhkan bantuan kiai.' 'Dan memang jalan keluar yang baik tetap meminta pertolongan kepada Allah.'
41 'Tayangan bau mistik laku; Mahluk halus sering mengganggu', *Majalah Film*, (13-27)-6-2003.

Pemburu hantu team would then set out to investigate the place and, should they indeed be present, capture the ghosts or other supernatural beings and cleanse the place and its surroundings of 'negative energies'. After the ghosts had been captured, a sticker would be glued on a wall with the image of a ghost and the words 'under observation' (*dalam pengawasan*). If the ghosts had not re-appeared after a few weeks, this sticker was replaced by another sticker showing the image of a ghost crossed out and bearing the words 'free of ghosts' (*bebas hantu*). The slogans associated with the programme sounded like commercials for a detergent: 'Ghosthunters, the supreme solution for overcoming ghosts!' (*Pemburu hantu solusi jitu atasi hantu!*) and 'Ghosthunters: contact us, we'll come, and we'll cleanse [the place]!' (*Pemburu hantu; hubungi kami, kami datang, kami bersihkan!*).

The *Pemburu hantu* team consisted of four persons: the supernatural expert (a *dukun kejawen*, or Javanese magic specialist) Pak Hariry Mak, Ustaz Aziz Hidayatullah, a young *kejawen/santri* (Javanese mystic/Islamic scholar), Ki Gusti Candra Putih, and a painter, who drew portraits of the beings with his eyes covered. During the programmes the team prayed and invoked God's help several times before, during, and after the ghost hunt. Its members also asked for the 'interactive prayers' (*doa interaktif*) of the viewers at home, beseeching God's support (*doa restu*) to ensure that the mission would be brought to a safe conclusion. When their mission was accomplished at the end of the programme, in a final comment Ustaz Aziz would confirm the existence of supernatural beings and explain that this also is acknowledged in Islam, for their existence is described in the Quran.[42]

The participation of religious leaders in *Kismis; Arwah penasaran*; the observance of religious rituals in *Percaya nggak percaya*; the emphasis on the authorization of Islam and the power of prayer in the hyper-real *Pemburu hantu* series –all are reminders of the influence of the Code of Ethics. During the New Order, a *kyai* figured prominently as the appropriate authority figure or expert to restore order in horror films which dealt with public taboos as a means to evade censorship. While many New Order censorship regulations and guidelines for film production became obsolete during Reformasi, within a few years the *kyai* resurfaced to deal with supernatural issues, or to speak on behalf of ghosts and other supernatural creatures, in a new formula for the mystery television series. There was now a subtle difference. The re-instated participation of religious figures in post-Soeharto mystery television

---

42 For a detailed description of an episode of *Pemburu hantu,* see Arps and Van Heeren 2006.

series implied a discourse about the supernatural which diverged from those discourses circulating during the New Order. In addition to the rise in reality TV, the socio-political climate of Reformasi set in motion a questioning of past dominant discourses of New Order rule. To unravel the authoritarian dogmas of the New Order, a widespread call for 'facts', 'truth', and 'authenticity' resounded. The search for post-Soeharto versions of the facts, realities, and truths of Indonesian society also impinged on mystery television programmes. Moreover, there were commercial grounds for such a call: reality shows cashed in on people's beliefs in the supernatural. In this setting, everything claimed to be true in horror infotainment programmes needed proof that it was 'real' and not caused by mere camera tricks or special effects. For example, a senior lecturer in criminology at the University of Indonesia in Jakarta, Prof Dr Tb Ronny Rahman Nitibaskara, proposed that in order to refute the idea that whatever occurred in the mystery programmes was fictitious, these programmes should be subjected to an analysis by an assembly of *ulama* and experts from different disciplines.[43]

Hence, the use of religious and other authorities in the new formulas devised for the mystery television genre during Reformasi functioned to authenticate what was shown on television as real. The tendency to define and authenticate the mysterious as part of present-day reality shifted the previous New Order boundaries, which had determined where the real and supernatural in Indonesian society should be placed and how they should be understood and exploited. In that sense, the *kyai* in horror reality shows after Reformasi challenged those discourses which rejected the mysterious as part of modern Indonesian society, marking possible new forms of imagining contemporary society. Nevertheless, the participation of religious leaders and the observance of religious rituals were presumably also re-instated to ward off anticipated objections by mainly Islamic groups, which may have felt disturbed, had the mysterious been allowed to hover undefined and uncontrolled. As such, the presence of a *kyai*, combined with an Islamic medium and religious observance on set as an integral part of these programmes, was intended to permit and legitimize the new themes in horror infotainment. Reminiscent of the old practices of evading censorship under the New Order, the use of these religious figures and symbols can once again be perceived as a safeguard enabling producers to show everything which might be construed as problematic, and still get away with it.

[43] 'Mengapa tayangan mistik digemari?', *Republika*, 12-4-2003.

CONCLUSION

In this chapter I examined the Indonesian horror genre as a forum for the representation of constituents of the nation and the formation of national identity. I showed that the genre itself, as well as certain formats and formulas employed in it, represented and imagined specific audiences and communities. New Order discourses about horror films produced for the cinema argued that the genre represented, first, the Indonesian film industry and Indonesian peoples, who, as part of Eastern culture, were close to mysticism. Second, horror films were seen as a genre for the lower classes and rural communities, because the films were screened mostly in rural or lower-class cinemas. Third, because of the *deus ex machina* formula which employed the intervention of a *kyai*, horror film was gradually equated with *film dakwah* and Islamic communities. When horror films were produced in another format, for the medium of television, and reached broader Indonesian audiences other connotations began to arise. The emphasis shifted to different ways of imaging and imagining the supernatural and rational in Indonesian society and raised the discourses about the horror genre to another level.

From this new perspective, discourses about the horror genre sought to find acceptable forms of representing the supernatural on Indonesian television without interfering with New Order conceptions of how to image and imagine the modern Indonesian nation. Mystical films or television series faced opposition if they did not reflect certain sanctioned formulas and dominant discourses about development and the rational – or reality based on Islamic teaching – of how to imagine the supernatural in New Order society. For example, in 1998 Minister of Information Hartono proscribed these series so as not to 'cause a rift in our nation with items which contest religion'. During fierce debates about mystery films, the definition of acceptable modes of representation of the supernatural and reality was discussed. Reformasi implied changes in both senses. The first shift occurred in the link between certain film formats and formulas and certain imagined audiences or communities. Changes in horror film formulas altered the specific association of horror with lower-class, rural, and Islamic communities. Several horror films produced for the cinema demonstrated a new freedom of expression among film-makers. In many cases the changes heralded the exit of the *kyai*. Also, a number of new Indonesian horror films were now screened in top-end cinemas, signalling that horror was no longer a genre confined to the lower classes only.

The second change could be found in the discourses of how to imagine the supernatural as part of Indonesian society. During Reformasi, television began to produce horror programmes according to new formulas. Within a few years new horror 'reality shows' or infotainment programmes emerged. These presented the supernatural as part of the everyday life of Indonesians. Such programmes contested the New Order discourses which had defined the mysterious as a realm outside reality. However, even though horror reality shows altered discourses about the supernatural, in due course old modes of representing the mysterious emerged again in some of the new television formulas. Personified by the *kyai*, past representations regained ground in an altered discourse. The *kyai* was an unrivalled asset in the exploitation of the supernatural in Indonesian audio-visual media. He increased the realism of horror reality shows and warded off censorship at the same time. I further explore the combination of commerce, censorship, and Islam in post-Soeharto media in the next chapter.

6

The celebrity *kyai* and phantoms of the past
Tussling with the bounds of Indonesian moralities, realities, and popularities

After two weeks of controversy the teen flick *Buruan cium gue!* (Kiss me quick!, 2004, Findo Purwono) was withdrawn from Indonesian cinemas on 21 August 2004. The film had passed the censors but after its release it had elicited strong protests from the famous *dai* (preacher), public figure, and businessman Abdullah Gymnastiar. Without actually having seen the film – basing his views simply on its title – AA Gym believed that it would encourage illicit premarital sex amongst teenagers. It did not take him long to round up support in Islamic governmental and mass organizations. After two weeks of loud protests from these groups the film was banned from cinemas. The producer, Raam Punjabi, retracted it so as 'not to destabilize the nation any further'.

Muslim protests stirred up by putatively inappropriate films were nothing new. Both under New Order rule and during Reformasi, films were banned, withdrawn from circulation, not publicly screened, or even not produced in anticipation of Muslim protests. Nevertheless, there were subtle changes in the socio-political environment under the New Order compared to after Soeharto's rule had ended. One significant difference was that during Reformasi, in response to the rise of freedom of expression in all kinds of fields, Muslim protests were expressed more loudly. Furthermore, in the freer atmosphere of Reform, images of Islam gradually achieved greater exposure in the Indonesian media. In the context of protests in the name of Islam, between 2003 and 2007 such outcries particularly attracted substantial media attention. It was not just film which elicited protests; music and dance performances and visual arts also drew the ire from some Muslim groups. In 2003 the uproar around *Buruan cium gue!* was preceded by a controversy about the famous *dangdut* singer and dancer Inul Daratista. Pious Islamic veteran *dangdut* singer and film star Rhoma Irama expressed his disgust with Inul's sexy dance movements. His objections to Inul's dances launched a heated debate about whether or not her provocative hip rotations could be defined as an act of pornography and be forbidden on the grounds of religious moral values. In 2005 another two cases which attracted ample media attention involved the militant Islamic organization Front Pembela Islam (FPI, Islamic Defenders Front). Like some other Indonesian Islamic paramilitary organizations, FPI can be linked to politicians or high-ranking members of the military and police.[1] Since its formation in August 1998, FPI had invariably been depicted in the Indonesian media as a fanatical Muslim group which would not shy away from violence to make its point. The first case which involved a protest from FPI in 2005 concerned the use of the Arabic calligraphic symbol for 'Allah' on the cover of the album *Laskar cinta* (Love army) of the rock band Dewa 19. FPI also objected to a television performance by the band because during the show, dancers trod on the calligraphic symbol which was painted on the studio floor. FPI accused Dewa 19 of blasphemy, reported the band to the Jakarta city police, and demanded a public apology. The second case which made the limelight was accompanied by FPI protests against a photograph on display at the 2005 CP Biennale art exhibition in Jakarta. It depicted a nude Adam and Eve. FPI repudiated this photograph on the grounds that it was pornographic and consequently reported photographer Davy Linggar, art curator of the Biennale Agus Suwage, as well as 'Adam', who was personified by popular television actor

---

1   Hefner 2002:14, 16. The FPI was formed in August 1998 and has strong ties with high-ranking members of the military and police. It was established with the direct assistance of the then commander of the armed forces, Wiranto (Hefner 2004:14), and now claims to have branches in 22 provinces. Based in Jakarta, FPI is led by Habib Muhammad Riziek Syihab, a religious teacher who was educated in Saudi Arabia. Many of the top FPI leaders, including Habib, have Arab blood. The stated goal of FPI is the full implementation of Islamic Syariah law, although it supports the current Indonesian constitution and avoids making demands for an Islamic state. FPI has a paramilitary wing called Laskar Pembela Islam (Army of Defenders of Islam), and is well known for organizing raids on bars, massage parlours, and gaming halls. FPI justifies these raids on the grounds that the police are unable to uphold the laws on gambling and prostitution. Sceptical observers suspect that the police turn a blind eye to, or are even complicit in, these activities, in the understanding that the victims will be encouraged to keep up payment of protection money to the police. In late 2001, FPI took the lead in threatening to evict Americans from Indonesia in retaliation for the US operations in Afghanistan, although the threat was not actually carried out; see http://www.aph.gov.au/library/intguide/FAD/sea.htm (accessed 19-11-2011). Even though FPI is sponsored by members of the military and police, the faction keeps a certain amount of autonomy. As Robert Hefner emphasizes, FPI cannot be seen as a mere puppet of an all-powerful military. There are significant groupings among the army, police, and the intelligence community who would be happy to see FPI suppressed. Since FPI is aware of the factions and divisions within the army and police itself, it can play this card to resist commands and achieve its own objectives (Hefner 2004:17).

Anjasmara, and 'Eve', the well-known model Isabella, to the Jakarta police. In February 2006, the four were named suspects who allegedly had displayed obscene art which affronted certain religious groups (Suryana 2006).

The growth in Muslim protests against films, music performances, and works of art in post-Soeharto Indonesia was linked to discourses about the position of Islam in the Indonesian public sphere and its role in the politics of Reform. This issue was a very old one, dating back to pre-Independence days. Then the discourses centred on the position of Islam in the Indonesian Constitution. The burning question at the time was whether the new Indonesian nation-state should separate state and religion or, alternatively, adopt a document known as the Jakarta Charter (*Piagam Jakarta*). This charter paved the way for the state to implement Islamic law among Muslims. The Jakarta Charter was rejected and in its stead the Pancasila was adopted as the state ideology on 22 June 1945. Reformasi and the concomitant bid it brought to change society reopened the debate on whether the Indonesian nation should be ruled on the basis of Islamic principles. Although in the period between 1998 and 2007 the general feeling was still that Islam should not be part of the Indonesian Constitution, in the public sphere and in regional politics Islamic values were gradually gaining ground. In particular, the law on regional autonomy, officially promulgated on 1 January 2001, strengthened the position of Islamic rule as part of regional regulations (*peraturan daerah*, Perda).[2] Between 2001 and 2005, the regional governments in Aceh, Tangerang, Cianjur, Padang, and South Sulawesi all implemented regulations based on Islamic law. Furthermore, in 2006 an important debate took place which involved questions about the position of Islam in ruling the nation. The majority of these discourses occurred in the context of the proposal for the drafting of a new law which would regulate public morality and boost the endeavour to ban pornography from the public domain. Under the presidency of Habibie (1998-1999), rightwing Muslim parties had proposed a new law on pornography. In 2006 their efforts bore fruit in the Rancangan Undang Undang Anti Pornografi dan Pornoaksi (RUU APP, Anti-Pornography and Porno Action Bill). Among the aims the law hoped to achieve, was to ban kissing in public, sensual dances, and the depiction of sexual activity in literature, paintings, photographs, and recordings.[3]

2   For more on regional autonomy, see Usman 2001; Jacobsen 2003.
3   Suryana 2006. For more background information on RUU APP, see 'Anti-Pornography Law- Indonesia' from *journeymanpictures*, posted on YouTube, http://www.youtube.com/watch?v=WFm2Y7CmoEA (accessed 19-12-2011).

Ideas about the implementation of Islamic values in the framework of the bill led to vehement protests from both non-Islamic and moderate Islamic groups. In the words of Muhamad Ali (2006), lecturer at the State Islamic University in Jakarta, the controversy between the proponents of the bill and its critics exposed 'the fault lines of a cultural war between the conservatives and the liberals, with the silent majority in the middle'. Next to the wider exposure and increased intensity of Muslim protests against films, performances, and visual arts, another difference between New Order Indonesia and Reform was that Islamic features became more frequent in audio-visual media after the fall of President Soeharto. To some extent this could be attributed to the growing number of Islamic groups and organizations which had begun to use audio-visual media as a tool for religious propagation and self-representation. As discussed in Chapter 4, this had led to the founding of the new film genre and movement of *film Islami*. The ideas and representations of Islam which the Islamic film movement had in mind with *film Islami* did not reach the Indonesian mass media. Instead, as discussed in Chapter 5, horror reality shows produced by commercial television stations were increasingly associated with religious propagation. In 2004, this trend of Islamic authority figures appearing on television increased yet again. A new television genre, called 'religious soaps' (*sinetron religius*), emerged. Although initially confined to the fasting month of Ramadan, these soaps, which had an outwardly Islamic appearance, were also screened on television after this time. Gradually, images of Islam managed to evade this framework, but the new religious series were still haunted by ghosts and, generally speaking, the stories still focused heavily on tearful repentance. As was the case in the horror reality shows, the religious soaps were imbued with elements of mystery, in the form of supernatural occurrences, and also reiterated the claim that they were based on true stories. Moreover, the religious soaps accorded a major role to heroes in the form of Islamic authority figures, as did films and series of the horror genre. *Kyai, ustaz, ulama,* or *dai* appeared in the soaps themselves, or celebrity *kyai* introduced the programmes and brought them to a close. Hence, even though Islamic films had broken free from the framework of Ramadan, most Islamic productions on television were a far cry from the envisaged *film Islami*.

The proliferation of images of Islam on television and the wider exposure of Islamic groups in their efforts to regulate audio-visual media, music, and art, could not but influence narrative practices in film and television. This chapter is an attempt to discover the way in which Islam was implicated in defining the bounds of post-Soeharto film and television narratives.

THE BAN ON KISS ME QUICK!: THE KYAI, THE FOREIGNER, AND INDONESIA'S MORALITY

On 5 August 2004, the film *Buruan cium gue!* was released in top-end cinemas of the Cinema 21 group in fifteen different cities. The film followed the average formula of 'ABG' (*Anak Baru Gedhe*, teenager) television soaps. It featured a simple love story about a young couple, Ardi and Desi, who are each other's first love. The girl, Desi, comes from a rich family. The boy, Ardi, is a poor orphan who works hard after school to pay for his education. Even though they have been dating for two years, Ardi has never kissed Desi on her lips. Ardi, who adheres to 'old-fashioned' principles, does not want to kiss his girlfriend before it is the right time to do so. Desi, on the other hand, dreams of being kissed by him. Most of her girlfriends at school have already been kissed. On a radio programme about 'the first kiss', Desi lies about her first kiss and it is this lie that stirs up a tempest of troubles. Because Ardi has never kissed her he wonders when and by whom Desi was kissed. After a plethora of misunderstandings all the problems are solved. In the end Ardi and Desi enjoy their first kiss.

Buruan cium gue! was produced by the 'king' of television soaps, Raam Punjabi. Since the beginning of the 1990s his production house Multivision Plus has been very successful in producing popular entertainment for Indonesian television. The film *Buruan cium gue!* strongly resembled the formula of Punjabi's other soaps, and it also featured actors and actresses who had played in one of his popular soaps, *Anak Baru Gedhe* (Teenagers). This soap had been launched two years earlier on the Indonesian private television station RCTI. In an interview, Punjabi mentioned that he had wanted to produce a version of the television series for the big screen, because '[t]here are things which actually do happen amongst teenagers but which cannot be shown in soaps; these are exposed in *Buruan cium gue!*'.[4] Only three days after its release the film sparked major controversy. On 8 August 2004, the then very popular *dai* Abdullah Gymnastiar raised objections to the film. He did so in his bimonthly Sunday sermon, which was broadcast live from the Istiqlal Mosque in Jakarta on private television channel SCTV, in a homily called *Indahnya kebersamaan* (The beauty of togetherness).

AA Gym was convinced that the film *Buruan cium gue!* contained pornographic elements, a conclusion which he extrapolated from its title alone; this inspired him to attack the film in his sermon. He said

---

4 'Ada hal-hal yang sebenarnya terjadi di kalangan remaja tapi tidak bisa ditampilkan dalam sinetron, itulah yang dimunculkan dalam Buruan Cium Gue!' ('Sekadar menjadi versi bioskopnya', *Kompas*, 8-8-2004.)

Buruan cium gue! was dangerous, as it would encourage premarital sex among teenagers. Gym said that according to Islamic doctrine it was a sin for a man and a woman who were not married even to touch each other, let alone kiss. Not only did such a kiss run counter to Islamic doctrine, it was one sure step on the road to premarital sex. Pursuing this theme, AA Gym asserted that the title of the film might as well be changed to *Buruan berzinah* (Hurry up, let's fornicate).

Soon after his televised sermon, AA Gym won the support from the MUI and several Islamic mass organizations. Some of these mass organizations initiated protests against the film, demanding that it be banned. The president of MUI, Amidhan, asserted that the film was not at all suitable to be screened in Indonesia. He too considered the title of the film to be an insuperable hurdle. It implied 'porno action' (*porno aksi*, meaning porn-related acts). Moreover, he believed that scenes of premarital kissing in the film destroyed the morality of the nation and should therefore be banned. Amidhan argued that additionally the film could be construed as an insult to religion. He felt personally offended that the film portrays the tale of how an initially deeply pious boy discards his religious moral values and in the end succumbs to kissing his girlfriend before marrying her (Yordenaya 2004a). Presumably stimulated by the support of MUI and the mass organizations, AA Gym began a tour around the city in efforts to gauge the popularity of *Buruan cium gue!* among film audiences. On Friday 13 August, in an interview before his visit to some film theatres, he laid heavy emphasis on the fact that he did not intend to watch the film personally. He reiterated that the title alone made it palpably clear that it ran counter to basic religious values and posed a serious danger to the younger generation of Indonesians. AA Gym declared that his sole purpose was to visit the cinemas to check on the popularity of the film. Precisely because of the controversy he had stirred up, the cinemas which screened *Buruan cium gue!* were packed. Many in the audience simply wanted to see what all the fuss was about and were curious about the risqué scenes. The majority came away disappointed after watching the film. It was an ordinary Indonesian soap or teen flick and there was nothing special to see.[5]

5   For example, in the wake of the controversy the ticket sales in Semarang rose. About 70% to 80% of the tickets were sold, which was not often the case when Indonesian films were screened. At first the pro-contra issue about *Buruan cium gue!* brought in lucrative business. However, when it became known that the film did not touch on any particularly controversial matters, ticket sales soon declined. See 'Mana yang perlu disensor?', *Minggu Pagi Online*, http://www.minggupagi.com (accessed 28-8-2004).

Nevertheless, AA Gym and his supporters continued their mission of protest against the film. Five days after his cinema visits, AA Gym and his associates set out to call on LSF. On 18 August they paid a visit to the head of the institute, Titie Said, in order to interrogate her about the institute allowing the film's general circulation in cinemas. In answer to Gym's questions, Titie Said explained that the kissing scene in *Buruan cium gue!* adhered to the censor's guidelines. It was believed that the scene portrayed a part of the daily lived reality of contemporary Indonesian youth. Moreover, Titie argued, before the making of *Buruan cium gue!* several other Indonesian films which had passed the censor had already contained kissing scenes. She explained that the title reproduced the trendy language used among teenagers. Despite her neutral explanation, after the visit by AA Gym, Titie Said commented in an interview that she believed that Gym's call on LSF was a sign that the institute had made an incorrect decision. As the film had already passed the censorship procedures, however, the institute was not entitled to withdraw it from cinemas (Yordenaya 2004b).

Surprisingly, four days later it was. On 21 August 2004, after a fortnight of controversy, the film was withdrawn from the cinemas. The institute, with the agreement of Punjabi's Multivision Plus, had decided to bow to the pressure of the public rejection of the film. LSF withdrew its approval of the film on the grounds that it had 'disrupted public order'. The Ministry of Culture and Tourism issued a letter revoking the distribution of the film and Multivision asked cinemas to stop screening it (Unidjaja 2004). The film copies were sent back to the production company, and it was decided that *Buruan cium gue!* would be re-released later that year after some editing and under another title. Raam Punjabi told the press that in revising the film, he would involve religious leaders in the production process in addition to the censor institute. Punjabi regretted that *Buruan cium gue!* had been banned, but believed that it was more important that the nation was not divided over it.[6] Punjabi clearly emphasized he had not retracted his film because of its content. The film, he argued, showed nothing but the factual lives of middle-class young people in Indonesian society.

The controversy did not stop there. In their turn groups of journalists, intellectuals, film-makers, writers, artists, and other public figures began to protest the banning of the film. The protest raised by these groups articulated a fear of the implementation of a new form of censorship on the basis of religious moral grounds. In the

---

6 'Mana yang perlu disensor?', *Minggu Pagi Online*, http://www.minggupagi.com (accessed 28-8-2004).

newspaper *The Jakarta Post*, cultural critic Zoso wrote that he was afraid that censorship on the basis of religion would be the first step on the path to political repression and restrictions on the freedom of expression. He recalled that the Indonesian media had already experienced such restrictions under Soeharto rule and nobody wanted to go back to this. Zoso (2004) emphasized that religion should not become an instrument of harassment. Others also probed the question of the role of religious pressure in the banning of *Buruan cium gue!*.[7] On 25 August the cultural centre Utan Kayu produced a petition signed by film-makers, intellectuals, artists, and other public figures. This petition addressed three points. Its first point was that the withdrawal of the film was an annihilation of the freedom of expression and could be seen as an anti-democratic action at odds with human rights. Its second objection was that religious authorities and symbols (in this case Islamic) should not be brought into the public sphere, but be reserved for the private sphere. The third objection raised was that this ban on a work of art was perceived as moralistic, dogmatic, old-fashioned, and not representative of the religious/Islamic community in Indonesia as a whole (Gaban 2004).

Ignoring such criticisms, Islamic pressure groups continued to stage protests against films and television programmes. Members of the Aliansi Masyarakat Anti Porno-Aksi (AMAP, Alliance of People against Pornographic Acts) complained about the programmes *Cowok cowok keren* (Handsome guys) on RCTI, *Nah ini dia* (Nah here he/she/it is) on SCTV, and *Layar tancep* (Mobile cinema) on Lativi. In their view, these programmes were merely a vehicle for selling sex. Even though each of the series had passed the censor, as far as AMAP was concerned they exceeded the boundaries of what was acceptable in the Indonesian media.[8] In this atmosphere, producers of films which might possibly elicit protests tried to pre-empt objections, usually by claiming that their films just represented reality. One of these films was *Virgin* (Hanny Saputra, 2004), which was released not long after *Buruan cium gue!* The film, which was noticeably inspired by the US films *Thirteen* (Catherine Hardwick, 2003) and *Coyote ugly* (David McNally, 2000), was said to depict daily life

7 Film director Ahmad Yusuf believed that AA Gym should have watched *BCG!* first before voicing his protests. The fact that the film was removed from cinemas after AA Gym's protests, he stated, recalled the atmosphere of the old regime. He considered the role of MUI to also be dubious, as the MUI member on the Censor Board had obviously let the film pass for release. Still, after AA Gym had raised an outcry, MUI had joined the protests against the film. 'Mana yang perlu disensor?', *Minggu Pagi Online*, http://www.minggupagi.com (accessed 28-8-2004).
8 'Mana yang perlu disensor?', *Minggu Pagi Online*, http://www.minggupagi.com (accessed 28-8-2004).

in contemporary Indonesia. In a television programme about the making of *Virgin*, producer Chand Parwez emphasized that the film showed what was actually happening in Indonesian society. According to Parwez, *Virgin*, which depicts teenage girls clubbing, using drugs, drinking alcohol, and selling their bodies to men to pay for trendy clothes and gadgets, was produced 'to inform and warn parents'. Parents, he said, should watch the film together with their children in order to make themselves aware of the dangers inherent in contemporary city life and, thus armed, teach the children right from wrong.

At the same time as protests about the moral value of *Buruan cium gue!* and similar films were occuring, an anti-pornography law was being drafted.[9] In 2006 discussion of the bill led to a huge controversy, which, according to lecturer Muhammad Ali (2006), was best understood in the context of the struggle of finding a fitting definition of the public morality of the Indonesian nation-state. Until 2006 any serious discussion of the law had mainly been conspicuous by its absence. The law was proposed under the presidency of Habibie and was brought up again a few times during the presidencies of Abdurrahman Wahid and Megawati Soekarnoputri. In 2003, new interest in an anti-pornography law was aroused by the enormous upheaval across the country caused by the erotic dance movements of the *dangdut* singer Inul Daratista. The hip gyrations of the rising star were compared to the working of a drill, giving her the title 'queen of the drill dance' (*ratu ngebor*). Inul's dance aroused the ire of celebrity, film star, and 'king of *dangdut*' Rhoma Irama. A devout Muslim, Rhoma Irama declared that Inul's drill dance posed a threat to the morality of the country and that such 'porno-action' – he was the one who launched the term – should be banned from the public domain. The row between Inul and Rhoma Irama received wide exposure in the Indonesian mass media and divided Indonesia into pro- and contra-Inul camps (Barendregt 2006; Wiwik Sushartami forthcoming). It did not take long for the controversy to enter the forum of social and political discourse and instigate discussions on public morality. Some were captivated by Inul's dance movements and viewed these as a form of art. Others were loud in their condemnation, as they believed Inul's dance movements downgraded the nation's morality. The discourses on Inul's drill dance as an expression of porno-action prompted some right-wing Islamic groups in the House of Representatives to

---

9 See the revealing title of an article in *The Jakarta Post* of 21 August 2004: 'Local teen flick withdrawn after Muslim leaders' protest; The House of Representatives is deliberating a bill on public morality, which bans kissing in public'.

push for the speedy enforcement of a law against pornography and porno-action. However, it was to be another two years before the Anti-Pornography Bill was discussed intensively.[10]

The case of *Buruan cium gue!* widened the scope of earlier discussions about the role of the government and Islamic values in the regulation of public morality. In an article posted on the Indonesian mailing list *Layarkata*, Farid Gaban, a journalist at *Kantor Berita Pena Indonesia*, wrote that the protests against *Buruan cium gue!* went far beyond this film. Farid interpreted these as a symptom of the Indonesian public being fed up with the existing trend in Indonesian mass media, which were completely dominated by mystery programmes, an obsession with private lives and the scandals surrounding celebrities, and vulgar criminal news programmes (Gaban 2004). In the same vein, in 2005, commenting on the controversy around the Anti-Pornography Bill, Muhammad Ali suggested that the drafters and supporters of the bill thought that the moral values in Indonesian society were being degraded by the rise of freedom of expression. Thinking particularly of the increase in pornographic materials in tabloids, art shows, literature, and films, Ali argued that such people saw these developments as a massive threat. Religious leaders and pressure groups, Ali believed, needed the bill as they found themselves powerless to impose their worldviews without a legal basis (Ali 2006).[11]

While some believed that freedom of expression had gone too far and blemished the Indonesian nation, others embraced it as part of the open and democratic society Indonesia had become during Reform. As mentioned earlier, some feared that religion would provide the new grounds on the basis of which the freedom of expression in Indonesian society would be restricted. Such commentators as Zoso (2004) compared the role of AA Gym and Islamic groups which had elicited the ban of *Buruan cium gue!* with 'the tyrannical authority' exercised by the Department of Information during the New Order. Gaban likewise expressed the fear that the case of *Buruan cium gue!* would lead to a new renunciation of freedom of expression. He was worried that the petition launched by Utan Kayu would trigger a polarization in which AA Gym would be supported by such groups as FPI, the Majelis Mujahiddin Indonesia, (MMI, the Indonesian Council of Defenders of the [Islamic]

---

10 In early 2005, President Susilo Bambang Yudhoyono declared he would call for maximum measures to ban pornography in Indonesian written and audio-visual media (Barendregt 2006:9-10).

11 In his paper on the use of mobile phones and debates on the RUU APP, Barendregt (2006:6) also refers to the fear of some that the liberalization of society had gone too far.

Faith), components of the Hizbut Tahrir (HT, Party of Liberation, an international Sunni pan-Islamist political party), or the Partai Keadilan Sejahtera (PKS, Prosperous Justice Party), which would fight with renewed vigour. Gaban (2004) was afraid that if that happened, the government would respond by reducing freedom of expression drastically.

Nevertheless, in the views of some others, among them noted psychologist Sartono Mukadis, comparing the ban on *Buruan cium gue!* to the limitations imposed on the freedom of expression during the New Order was inaccurate. Mukadis was adamant that the protests of one person backed by a number of groups could not be compared to the rigid control exercised by institutions which was implemented under the New Order. He was not at all convinced that the case of *Buruan cium gue!* reflected the birth of a new system which would curb the freedom of expression on the basis of religion because, he argued, when Rhoma Irama spoke on behalf of religion in his attempts to stop Inul from performing, he had failed to achieve his purpose (Mukadis 2004). In a similar comparison, Jujur Prananto went a step further. He did not think the cases of *Buruan cium gue!* or Inul were connected to the question of whether Islam was at the basis of new censorship regulation in Indonesia. Instead, he saw both cases as evidence that control over the nation was in the hands of those people who wielded great influence. In the era of Reform, Prananto argued, power was in the hands of the most popular celebrities: at the time, Inul Daratista and AA Gym (Prananto 2004). Even so, Inul owed her victory over Rhoma Irama not only to her popularity, but also to the fact that she was supported by prominent Nahdlatul Ulama (NU, Revival/Awakening of Islamic Scholars, a 30-million-strong Muslim organization) figures such as former Indonesian president Abdurrahman Wahid and Ahmad Mustofa Bisri (Islamic leader and teacher as well as painter and poet, well known as Gus Mus).

Prananto did address two valid points. Firstly, it was true that in post-Soeharto Indonesia celebrities dominated the mass media and, secondly, that the use of religion as grounds to control censorship was not irrefutable. The victory of AA Gym and religious groups in the case of *Buruan cium gue!* was based not purely on religion. It was a mixture of stardom, popularity, and religion, all on the side of the popular real-life *kyai*-celebrity AA Gym, which turned the case into a non-contest for Raam Punjabi, the film's producer. The latter was of Indian descent and therefore open to accusations of being a 'foreigner' and 'capitalist' promoting non-Indonesian secular realities. As said, the withdrawal of a film in response to Muslim protests was not something new. Under the New Order there had also been some cases in which Islam was used as grounds to ban or retract films. The next section gives a broader overview of the role of Islamic authorities and mass organizations and the fear of Muslim protests in film production, exhibition, censorship, and self-censorship during the New Order and Reform.

CENSORSHIP FROM THE STREET: THE AUTHORITY OF RELIGION

Under the New Order, influential censorship of the media was based on the principle of SARA. The mass media were not permitted to cover SARA-related subjects in any critical way, as there was a fear that this would destabilize the nation. Besides the guidelines for SARA, rules and regulations were drawn up specifically for film administered by the Film Censor Board/Institute (BSF/LSF.) The members consisted of representatives of the government, the legal profession, the army, film producers, and several religious organizations, among them the Indonesian Ulama Council, Nahdlatul Ulama, Muhammadiyah, Dewan Gereja-Gereja di Indonesia (DGI, Council of Churches in Indonesia), Konferensi Wali Gereja Indonesia (KWI, Bishops' Conference of Indonesia), and Parisada Hindu Dharma Indonesia (PHDI, Hinduism Society).[12] Both domestic films and imported products had to pass the board of censors before they could be released in cinemas or on television, or distributed in the format of video cassettes, VCD, and DVD. As mentioned in chapters 2 and 5, besides the official censorship regulations laid down in Indonesian film legislation, a special Ethical Code for Film Production was created in 1981. Despite the involvement of a special commission for administering religious principles in the creation of the Ethical Code for Film Production and the co-operation of representatives of religious mass organizations in the censorship system, from time to time there were protests about films, which were led by religious, mainly Islamic, communities and (mass) organizations. These protests interfered directly in censorship proceedings, or were raised to demand the withdrawal of films which had already been released by the board. However, such protests were apparently random: not all films which might conceivably have been rejected on the grounds of religious sentiments raised objections, and at times protests were elicited by films which contained nothing that could be construed as contrary to religious teachings.

12 'LSF diminta meniadakan tontonan kekerasan, seks dan mistik', *Suara Karya*, 21-6-1995.

Between 1993 and 1997, such groups as Forum Komunikasi Lembaga Dakwah, (FKLD, Communication Forum of Dakwah Institutions), Himpunan Mahasiswa Islam (HMI, Association of Islamic Students), Komite Indonesia untuk Solidaritas Dunia Islam (KISDI, Indonesian Committee for Solidarity in the Islamic World), and branches of MUI in different provinces of Indonesia all lodged protests about films.[13] The greatest objections were raised against 'pornographic' images in Indonesian films. Ever since the 1970s, various Indonesian films had toyed with an impression of female nudity and sex. Members of Muslim organizations in particular feared that these films would have a bad influence on the young generation and lead them to stray from religion. The films were deemed to be unacceptable from the point of view of religion and to oppose the essence of Indonesian cultures and traditions. Anwar Sanusi of Lembaga Pengkajian dan Pengembangan Dakwah (LPPD, Institute for the Study and Development of Dakwah) and Ahmad Suaidy and Husein Umar, respectively head of and spokesperson for FKLD, argued that Indonesia was a pious nation.[14] Even though the majority of those protesting about films were members of Muslim groups, leaders of other religious groups upheld the same ideas about pornography. They also argued that films which contained nudity or sex should be forbidden: 'The sentiments of the Islamic community are also those of the Roman Catholic, Protestant, Hindu and Buddhist communities'.[15]

Alongside regular protests about the circulation of both legal and illegal pornographic films and videos, or the qualms voiced about sexy film posters, which mainly tended to be lodged during the fasting month of Ramadan, under the New Order there were three particular cases in which protests about films sparked heated controversy.[16] In all three cases, Muslim protests interfered in the work of the film censor. Twice the controversy involved imported

13 '12 lembaga dakwah protes keras film "Bagi-bagi Dong"', *Pelita*, 31-12-1993; 'Kelompok Islam di Yogya protes film porno', *Pikiran Rakyat*, 2-8-1994; 'MUI Jatim minta sensor film dan iklan TV diperketat', *Berita Yudha*, 28-7-1995; 'MUI Jatim minta film & iklan jorok dilarang', *Berita Buana*, 26-1-1996; 'Ulama Jatim protes tayangan sadisme di TV', *Republika*, 4-3-1996; Yaya Sutara 1994.
14 '12 lembaga dakwah protes keras film "Bagi-bagi dong"', *Pelita*, 31-12-1993; '"Bagi-bagi dong" diprotes 58 ormas Islam', *Harian Terbit*, 7-1-1994; Anwar Sanusi 1993.
15 'Tindak tegas distributor', *Suara Karya*, 21-7-1996.
16 For accounts of various protests, see 'Umat Islam Jabar; Habisi film porno', *Republika*, 25-7-1994; 'Kelompok Islam di Yogya protes film porno', *Pikiran Rakyat*, 2-8-1994; 'Puluhan ormas Islam protes film porno', *Merdeka*, 2-8-1994; 'Keberatan pemutaran film porno; HMI Ciamis datangi DPRD', *Pelita*, 17-2-1995; 'Ketua LPLI Sunan Ampel; Hentikan film panas selama bulan puasa', *Sinar Pagi*, 18-1-1996; 'MUI Jatim minta film & iklan jorok dilarang', *Berita Buana*, 26-1-1996; 'Di bulan Ramadhan poster porno masih marak', *Berita Yudha*, 28-1-1997.

films from the US. The first of these was *True lies* (James Cameron, 1994), which was perceived to be an insult to Muslims as they were represented as terrorists. Even though *True lies* had passed the censor, Muslim groups demanded it to be withdrawn from circulation. The upshot was that its popularity soared and it was transformed into an item very much in demand in pirated-video sales. The second film which upset Muslim sensibilities was *Schindler's list* (Steven Spielberg, 1993), which never reached Indonesian cinemas. Before they had even watched the film, some Muslim groups were convinced that it contained Jewish propaganda and protested against its release in Indonesia. In order not to incite Muslim protests further, but also because it did not get permission from the film-maker to cut any scenes, LSF decided not to release the film.[17] Again this film proved a popular item which was widely available in piracy networks. A third controversial case involving the efforts of Muslim groups to override state censorship. was sparked by the Indonesian film production *Pembalasan Ratu Laut Selatan* (Revenge of the Queen of the Southern Sea, Tjut Djalil, 1988). This film was a horror story about a legendary goddess who harbours a snake in her vagina which bites off the vital organs of men who have sex with her. *Pembalasan Ratu Laut Selatan* had passed the censor, but after its release Islamic organizations strongly objected to the film's content. The organizations objected to the pornographic theme of the film and singled out particular scenes for especially hard criticism. Because of the uproar caused by these protests, after a few days the film was withdrawn from cinemas.

During and after Reformasi a huge wave of new developments in the world of film came about. Just as various groups and film-makers were experimenting with testing the boundaries of Reformation's new freedom of expression, some Islamic groups were gauging the extent to which they could have their say in the restriction of these liberties.[18] Such Islamic groups as FPI, PKS, and the *laskar* (paramilitary unit) of Masyarakat Anti Pembajakan dan Pornografi Indonesia (MAPPI, Indonesian People Against Piracy and Pornography), a special force consisting of some 750 people, the majority of whom were part of the *banser* (paramilitary wing) of NU, organized themselves to win victories over what they considered amoral, anti-Islamic film products. MAPPI instigated raids to halt the sell-

---

17 'Schindler's List & sensor kita', *Pikiran Rakyat*, 10-7-1994.
18 These discourses recall the early years of Independence in the 1950s. At that time debates were also imbued with a spirit of great enthusiasm about the future of Indonesian cinema and also covered the questions of American film imports, censorship, and Islamic morality (Sen 1994:19-20, 22-3).

ing of pirated or banned films, which involved demolishing stalls of street vendors.[19] FPI mainly confined itself to threats. Television stations and organizers of film festivals, for example, were left in no doubt that their offices or cinemas would no longer be safe if the screening of certain films was to go ahead.[20]

In post-Soeharto Indonesia, the fear of protests from Islamic groups not only restricted the distribution of films, but at times also hindered the production process. In 2001 film director Garin Nugroho planned to make a film, called *Izinkan aku menciummu sekali saja* (Let me kiss you just once), about a young boy in a *pesantren*, who dreams of kissing a beautiful Chinese girl whom he happens to see walking by every day. However, after protests from *pesantren* representatives the producer retracted funding for the production of the film (Wardhana 2001b). Garin relocated the setting to Papua, where Roman Catholics are in the majority. In 2003 the film was released under the title *Aku ingin menciummu sekali saja* (I want to kiss you just once).[21] Garin Nugroho found himself contending not only with protests from Muslim groups. In 2005, during the pre-production of his film *Sinta obong* (The burning of Sinta), the Gerakan Perempuan Hindu Muda Indonesia (GPHMI, Indonesian Young Hindu Women's Movement) repudiated the film because it believed the screenplay was offensive to the Goddess Sinta and the true story of the Ramayana. GPHMI also emphasized that even though Hinduism was a minority religion in Indonesia, the nation should be aware that one billion Hindus worldwide believed in the Ramayana. Moreover, they declared, Bali, Hinduism, and its symbols and sacred books should neither be attacked by bombs (referring to terrorist attacks that were committed in the name of Islam

---

19 'Laskar MAPPI siap menggeledah Glodok', *Media Indonesia*, 16-4-2000.
20 In 1999, violent threats by FPI to disrupt the screening of the Israeli film *Kadosh* (Sacred, Amos Gitai, 1999) caused the committee of the Jakarta International Film Festival not to show it. In 2000, protests by FPI led to the end of the screening of the highly popular Latin-American soap *Esmeralda* on SCTV. FPI demanded that the soap be banned because the antagonist was called Fatima, the name of the daughter of the Prophet Muhammad, and giving an antagonist her name was perceived to be an insult to Islam. In 2003, members of PKS organized protests in all cities during the road-show of the independent film production *Novel tanpa huruf R* (Novel without the letter R, Aria Kusumadewa, 2003). However, the film-maker refused to stop screening his film and in a counter-move opened a debate with the people who had protested against his film at a film screening in Bandung.
21 In the same year, Garin Nugroho encountered another protest from Islamic groups. This time the trouble was caused by his production of a Public Service Announcement (PSA) called *Islam warna warni* (Different hues of Islam). The MUI protested against this PSA and demanded a ban, alleging that mentioning the 'different hues' of Islam represented Islam as something ambiguous. In the opinion of MUI, there was only one Islam, and different interpretations of the religion were not possible. To represent Islam as something unfixed was perceived as an insult (Abidin 2003).

in 2002 and 2005), nor treated with contempt (*pelecehan*).[22] In the end Garin produced the film after judiciously changing the title to the more comprehensive *Opera Jawa* (Javanese opera, 2006).

In addition to these examples, generally speaking between 1999 and 2004 the religious protests, the majority of which were launched by Muslim groups, were not markedly different from those staged under the New Order. In the outcry concerning film and VCD and DVD productions most protests targeted 'amoral' films depicting what was interpreted as pornography as well as female nudity. On television in particular, Latin-American telenovelas and such American series as *Baywatch*, *Melrose Place*, and *VIP* were considered to be incompatible with Islamic values, which were often cited as forming the basis of Indonesian culture and civilization. As a sop to accommodate members of the Islamic community, programmes which may have been construed as offensive were put on hold during the Islamic fasting month. But as soon as Ramadan was over, they simply resurfaced.[23] Again, notwithstanding the various examples which may be adduced, it must be emphasized that religious protests about films were sporadic and did not cover all films which might have incited controversy from a religious-moralist point of view. For example, a kissing scene in the teen flick *Ada apa dengan Cinta* (What's up with Love, Rudi Soedjarwo, 2002), and a kiss by a gay couple in *Arisan* (Gathering, Nia Dinata, 2003) did not generate a murmur of dissent.

After the ban on *Buruan cium gue!* and protests against various television programmes by AMAP at the end of August 2004, discourses began to address the need for the involvement of religious authorities in film and television production. Because of the controversy aroused by *Buruan cium gue!*, both the strengthening of the role and representation of Islamic authority figures in the LSF and a revision of censorship rules in the near future, including the assessment of film titles, was on the cards.[24] Some favoured the involvement of Islamic authority figures, not as any official part of the state system but in the form of pre-censorship or self-censorship in the production process. In early August 2003, a year before the controversy about *Buruan cium gue!* erupted, a representative of film professionals in the censor institute, Tatiek Malyati Ws, had already put

---

22 'Film Sinta Obong diprotes di Bali', *Bisnis Indonesia*, 9-12-2005.
23 'Libatkan para ulama dalam Badan Sensor Film', *Terbit*, 18-1-2000; 'MUI; Pemerintah harus tegas tertibkan pornography', *Warta Kota*, 13-11-2001; '90% tayangan teve langgar kaidah agama', *Republika*, 13-3-2002.
24 'Mana yang perlu disensor?', *Minggu Pagi Online*, http://www.minggupagi.com (accessed 28-8-2004).

in a request for stronger self-censorship on the part of film producers and television stations. Moreover, she had called on the leaders of the nation, parents, and religious authorities to be pro-active in lodging complaints against pornographic films and participating in censorship.[25] In the controversy which blew up around *Buruan cium gue!*, it seems her ideas were implemented. Besides pro-active protests leading to a ban on a film, king of soaps Raam Punjabi announced that he intended to involve religious leaders in the revision of *Buruan cium gue!*.[26] It is difficult to obtain any clarification on the ways in which and extent to which Raam Punjabi proceeded in honouring this promise of involving Islamic authorities in his film and television productions. It is remarkable, however, that after the ban on *Buruan cium gue!*, religious soaps appeared more frequently on television and were no longer confined to the framework of Ramadan.

The boom in the production of religious soaps commenced in February 2004, when the private television station TPI began to broadcast the series *Rahasia Ilahi* (God's secret).[27] The series was based on true stories of people who had experienced the wonders of God, accounts of which were published in the magazines *Hidayah* (God's guidance) and *Allah Maha Besar* (God is great). *Rahasia Ilahi* was hosted by Ustaz Arifin Ilham, a young, fairly popular *dai*. Television viewers loved the series and it brought TPI to the number one spot in the AC Nielsen ratings with a share of 15.8%. Sensing a successful formula, other television stations were quick to follow suit with similar programmes.[28] While most of the series drew their stories from among the common people, some religious soaps were based on stories from old Islamic sources.

---

25 'Sensor segera tayangan televisi…!', *Republika*, 6-8-2003. At the beginning of 2003, when 45 new members of the Film Censor Institute were appointed for the period 2002-2005, the secretary of MUI, Ichwan Sjam, stated that he regretted that the number of representatives of religious mass organizations in the board that year had declined from two persons per organization to only one ('Cyber Media', *Kompas*, 28-1-2003). Before 2003, the Islamic mass organizations Muhammadiyah and NU were both represented by two persons on the board.
26 'Mana yang perlu disensor?', *Minggu Pagi Online*, http://www.minggupagi.com (accessed 28-8-2004).
27 For more on the popularity of religious series in for example Egypt and India, see Abu-Lughod 1993 and Mitra 1993 respectively.
28 SCTV produced *Astaghfirullah* (May god forgive me!; also an exclamation used when one is shocked by immoral behaviour), based on true stories from the magazines *Ghoib* (Mysterious, pertaining to the invisible (divine or supernatural) sphere) and *Kuasa Ilahi* (God's power). Trans TV had *Taubat* (Repent and foreswear), taking its stories from the magazine *Insting* (Instinct), and the series *Insyaf* (Aware) and *Hidayah*. Lativi screened *Azab Ilahi* (God's wrath) and *Sebuah kesaksian* (Witness to faith), both based on stories of people who had experienced or witnessed miracles which they attributed to God.

These sources, mainly *hadits* (traditional collection of stories relating to words or deeds of the Prophet Muhammad, the chief source of guidance for understanding religious questions), were adapted to a present-day setting. To name one, TPI's *Takdir Ilahi* (God's divine decree) used *hadits* taken from Bukhari and Muslim, which were inserted in the books *Mi'ah qishshah wa qishshah fi anis al-shalihin wa samir al-muttaqin* (One hundred tales and the tale of the righteous), written by Muhammad Amin Al-Jundi Al Muttaqin, and *Madarij al-salikin* (The path of the mystic traveler), written by Ibnu Qayyim Al-Jauziah.[29] In advertisements, TPI went to great lengths to emphasize that *Takdir Ilahi* was an 'actualization of occurrences which had once taken place in the time of the Messenger of God' (*aktualisasi dari peristiwa yang pernah terjadi di zaman Rasulullah*) (Ruslani 2005).

The above-mentioned religious television series featured both supernatural occurrences and an Islamic authority figure. A *kyai, ustaz, ulama*, or *dai* would appear at the beginning or the end of the episode either to introduce and explain the programme, or to play a role in the story itself. For example, the young *ustaz* Jeffry al-Buchory, who was very popular among teenagers, hosted the programme *Azab Ilahi*. Each episode of *Astaghfirullah* featured an *ustaz* in its storyline, and the series *Takdir Ilahi* always ended with pronouncements by Ustaz Ali Mustafa Yaqub from MUI. Mustafa not only explained the *hadits* on which the series was based to round off the programme, he also supervised every stage of production. To conclude, Mustafa would present a disquisition on the solution by which the evil forces which had exerted a baneful influence on the main character could be exorcised. The director of the series, Chaerul Umam, emphasized that in the series the *ustaz* used the Islamic *ruqyah* method, a sanctioned instrument to expel evil, consisting of prayers which are consonant with the Syariah. As most of the religious series either contained elements of mystery or the intrusion of supernatural occurrences, the mission of the authority figures was to link these specifically to religious teachings. The producer of *Takdir Ilahi*, Dondy Sudjono, and Chaerul Umam explained that the appearance of Islamic authority figures in their series was to ensure that proper information was disseminated about how to deal with the supernatural. Without the explanations provided by Islamic authority figures, people might not interpret the series cor-

---

29 Bukhari and Muslim were Arab Islamic scholars who lived around AD 800/200 Shawwal. Their books, both called *Sahih*, are still highly celebrated among the collections of traditions (Gibb and Kramers 1974).

rectly, and there was the lurking danger that these series would only feed people's superstitions.

In fact, the religious programmes did not differ greatly from regular television horror programmes. Cultural critic Taufiqurrahman (2005) described the contents of the religious series

> as regular soap operas with God's name attached to their title [which] carry a formulaic story line in which sinners of all kinds, from corrupt state officials and gamblers to a misbehaving son, will be punished by God with a very painful death, ranging from literally being burnt in hell, eaten by flesh-eating worms to being swallowed alive by the earth. By the drama's end, after a noisy commercial break, a preacher will appear on screen to give a sermon about what sinners will face in the afterlife in return for their misdemeanors and will remind viewers not to commit sinful acts.

Moreover, Taufiqurrahman (2005) pointed out, as time passed some religious soaps deteriorated into campy horror shows featuring 'devout religious leaders [who] become engaged in Armageddon-like battles against demons (portrayed with red skin and two horns on their heads) and ghosts of all kinds'.

Only a few 'Islamic' soaps did not contain elements of mystery or supernatural occurrences. The actor and film producer Deddy Mizwar, who had produced and directed the Islamic film *Kiamat sudah dekat* (Judgement day is nigh, 2003) and played a role in its soap version, regarded the religion-inspired series as a mere extension of the horror and mystery programmes. In his opinion, the only difference was that these programmes now were packaged as if they were about Islam. The soaps, he argued, actually just repeated the success of mystery films in Indonesian cinema in the 1970s. This was the reason Deddy claimed that 'our nation has now stepped back again to the 1970s' (*masyarakat kita sekarang ini mundur ke zaman 1970-an lagi*) (Fitrianto 2005). Despite the dubious quality of the majority of religious programmes, MUI embraced them wholeheartedly. In 2005 its secretary general, Din Syamsudin, was quoted by the weekly *Gatra* as saying that there had been an internal discussion about the possibility of handing out awards to television channels which ran religious series.[30] Ismail Yusanto, spokesperson of Hizbut Tahrir, also believed that the religious shows breathed a breath of fresh air into TV programming (Taufiqurrahman 2005).

---

30 Taufiqurrahman 2005. As mentioned in Chapter 4, MUI had given awards in recent years to television stations which contributed to enlivening the Ramadan fasting month.

THE POST-SOEHARTO DISPUTE OVER CENSORSHIP: SPIRITS OF REFORM AND GHOSTS FROM THE PAST

With the twin phenomena of the growing fear of Muslim protests taking control of the film industry and the rise of religious soaps, it is fair to say that Islam increasingly directed narrative practices of post-Soeharto audio-visual media Along the lines of the earlier controversy about the Anti-Pornography Bill in January 2007, the juxtaposition of religious sentiments supporting conservative forces in society against those defending more liberal views also affected the world of film. At the end of December 2006 a new film movement, Masyarakat Film Indonesia (MFI, Indonesian Film Society) was founded. MFI represented a group of film professionals who wanted to initiate a belated reform of the old power structures in the film industry. It soon found itself in opposition to an old New Order film institution, LSF. In the disagreement between the two, LSF found support in its former opponent, the militant Islamic organization FPI. The commitment of FPI to the censor institute and its opposition to MFI reflected the wider conflict between conservative and liberal forces in the contest to rule the nation, bolstering public allegations that Islamic pressure groups were being put to use in a game of power play manipulated by the state.

The controversy was sparked off by the tremendous upheaval about the awards which were handed out at the Indonesian Film Festival (FFI) at the end of December 2006. After the fall of Soeharto, the production of films had grown because of the rise of mainly independent film-makers. In 2004 the state responded by reviving the Indonesian Film Festival. FFI, which had been held for the last time in 1992, was organized by a committee chosen by the Badan Pertimbangan Perfilman Nasional (BP2N, National Film Assessment Board). Since 1992 the BP2N had been the umbrella organization of all official New Order film organizations. As discussed in chapters 1 and 2, notwithstanding Reform and the dismantling of the Department of Information under the presidency of Abdurrahman Wahid, the New Order organizational system pertaining to film and its mediation practices had not been dislodged. Between 2004 and 2006, FFI, which was composed mainly of long-established figures in the film industry, handed out awards for best film and television productions. As an institution, FFI can hardly be said to have represented contemporaneous developments in the film industry. In inner circles of young film professionals who had emerged during Reform, FFI was criticized for being a bureaucratic body run in the spirit of the New Order. There was deep suspicion that FFI sidelined new talent in the industry and favoured the old guard and, much like New Order *arisan* film festivals, preferred to present awards to all participants rather than truly evaluating films (Sasono 2007). In 2006 the accumulated disappointment with FFI among young film-makers resulted in widespread controversy.

On 3 January 2007, twenty-two film-makers, actors, and professionals, mainly of the younger generation, symbolically returned the Citra trophies awarded to them between 2004 and 2006. In doing so, they protested against the jury's decision at the FFI 2006 to grant the award of Best Film to *Ekskul* (an abbreviation of *Ekstra kurikuler* (Extra-curricular, Nayato, 2006), and the jury's refusal to explain the selection process. The film *Ekskul*, produced by soap opera production house Indika Entertainment, was a campy high-school drama barely distinguishable from run-of-the-mill Indonesian soaps. It was inspired by the Emmy-award winning American television film *Bang bang you're dead* (Guy Ferland, 2002). Based on a true story, *Ekskul* recounts the tale of a student who takes his schoolmates hostage at gunpoint. In terms of the number of votes it received at FFI, the movie outdid the films *Berbagi suami* (internationally distributed under the title *Love for share*, Nia Dinata, 2006), a film dealing with problems of polygamy, and *Denias; Senandung di atas awan* (Denias; Singing above the clouds, John de Rantau, 2006), which was about a Papua farmer's son who pursues his dream to go to a real school. Both were widely acclaimed by film critics and film-makers alike (Taufiqurrahman 2007). The surprise victory of *Ekskul* unleashed a storm of discontent among film professionals of the *film indie* generation and beyond, who were exasperated by the hidebound Indonesian film industry.

Between 24 and 29 December 2006, around forty film professionals founded the new film movement MFI. Approximately 200 people, among them directors, producers, actors and actresses, film crew members, festival organizers, curators, journalists, members of film communities and organizations, and others who wanted to see changes in the Indonesian film industry supported the movement. MFI used the protest against FFI awarding a Citra for Best Film to *Ekskul* as the point of departure from which to criticize and call for changes in the official system in the Indonesian film industry.[31] In an interview, film producer, member of MFI, and chairman

---

31 In a press-statement issued on 3 January 2007, the movement called attention to the fact that the film *Ekskul* illegally used the music score of several Hollywood films, which constituted a breach of copyright. Pointing out that this was not noticed by the FFI jury, MFI concluded that this was an indication of the poor management and lack of competence on the part of the festival organizers.

of Jiffest Shanty Harmayn commented: 'We use this moment to call for changes to the system in our film industry. That is our main agenda' (Hari 2007). In a petition addressed to the State Minister of Culture and Tourism, the president, leaders of BP2N and other film-related organizations, and the House of Representatives on education and culture, MFI insisted that the organization of the 2006 FFI withdraw the award for Best Film and give a public explanation of the selection process used by the jury. MFI also petitioned for the temporary disbanding of FFI as well as the shutting down of all old film organizations and institutions and for replacing these with new, more democratic and more transparent equivalents. Turning to the legal side of things, MFI called for a revision of the 1992 Film Law and for a fundamental change in the rules and implementation of film censorship, as it was convinced that film should be regulated by a system of age classification rather than censorship, as was the case now. MFI vowed that if these demands were ignored, its members would boycott future state-organized festivals and consistently reject all activities organized by the government in the name of the Indonesian film industry.[32]

The controversy surrounding the 2006 edition of FFI exposed the tensions straining the relationship between the surviving New Order film institutions and the fresh sentiments pervading the industry espoused by newly emerging film-makers in the era of Reformasi. In 2006, the same system, institutions, and people that had been in place under the New Order still officially ran the film industry. Now, under the supervision of the Department of Culture and Tourism, old hands, mostly retired film professionals, were in charge of the BP2N film organizations. Although Reform had led to new press legislation and a new broadcast law, the film industry was still regulated by legislation dating back to 1992. As mentioned in Chapter 2, since the production of *Kuldesak*, in practice film-makers had not abided by all the rules and regulations of the New Order film law. Most film-makers whose talents emerged during and after Reform no longer bothered to observe all the stages of film mediation scrupulously set out by the New Order regime, and did not subscribe to any of the official film organizations authorized by BP2N. The only New Order film institution still carrying considerable weight was LSF. When producers chose to distribute their films through official channels for film exhibition, such as cinemas or through legal VCD or DVD productions, they were required to hand in a film copy to the censor beforehand.

---

32 See 'Pernyataan sikap MFI', http://masyarakatfilmindonesia.wordpress.com/pernyataan-sikap (accessed 19-12-2011).

6 The celebrity kyai and phantoms of the past

The state censor institute was notorious for both its ultra-conservatism and its arbitrariness. The criteria for censorship imposed by the board were extremely blurred.[33] The main explanation given for censoring a film was fear of social unrest, which meant the board was highly receptive to protests from religious groups, bureaucrats, and people in powerful positions.[34] Although many believed that censorship in Indonesia was redundant given the widespread availability of pirated VCDs and DVDs and the Internet, LSF's director, Titie Said, claimed that without censorship there would be 'more damage to society' (Diani 2005). Commenting on censorship, Titie argued: 'It's not undemocratic, we're not against artistic freedom. But there is a bigger interest here, that of the nation' (Diani 2005). The gist of the protest launched by MFI against FFI was that the latter was representative of both the state film system and state support for specific narrative practices. MFI argued that the time had come to revise the New Order 1992 Film Law, the film institutions, and particularly the *modus operandi* of LSF.

MFI encountered both support for and opposition to its ideas. Activists and practitioners who wanted to change film legislation, members of Karyawan Film Television – Asosiasi Sineas Indonesia (KFT-ASI, Film and Television Employees – Association of Indonesian Cineasts), and even the cinema network Cinema 21 supported MFI (Imanda 2007; Adityawarman 2007). Its challenge rocked most old film organizations, which sensed that their power was being contested and which preferred to hold on to the status quo.[35] Religious communities were also far from happy with the idea of reforming the film industry. Some conservative groups were particularly worried about the appeal to change the working method of the censor institute. They interpreted this as a call to abolish film censorship altogether, and accused film-makers of wanting to dis-

---

33 For example, in kissing scenes sometimes even a mere peck on the lips was cut. However, as mentioned earlier, the kissing scene in the teen flick *Ada apa dengan Cinta* and, to great surprise, a gay kissing scene in *Arisan!*, and even a masturbation and lesbian sex scene in the film *Detik terakhir* (Last second, Nanang Istiabudi, 2005), passed the censor board uncut (Diani 2005).

34 In addition to the 2004 example of *Buruan cium gue!*, in 2005 the censor institute withdrew the action film *Bad wolves* (Richard Buntario, 2005) because the police objected to the portrayal of corrupt officers in the film. The police said it would tarnish the image of the force, which, as journalist Hera Diani (2005) commented, was in fact already at an all-time low.

35 Likewise, the FFI organizers, who initially failed to comprehend the wider objective of MFI, did not see the protests as a positive effort to bring about change. In the mass media, they criticized the returning of the Citra as an act by ill-mannered youngsters who could not accept their defeat. Veteran film-maker Chaerul Umam, a member of the FFI jury who himself had won a Citra for his film *Ramadhan dan Ramona* (Ramadhan and Ramona) in 1992, dismissed the young film-makers as childish for staging a protest: 'It shows that they can't accept their defeat. If they thought there was a problem, they should have informed us as soon as possible' (Hari 2007).

band film censorship in order to be free to produce pornographic films (Imanda 2007).

In the middle of all this commotion, FPI decided to show its support for film censorship. On 17 January 2007, an FPI delegation visited the LSF office and was given a tour which included an explanation of the work of the institute. After the tour, the leader of the delegation and secretary general of FPI, Ustaz Jafar Sidik, stated that FPI would join and monitor the work of LSF and protect it in view of the threat posed by some groups which wanted to disband it.[36] Sidik was convinced that the censor institute was desperately needed: 'LSF must stay. Look at what is screened on television and in cinemas, it has been censored but is still outrageous. It would be even worse if there were no censor. In our position as a mass organization we are going to monitor this institution, and simultaneously broaden the work terrain of FPI.'[37] Sidik planned to hold conversations with members of the House of Representatives and the government in preparation of an appeal for the intensification and broadening of film censor criteria. He was in no doubt that films now screened in cinemas and on television contaminated the religious values and morality of the Indonesian nation. In particular, Sidik would have liked to add a ban on showing elements of mysticism to the existing criteria. In response to the visit of the FPI delegation, Titie Said commented that she had explained to FPI that the board censored films on the basis of criteria drawn from religion, politics, culture, and public order: 'LSF is a guardian of the nation's morality, protecting it from bad influences, just as FPI'.[38]

The involvement of the Islamic pressure group FPI in supporting LSF and opposing the MFI petition revealed two separate issues. The case can be seen as representative of the wider conflict between conservative and liberal forces in their jockeying to gain the upper hand in ruling the nation. MFI's call for changes to the system in the film industry represented another bid to reform Indonesian society. LSF and FPI both represented groups which were determined to hold on to their status quo and by doing so 'protect the nation's morality'. Secondly, the MFI versus LSF and FPI case provides a good example of discourses on the state's deployment of Islamic pressure groups in its bid to cling to power. Media

36 'Keberadaan sensor film didukung FPI', *Bisnis Indonesia*, 17-1-2007.
37 'LSF harus tetap ada. Lihat saja tayangan televisi dan bioskop, disensor aja gila, apalagi kalau lembaga sensor itu nggak ada. Selaku Ormas, kami akan memantau kelembagaan ini, sekaligus memperluas bidang kerja FPI' ('Keberadaan sensor film didukung FPI', *Bisnis Indonesia*, 17-1-2007; Hadysusanto 2007).
38 'LSF harus dipertahankan'. Posted on Layarkata-Network@yahoogroups.com, Layarkata-Network, 'FPI siap melawan sineas muda?', 19-1-2007.

watcher Veven Wardhana suggested that there was a widespread belief that the censor institute itself had actually invited FPI. Wardhana intimated that the board invited the Islamic mass organization to provide a justification and legitimization for the existence of the institute. He speculated that in all probability during the tour and the concomitant explanation of the working methods of LSF, the FPI delegation was deliberately shown sensual and violent film scenes which had been banned by the board in order to elicit FPI's response that censorship was crucial. Wardhana pins his arguments on the fact that by means of the statements made by the FPI delegation before the invited press, LSF ensured that it secured its authority on the basis of popular support.[39]

In addition to Veven Wardhana, film-maker and festival organizer Dimas Jayasrana also believed that FPI was used as a strategic partner by the censor institute. Just as Wardhana, Dimas suggested FPI was manipulated by the board to substantiate the fact that it had 'the voice of the people' (*suara masyarakat*), which supported the existence of the institute and its censorship decisions. Dimas stated that this alliance, in which FPI reinforced the position of the state-sponsored LSF, extended beyond the bounds of film. He was convinced that it was just one more example of the broader power play instituted by the state. In his view, contemporary Indonesian Islam is used as a commodity and political tool either to perpetuate or alternatively to seize power. The state manipulated FPI and other militant Islamic organizations in the same way LSF had, assisting it in its efforts to preserve the status quo and consolidate its own power. Dimas pointed out that the government had never intervened to quell any of the aggressive protests launched by FPI or any other militant Islamic groups. In fact, these groups had been fostered by the state to make sure that the atmosphere remained unstable and chaotic, which in turn supplies the state with a *raison d'être*. Dimas was convinced that Indonesian politics were still built on generating fear of the recurrence of political, social, and economic instability. Fear of militant Islam has now replaced the fear of communism so as to legitimate strict state control of society. If necessary, fear of radical Islam would give leeway to the state to seize all power if this were deemed essential to national security.[40]

---

39 Personal communication with Veven Wardhana via e-mail on 22 January 2007. In an interview, Titie Said denied the charge that FPI had been invited by LSF. She stated it was a visit similar to those made by many other Indonesian social communities and groups to the institute. The censor institute, she emphasized, 'always opens its door to the people' (Hadysusanto 2007).
40 Communication via e-mail with Dimas Jayasrana on 23 January 2007, and personal communication in Jakarta in March 2007.

Other film professionals, such as directors Aria Kusumadewa and Tino Saroenggalo as well as film critic Ekky Imanjaya, have supported this point of view.[41] Pursuing this line of argument and taking account of the wider notion of the state, the support of Islamic groups for the state film censor has been perceived as an example of the way in which Islam was used as a device to control Indonesian society.[42]

CONCLUSION

In both post-Soeharto audio-visual media and Indonesian politics there has been a perceptible growth in representations of Islam. However, the fact that Islam has been garnering a large amount of publicity does not mean that it has actually gained in terms of political clout. Instead, Islam is but one part of a complex discourse about the organization, principles, and representation of the post-Soeharto Indonesian nation. The two specific cases of *Buruan cium gue!* and of MFI versus LSF/FPI have revealed debates about what social norms, religious beliefs, and realities are acceptable in narrative practices in post-Soeharto Indonesian audio- visual media. These debates have certainly been tied into the endeavours by some Islamic groups to implement national moral codes based on the application of Islamic principles in society. Moreover, they have clearly revealed the divide between conservative and liberal forces in their efforts to rule the nation.

In his study on the historiography of modern nationalism in East Asia, the historian Prasenjit Duara has called attention to the different 'nation views' which nationalism in each nation encompasses. As Duara argues, nationalism as an ideology and politics are neither uniform nor monolithic. Such different groups as political parties, women, workers, farmers, the majorities as well as the minorities in a nation-state have different conceptions of the nation, for which Duara has coined the term 'nation views'. Different nation views moreover compete to define the 'authentic' history and traditions – regimes of authenticity – of the people of a nation-state. Generally speaking, it is the state which directs and determines which regimes

---

41   Personal communication with Aria, Ekky and Tino in Jakarta in March 2007. Moreover, they pointed out rumours which insinuated that FPI was an organization run by Governor of Jakarta Sutiyoso, or the police forces.
42   For more on the utilization of the threat of Islamic fundamentalism in Muslim countries to justify repressive state measures, see Esposito 1999:172.

of authenticity will form the foundation of the nation. However, at many points non- state movements and the force of their ideas test and transform the structure of the regimes of authenticity and the nation-state (Duara 2008). The debate about filmic moral bounds that I described above can be seen as part of a process in which multiple nationalisms test the structure of the nation. To the filmmakers who joined MFI, democratic rights-based individualism and freedom of expression overrule moral bounds determined by religious nation views. To the religious groups, Islam represents the basis of the Indonesian nation and identity, and this foundation should direct the content of domestic film and television. Secular images and representations are discarded and shrugged off as influences of foreign culture and propaganda.

Muhamad Ali's reading of the controversy about the Pornography Bill, which took place in the interval between the *Buruan cium gue!* furore and the MFI versus LSF/FPI clash, offers a constructive analysis of the context in which these different nation views surfaced. Ali has suggested that the anti-pornography controversy is best understood in the context of power relations. In his opinion the controversy reveals a power struggle about the definition of what forms a morally upright society in the context of the Indonesian nation-state. The struggle about what constitutes public morality, he argues, addresses the questions of which views, practices, and traditions should be maintained in Indonesian society, and which should be discontinued. It also sheds light on the matter of how to deal with religious beliefs and social norms and how to relate these to the state. Ali thinks that this power struggle has been greatly influenced by the fact that the post-Soeharto definition of an Indonesian nation-state has never been formulated in unequivocal terms. In his words: 'Within the context of an ambiguous definition of an Indonesian nation-state, pressure groups continuously want to move the pendulum toward a nation based on religious dogma' (Ali 2006).

Being rooted in different 'regimes of authenticity', the opposition of secular and religious groups in the two cases of *Buruan cium gue!* and MFI versus LSF/FPI also exposed the divide between the secular and religious conceptions of daily reality. In a Foucauldian sense – each society causes certain types of discourse to function as true – the claim by Raam Punjabi that his film merely represented social reality as opposed to AA Gym's argument that it encouraged immoral behaviour at odds with Indonesian religious values and culture, exposed a power struggle over the 'true' representations of Indonesian realities. Nevertheless, the fact that AA Gym won the controversy over *Buruan cium gue!* cannot be perceived as a victory of religious authority over secular Indonesian nation views and realities. Instead, as such cultural commentators as Prananto have put forward, it was a victory of stardom: the most popular celebrity of the moment rules the nation, in this case the widely celebrated celebrity-*kyai* AA Gym.

In the struggle to define the representations and realities of contemporary Indonesian society, to a large extent Islam as a religion has taken centre stage in the debates. Islam was increasingly transformed into a commodity; not only as part of the framework of Ramadan, as discussed in Chapter 4, but also in the new television genre of religious soaps, which proved just as adept at using the outward appearances of Islam to attract viewers. Ironically, and in a way similar to the narrative practices employed to address Islam under the New Order, religious soaps have waved the banner of Islam to depict all sorts of controversial social norms or realities and still escape unscathed. In other words, television producers have juggled with images of Islam to sell their productions and to safeguard these from protests. In the same vein, Islam has been progressively used as a political tool. The government, political parties, and mass organizations have not hesitated to invoke the spectre of Islam in their play for power. Moreover, according to some film-makers the state has fuelled a fear of domination by extremist Islam to guard the status quo. The cases of *Buruan cium gue!*, LSF and FPI versus MFI, and 'religious soaps' show how Islam has been used by Indonesian film and television producers as well as groups active in the socio-political field to acquire assets and power. In this context, the rise of Islam in the post-Soeharto audio-visual media and in Indonesian society can be understood as a tactic employed by different parties to use this religion as an instrument to try to have it their way.

Conclusion

On Thursday 24 January 2008 at 10.00 a.m. I was present at the Constitutional Court in Jakarta to attend the fourth MFI trial of a judicial review of the 1992 Indonesian Film Law. In this concluding chapter I discuss this court case in detail, as it brings together a variety of issues that were brought up in different chapters in this book. When opening the trial Prof Dr Jimly Asshiddiqie, chief justice of the Constitutional Court, remarked it was unusually crowded that morning. He added that this case brought before the court indeed was extremely important as it involved the checks and balances of the validity of the film law with respect to the Indonesian Constitution of 1945. According to MFI, the articles on censorship of the New Order film law were neither in agreement with the new era of Reform nor with Article 28F of the Constitution, which pertains to free communication and free access to information, as it was maintained by members of Indonesian parliament and state film institutions. According to Asshiddiqie, this case would test 'the norms of the law that bind [all the members of] the Indonesian nation' (*Risalah sidang perkara* 2007:9).

At the hearing, the claimants – film directors and producers Riri Riza, Nia Dinata, and Tino Saroengallo, together with Jiffest director Lalu Roisamri, movie star Shanty – and the state and its related film institutions – LSF, Parfi, Parsi, BP2N – both brought in experts and witnesses to plea their case. The claimants invited five experts and two witnesses, the state and related film institutions fifteen. Among both parties were prominent public figures. The claimants had called on renowned writers and intellectuals Goenawan Mohamad and Seno Gumira Adjidarma prominent film producers Budiyati Abiyoga and Mira Lesmana, political activist Fadjroel Rahman, legal expert Nono Anwar Makarim, and famous actress Dian Sastrowardoyo. The state and related film institutions had mainly invited prominent leaders representing all religions acknowledged by the state, as well as celebrated writer and poet Taufiq Ismail, Mudzakir, a law expert, Fetty Fajriati Miftah, an expert from Komisi Penyiaran Indonesia (KPI, Indonesian Broadcast Commission), Masna Sari, spokesperson of Komisi Perlindungan Anak Indonesia (KPAI,

Children Protection Commission), and Fadloli El Muhir, head of Forum Betawi Rempug (FBR, Betawi Brotherhood Forum), a people's organization which was widely regarded as consisting of thugs operating in the same loud and aggressive way as FPI in 'defending' morality.

At the court case, several well-known film directors, actors and actresses, artists, writers, and other public figures were also present, most of whom showed their support for MFI. The famous attracted a lot of attention from the mass media. Journalists from infotainment programmes were frantically running around in front of the building and courtroom, with their cameras rolling to get shots and soundbites, whether applicable to the case or not, of the popular and the famous. Inside the courtroom the presence of artists and public figures who either supported MFI or the official film institutions was also apparent. The hearing was quite spectacular. Often the formal atmosphere of the Constitutional Court was stirred. The experts and witnesses on both sides pled their case with vigour, and, I may be biased here, some of the experts speaking on behalf of the state in particular gave quite a performance. They often adorned their statements with trembling voices, dramatic sobs, or deep sighs to indicate their deep-felt concern and fear of the deterioration of Indonesian reputable values and tradition. Above and beyond the theatrical presentation of some of the experts, the audience, consisting of supporters of both sides, noisily commented on the testimonies. Sometimes the public responded to what was said with genuine or cynical laughter, applauding or booing out loud.

In short, the arguments were a cry for freedom against the desire for protection. Those pleading on behalf of MFI called for free access to information and freedom of expression set within the limits of individual choice and responsibility. The film-makers petitioned to be freed from the shackles of the New Order and to be enabled to explore artistic creativity and further develop film expertise. State film censorship, they argued, should be replaced by a system of film rating in which it was up to individuals to set their boundaries. MFI defended the film-makers' individual and democratic rights by referring to Article 28F of the Indonesian Constitution of 1945: 'Everyone is entitled to communicate and obtain information for their personal development and that of their social environment, and the right to seek, obtain, possess, store, process and convey information using all types of channels available.' Those pleading on behalf of the state defended censorship on the basis of ethical bounds, particularly those set by religious values. Miftah, representing the Indonesian Broadcast Commission, also reverted to the 1945 Constitution. She argued that Article 28 had two more clauses, which in her opinion supported censorship (*Risalah sidang perkara* 2007:51). Article 28J (1): 'Every person shall respect the human rights of others in an orderly society, nation and state,' and (2): 'In carrying out one's rights and freedom, every person shall be subject to the restrictions set by law solely for the purpose of ensuring the recognition and respect for rights and freedoms of others and to meet the demands which are appropriate to the consideration of moral values, religious values, security and public order in a democratic society.' Absolute freedom of expression and human rights, some of the defenders of censorship argued, may be a valid concept in the West, but is certainly not applicable to Indonesia, where religious principles and 'Asian values' are more important. In the same vein, Kyai Haji Amidhan from MUI, at the court case representing one of the religious experts on the side of the state, emphasized that clause 28J-2 legally curbed the freedom of expression and limitless right to information in Indonesia for the sake of general stability and religious, moral, and cultural values (*Risalah sidang perkara* 2007:38). Moreover, some pleading on behalf of the state film institutions emphasized that the majority of Indonesians, mainly consisting of the poor and uneducated, were not ready to make appropriate choices in media consumption.

The divide between MFI and the state was clearly represented in the accounts of renowned writers and poets Taufiq Ismail and Goenawan Mohamad. Taufiq Ismail, in his support of state censorship, argued that over the past few years Indonesian culture had come under attack of permissive, addictive, brutal, and violent behaviour. As Ismail saw it, particularly since Reformasi people had begun to transgress accustomed rules and morals resulting in a celebration of hedonism and materialism. People supporting this trend, in his view, disregarded all religious principles and deliberately bred an industry which harboured the flow of free sex and other, in his view interrelated, dangers like rape and drug abuse. This tendency, which some believe is part of the 'ideology' of neo-liberalism,[1] also influenced Indonesian cinema. Ismail did not explicitly refer to it, but some films produced by film-makers supporting MFI, like Nia Dinata or Joko Anwar, had been condemned for promoting Western ideologies, such as the rights of women and homosexuals.[2] Ismail particularly problematized sex. He came up with no less than ten examples of how, why, and to what degree permissive sex

---

[1] See, for example, http://yherlanti1971.multiply.com/journal/item/23 (accessed 19-12-2011).
[2] See, for example, http://yherlanti1971.multiply.com/journal/item/23 (accessed 19-12-2011).

| *Conclusion*

was destroying Indonesian society (*Risalah sidang perkara* 2007:34-5). In a poem, which Ismail read out loud at the end of his statement, the poet symbolically expressed that censorship functions as a fence protecting the ignorant and reckless young from the abyss of free media, the danger of which they can or will not understand (*Risalah sidang perkara* 2007:36-7).

The metaphor of the ignorant young was a reference to MFI. In the analysis of Indonesian film scholar Intan Paramaditha, ever since MFI's protest at FFI's award ceremony in December 2006, members of official film organizations and the establishment endeavoured to 'infantilize' the movement. MFI's action was dismissed as 'childish' (*kekanak-kanakan*) and 'arrogant', and its members were called a bunch of 'young protesters' (*anak-anak muda protes*). The late actor Sophan Sophiaan, who was a member of the House of Representatives, even stated that 'They are like monkeys that have just been unleashed from the cage, a consequence of this democracy'.[3] In addition to the imagery of children and monkeys, at the court case Amidhan from MUI alluded to supporters of MFI as cronies of the Devil (*Iblis*). Amidhan argued that based on Qur'an teachings the diabolic nature of the Devil was not that it did not believe in God and religious doctrine. Its devilish bearing was that it felt superior and dared to rebel and oppose God. Up to this day, Amidhan believed, the Devil recruits cronies who have a mentality to rebel and show contempt for religious values and order. He went on to say that although the Devil's cronies are particularly well aware of what is right and wrong, they deliberately endeavour to twist data and facts to make wrong appear right (*Risalah sidang perkara* 2007:38).

On behalf of MFI, and questioning the existence of but one single notion of right and wrong as well as the established order, writer Goenawan Mohamad defended the freedom of expression. Responding to the call for protection by Taufiq Ismail, Mohamad addressed the intricate convolution of protection and repression. He raised examples from his own experiences dealing with censorship under the New Order. On the one hand, he had been a member of the Censor Board from 1969 to 1972. On the other hand, he had experienced severe censorship himself as the founder and editor of the critical news magazine *Tempo* (Time). His experience as a member of BSF had made him fully aware of the subjectivity and slippery

---

3   Paramaditha 2010:4, 7. Paramaditha wrote a constructive paper on the shifting performance and changing descriptions of the film-makers as cultural actors. She also explored the new roles and imagery adopted by the state within the rhetoric of 'change' that characterizes Reformasi (Paramaditha 2010).

nature of censorship. As ideas about morality were highly subjective, he believed no one should have the right to decide what is right or wrong for others to watch. Furthermore, Mohamad had experienced first-hand what the lack of press freedom under Soeharto rule entailed. *Tempo* was banned twice by the regime because of its vocal criticism, and in lawsuits Mohamad had to face the delusion of justice under an authoritarian regime. In his opinion, in post-Soeharto Indonesia all forms of repression should come to an end.

Mohamad proceeded by mentioning a recent statement by Malaysia's Minister of Information, who had criticized Indonesia's post-Soeharto press for over-exuberance with the freedom afforded them. Mohamad spoke out vigorously: 'To me that is an insult. Press freedom in Indonesia, our basic rights to freedom, were not given to us, we have fought for them. Munir [a human rights activist poisoned in 2004, allegedly by Indonesian intelligence, KvH] died for it, let us not forget that. How many students have been locked up and killed? Abducted? Can we forget that?' (*Risalah sidang perkara* 2007:58-9). Mohamad went on to comment on the universality of human rights. He reminded the addressees that in June 1945, in the Panitia Persiapan Kemerdekaan Indonesia (PPKI, Preparatory Committee for Indonesian Independence), one of the founding fathers of Indonesia, Muhammad Hatta, had already included articles on human rights. He had done so even a few years before the Declaration of Human Rights was proclaimed in 1948. 'Not Malaysia, Saudi Arabia, or America, but Indonesia was first' (*Risalah sidang perkara* 2007:58-9). Those who forget that, Mohamad argued, do not believe in the capability of the young generation and the capability of the Indonesian nation. To him the argumentation that most Indonesian people are poor and stupid and therefore cannot handle freedom is colonial: 'If back then we [had believed we] were not ready for freedom, we would not be independent now, we be free when we are free'.[4]

In a nutshell, the court case and accounts of both writers summarize several issues which have run through the different chapters of this book. To begin with the origin of the case, the film-makers' protest against the FFI jury's decision to name *Ekskul* Best Film: the fact that supporters of MFI returned their Citra was a strong reaction against entrenched interests and established parties of the Soeharto era to continue to control film mediation practices, connecting Chapter 6 to Chapter 1. Since the return of FFI in 2004, young film-makers had felt disturbed with the revival of old *festi-*

---

4 *Risalah sidang perkara* 2007:59. 'Kalau kita tidak siap merdeka pada saat itu, kita tidak akan merdeka, kita merdeka sampai merdeka.'

val arisan sentiments. Many of them had visited or been invited to foreign film festivals and all were in favour of applying more professional, international standards to the process of awarding films. They wanted to take national film to another, more 'objective' and transnational competitive level. MFI's questioning of FFI led to a questioning of the existence and function of all New Order film institutions, which eventually targeted censorship and the law in particular.

In addition to revisiting the predicaments of New Order film institutions, Taufiq Ismail's 'fence' argumentation recalls another issue conveyed in the first chapter. In the 1990s, the 'cultural fence' rhetoric had been used in the context of *layar tancep*. Then, too, it was argued that the poor and ignorant must be protected against the destructive influence of the medium of film. Ismail's argument once again ignored the day-to-day reality that everyone can get their hands on all sorts of cheap, uncensored, and illegal pornographic, violent, and supernatural material via pirated VCD's and DVD's. It also disregarded the existence of alternative networks of film distribution, such as the independent-film screenings and festivals. Ismail believed that the state should protect Indonesian values and culture through censorship. Period. However, as writer and short-film-maker Seno Gumira Adjidarma argued in his statement before court, how could that ever really work? LSF in Adjidarma's opinion was like a little island in a sea of national and transnational media networks and modes of access. The institute pointlessly tried to censor all that was already freely and uncensored available in society (*Risalah sidang perkara* 2007:23). Adjidarma believed a system of film rating would be more functional, as it would at least bring some clarity to the audiences as to which films to choose from. However, practicality was not necessarily at stake at the court case. Just as the earlier discussions on *film independen*, historiography, *film Islami*, horror, and the supernatural, the debate at the court case centred on the drawing and endorsement of local, national, or transnational identities and realities. It questioned the position within the nation-state of the universality of individual rights within the ideology of democracy on the one hand, and religion and communal 'Indonesian values' and indigenous society on the other.

The contemporary dialectic of different worldviews, ideologies, and identities of secular and religious groups in the Indonesian mediascape are part and parcel of a universal development marked by the resurgence of religion in the public sphere.[5] Rosalind Hack-

---

5   For more on this subject, see Casanova 1994; Robertson 1992; Beyer 1998; Hoeber Rudolph and Piscatori 1997.

ett, a scholar of comparative religion, has emphasized that in today's mass-mediated world, religion forms a new primacy of identity politics. She analyses the contemporary resurgence of religion in the public sphere as 'the drive to claim recognition for, and the possibilities for implementation of, religious ideas, values, practices, and institutions in the governance of nation states and the lives of their citizens' (Hackett 2005:63). Moreover, she asserts that '[a]gainst the backdrop of the forces of democratization, mediatization, and the global market, religious groups are compelled to justify their existence to state and consumers alike' (Hackett 2005:76). In Indonesia, Islamic identity was often explicitly connected to state nationalism and policies. In the discourses discussed in Chapter 5, on whether or not the supernatural was part of Indonesian society under New Order rule, several Islamic groups supported the state vision that Indonesia was to be or to become a modern and developed nation. Hence, they endorsed the supernatural only if it were imagined in a framework of the past, or else it should be discarded as foreign culture. After the fall of Soeharto, a number of Islamic groups came out on the side of the state again, in their backing of state censorship and the existence of LSF. Religious studies scholar Peter van der Veer has linked the rise of religious movements in India to debates on and identifications of national identities. He argues that religious movements can best be designated as 'religious nationalisms', because many of them 'articulate discourse on the religious community with discourse on the nation' (Van der Veer 1994:195).

In the opinion of some Indonesian Islamic communities, Islam is what lies at the foundation of the Indonesian nation-state. Still, it must be noted that the interests of some factions of Indonesian military, police, and political parties also can be an important component in drawing the Islamic card. Taking into account that Islamic paramilitary organizations like FPI or FBR have strong ties with high-ranking members of the military and police, or at times are paid to collaborate with political and civilian sponsors, the backing of such groups seems to be based on a continuation of controlled thug rule of the New Order in an Islamic veneer, rather than on the corroboration of radical religious nationalisms. However, as Robert Hefner emphasizes, Islamist paramilitaries cannot be seen as mere puppets of an all-powerful military. There are significant groupings among the army, police, and the intelligence community, who would be happy to see FPI suppressed. Moreover, there are hundreds of Islamist paramilitaries operating across Indonesia, among which many are less disciplined, freelance groups, independent of any national organization. Also the precise measure of collaboration with civilian and, especially, military sponsors varies from group to group. Some groups work closely with military sponsors but others reject such collaboration (Hefner 2004:16). Importantly, even the groups that are sponsored by the armed forces, such as FPI, keep a certain amount of autonomy. Since FPI is aware of the factions and divisions within the army and police itself, it can play this card to resist commands and achieve its own objectives (Hefner 2004:17). The presence of El Muhir from FBR at the court case speaking on behalf of the state inconspicuously seemed to imply that the state now acknowledges authoritative participation of radical Islamic paramilitary groups.

MFI also connected with the nation-state but did not resort to religious nationalism. Rather, it appeared to support universal ideas about secular humanism and democracy. The post-1998 film-makers who are part of MFI are much aware of the global influences in their work and thinking. They find inspiration for their films in encounters with transnational lifestyles, products, and trends, and they nourish transnational networks especially through film festivals. However, notwithstanding what members of the state film organizations tended to believe or tried to contend, MFI was not against morals or Indonesian culture, nor was it opposed to the state. The fact that the contributors strove for a revision of the film law showed they believed in a more democratic state, with, in the words of Paramaditha (2010:8), 'the desire for a more cohesive structure, more top down rather than bottom up, to develop national cinema'. Agus Mediarta, associate at Konfiden, emphasized that the court case was not about free media access or more possibilities of communication per se, as it was fairly easy to illegally produce and screen films and even organize uncensored film festivals. Rather, MFI's endeavour to reform New Order film institutions was about the acknowledgement of artistic freedom, about the future of national cinema, and about the question where Indonesia stands as a democratic nation.[6] MFI's approach differed from the emphasis placed on local culture and identities, and the evasion of and opposition to national political power of mainly the *film independen* groups between 2001-2003; in this respect MFI was on the same level with *film Islami* ideas about national cinema, emphasizing the role of the state therein. As Paramaditha (2010:8) sees it: 'Using the rhetoric that addressed the nation rather than communities, the filmmakers envisioned the ideal roles of the state in creating and facilitating a well-planned structure while inviting them to participate within it'.

6   Personal communication with Agus Mediarta, 25 January 2008.

In a new phase of negotiations about the formation of a new film law, MFI even began to use arguments and jargon which reproduced state discourses. Between April 2008 and September 2009, after the Constitutional Court had ruled that censorship should endure but that there was a need to revise the film law, MFI began to further emphasize the connection of film with the nation and resorted to the UNESCO Convention for the Safeguarding of the Intangible Cultural Heritage (2003), which was drafted to protect cultures from processes of globalization. MFI accused the 1992 Film Law of failing to sustain Indonesia's 'cultural preservation', 'cultural heritage', and 'national identity' in film. Furthermore, in a hearing session with the House of People's Representatives, MFI member and film-maker Abuh Azis criticized the law for not containing a 'cultural strategy' for film while other countries 'have a clear mission statement: it (film) is designed to fight the cultural hegemony of the developed countries' (Paramaditha 2010:9). To Paramaditha, MFI's emphasis on national identity and use of state jargon was quite remarkable in the light of the post-1998 film-maker's awareness of transnational influences in their films and networks. In Paramaditha's words (2010:9): 'The terms "cultural preservation" and "cultural hegemony" were quite surprising to me as they show how, in performing the role as an important stakeholder of cinema (and nation), the new generation downplays their agency in the transnational circuit and resort to cultural essentialism as a strategy to find a common language they could share with the state.'

MFI's choice to defend and represent national identity over universal transnational identities, which Paramaditha explains is informed by a strategy to draft in the state, does not automatically deny the group's transnational linkages. As outlined in Chapter 2, the film communities that emphasized the representation of local or national identity in their opposition to national and transnational hegemonic mainstream media were not tied to only these identities either; they, too, engaged in supranational fora of identity formation and community affiliation. Firstly, the communities of independent film identified themselves with international movements of independent and alternative film: I-Sinema was inspired by the Danish Dogme '95, and the production of *Kuldesak*, the first Indonesian 'independent' film ever, was modelled on American Robert Rodrigues' *Rebel without a crew*. Moreover, *Kuldesak* greatly resembled American independent film-maker Quentin Tarantino's *Pulp fiction*. Secondly, the members of the community of Islamic film explicitly defined themselves as a film movement which was part of Third World oppositional cinemas. Over and above this, the members asserted they belonged to the worldwide *umat* of Islam. They founded the Islamic film genre to challenge what they considered to be universal misrepresentations of Islam in transnational media.

The emphasis on local or national identities of the independent and Islamic film communities is, as Dirlik (1996:35) has put forward in another context, part of a 'politics of difference', which produces a modern notion of the local. The film communities presented the literal and metaphorical local differences – or in the case of Islamic film, national ones – as their identities in the contemporary international mediatized world. This modern local or national identity constituted, in the words of Dirlik (1996:35), 'the local that has been worked over by modernity'. Importantly, this transcended notions of local or national boundaries. Dissanayake (2003:222) emphasizes that where the local and the global meet, processes of 'transnationalization and deterritorialization of consciousness' are likely to occur. This in turn results in the coming into existence of 'new communitarian cultural imaginaries'. Dissanayake states that this does not imply that community in its traditional sense no longer exists; rather, he points to the rise of 'more decentred, contested, and hybridized forms of community'. In the realm of the independent and Islamic communities, modern local or national identity was not confined to notions of the local or national attributed to the Indonesian nation. Rather, the conception of the local was part of a supranational affiliation of localism, but one which opposed global hegemonic mainstream media networks worldwide.

While MFI and *film Islami* both positioned themselves as advocates of national culture and identity in the context of the nation-state, they were on different sides of the debate on religious and secular identities and realities of Indonesian society. In this context, MFI stood closer to the worldviews of the members of *film independen* communities. As discussed in chapters 2 and 4, before the case of *Buruan cium gue!* and MFI versus LSF with the backing of FPI, the differing views of Indonesian society entertained by secular and religious groups had already surfaced in discussions held by the Islamic film movement and independent-film communities on the formation of oppositional cinemas. Both groups shared many viewpoints in that they criticized New Order and national and transnational commercial film mediation practices. However, the movements of Islamic and independent film adhered to different worldviews. The imaginations and claims to specific worldviews were derived from different positions in national and transnational contexts. Like MFI did later on, members of the independent-film communities were mainly concerned with total freedom of expression and representation in film. They endorsed the values of universal human rights, individuality, and democracy. Claims by Islamic groups about how to image and imagine Indonesian society, on the other hand, were related to particular conceptualizations of Islamic identities in the Indonesian nation and internationally. Muslim groups felt that both nationally and globally, Islam was not simply underrepresented; it was misrepresented. In their opinion, worldwide there were hardly any film and television productions which endorsed Islamic views. In contrast, the representations of secular thought, which were disseminated in film productions from the West as well as from China, India, and Latin America, spread all over the globe. Some Islamic communities feared that the hegemony of national and transnational media, in which the US and Hollywood played such a prominent role, was part of a scheme to conquer the world by spreading either secular or Jewish propaganda, or a combination of the two. To the communities of Islamic film, Indonesian culture and Eastern values both had deep roots in Islam. Consequently, representations of social realities in film should be based on religious teachings.

However, even though the majority of Indonesians are Muslims, as a group they are a minority in both media ownership and in the production of successful films and television programmes. Instead, national and transnational commercial media and their relationship with consumer culture have dictated the Indonesian mediascape. Typically, despite both *film indie*'s and *film Islami's* opposition to mainstream media, in the post-Soeharto mediascape commercial television soon hijacked the genre of independent film and usurped images of Islam. Three years after the rise of the independent-film genre, the private television station SCTV opened a contest for independent-film productions. The television programme was very successful in that it attracted many contestants, but it ushered in the decay of the independent-film movement. Films produced by the movement of Islamic film never reached the public eye. In contrast, after the fall of Soeharto private television stations, which the Islamic film movement asserted were driven by foreign capitalism, annexed images of Islam. As Dissanayake (1993:222) has postulated, social values, social practices, the cultural imaginary, and notions of identity and citizenship in cinema are increasingly defined in terms of consumption and the power of the market: 'As such identity is becoming a function of commodity consumption and not the other way around'.

In response to the development of an increasing domination of the market by and the strong advancement of commodity consumption, political commentator Farish Noor believes that communities that hold on to an ethical code which resists the hegemonic influences of capitalism and neo-liberalism must be recognized as counter-hegemonic communities in their own right. Particularly addressing Islamic communities, Noor (2009) argues:

> Islam, Islamism and Muslims are today – by virtue of their attachment to a moral logic that is transcendental – one of the few remaining forces of counter-hegemony by default. By simply insisting on their right to be Muslims, Muslims demonstrate that for some people living in a globalised world does not entail the abandonment of ethics or moral values. One may not agree with some aspects of Islamism and some of its manifestations, but the deeper point that has to be made is the defence of any transcendental ethics that transcends the logic of commodification and the free market.

Noor (2009) goes on to say:

> while such forms of cultural resistance may be based on the discourse and symbols of cultural-religious essentialism, they are nonetheless important by virtue of the symbolic power they wield as tools of social mobilisation and counter-hegemonic identity politics. Muslims are living proof of the possibility of a radically different social order where Ethics informs and controls the workings of the market.

Under the New Order, Muslim ethics also have been commended. The regime particularly applied the symbolic power of Islam to its discursive politics to counter communism. As described in Chapter 3, with the aid of the United States Information Agency (USIA) film discourse practices under the New Order revealed influences and concerns of transnational Cold War politics. USIA policy particularly materialized in topics, generic conventions, and narrative traits in films which were representative of the New Order regime. Hence New Order history films, development films, and propaganda films featured heroes, the blessings of modernization, and the opposition of 'evil' communism versus 'good' Islam. Noor's assertion on the symbolic power of Muslim ethics is made in the context of the post 9-11 'war on terror', which has radically altered the image of Islam worldwide. It seems that the 'war on terror' rhetoric stepped into the void left by former Cold War politics. Today Indonesian Muslims have to deal with a transnational political discourse which has replaced the fear of communism for a fear of radical Islam which battles the values and ideologies of democracy and neo-liberalism. Noor disconnects anti-neo-liberalism sentiments from a denunciation of democracy, at the same time denying that anti-neo-liberalism is an ideology of radical Islamists alone. Still, his argument is slightly one-sided as he does not mention or problematize the important development of the commercialization of Islam. Commercial Islam can be seen as a fixed part of the hegemony of neo-liberalism, which has seized and commodified the religion too. But it can also be perceived as a trend of Muslims freely choosing to blend religious dogma with transnational humanism and consumption without this posing any major ideological problems.

Evidently, worldwide media trends have reached contemporary Indonesian audio-visual media, and in this setting both Muslims and non-Muslims consume the stories about celebrities, ghosts, heroes, preachers, common people, and victims which appear frequently on TV and in cinemas all over the world. However, as McKenzie Wark (1994) and Trinh T. Minh-ha (1993) have argued, people brought up in different cultural frames have a repertoire of quite different stories with which they read the genres or the content of audio-visual media. The form and content of audio-visual media and the configuration of power relations and access to media resources impinge on the discourses about representations of the nation, communities, and social realities circulating in society. In this sense Noor raised a valid point, which connects to debates on the emergence of Islam in transnational politics and media networks on the one hand, and the display of different views on social realities on the other hand. These debates were highlighted in Chapters 5 and 6.

Chapter 5 considered discourses on representations of the supernatural and ghosts in modern Indonesia. In debates on the use of certain formulas within the horror genre, the discourses disclosed a contention about whether or not the supernatural in Indonesia was part of modern life and daily reality. What representations of reality and modern times were possible in Indonesian society, and where should the moral lines be drawn? To some, the supernatural was seen as part of modern Indonesian society and daily life. To others, it was not part of national culture and reality, or it was confined to Indonesia's imaginations of the past only.

Furthermore, the cases of AA Gym and *Buruan cium gue!* and MFI versus LSF/FPI in Chapter 6 showed that a gap existed in representations of society between commercial film-makers and filmmakers and persons who joined MFI, and groups and individuals who based their platform on religious conviction. Both groups wanted to define the bounds of narrative practices in film, but both groups espoused fairly diametrically opposed 'nation views' (Duara 2008) or imaginations of what was part of Indonesian society and daily reality. In claims of what was part of Indonesian culture and society and what not, each group put forward and defended different filmic representations. These representations encompassed cosmopolitan secular and global consumerist lifestyles and cultures, juxtaposing the realities of religious and so-called Eastern values, lifestyles and cultures. The opposition of religious and secular media ownership was represented by Indonesian Islamic authority figure and celebrity *kyai* AA Gym versus the king of soaps, Raam Punjabi. AA Gym had built up a very successful business emporium selling Islamic television programmes and soap operas, VCDs, religious text messages for mobile telephones, books, audiocassettes, and other merchandizing at his headquarters in Bandung. Gym and his Bandung-based media emporium stood for local culture, local leadership, and local identity. Raam Punjabi is also a very successful businessman. He owns one of the most profitable Indonesian television production houses in Jakarta and in the past has produced extremely popular soaps. However, Punjabi represents, in the eyes of many, foreign culture, foreign domination, and foreign identity.

Taking Duara's concept of 'regimes of authenticity' and viewing the situation in a Foucauldian sense, in that each society has its own regime and general politics of truth, the juxtaposition of AA Gym and Raam Punjabi also represents two different views on Indonesian society and its realities. Raam Punjabi stands for global consumer culture and secular realities, whereas AA Gym advocates that consumerism and freedom of expression should be controlled and restricted by religious norms. In the case of *Buruan cium gue!*, AA Gym believed that only religious norms should define 'authentic' Indonesian realities and the narrative practices in film and other media. Conversely, in their attempt to resist the religious bounds for audio-visual media, film producers have explicitly emphasized that their film narratives are representative of Indonesia's daily realities. Raam Punjabi is not alone; Chand Parwez, who produced the film *Virgin*, and the producers of horror reality shows have all stated that their films and programmes simply represent the reality of, and the true stories circulating in, contemporary Indonesian society.

In view of the emergence of the hyper-real reality television programmes and their representations of Islam, the references to social realities by Islamic groups in debates about representations of Indonesian society have become quite complicated. Particularly in the context of representations of reality and the moral bounds set by Islamic groups, reality television has undermined both. While Muslim protests about certain domestic films were founded on the argument that their narrative practices did not represent Indonesian culture, values, and realities, commercial television co-opted

Islam in reality ghost shows and religious soaps. The call for moral bounds by Muslim groups has contrasted starkly with the lack of bounds in the reality-based programmes and soaps, which featured Islam in a seething brew of all sorts of evil and ghosts.

While truth and ghosts appear to be particularly liberally coupled with Islam, in the context of historiography both claims to truth and reality are crucial, as well as the hovering of ghosts. Goenawan Mohamad's appeal at the MFI court case not to forget Munir and others who were killed fighting for a just and democratic society in the past can not only be linked to his plea for an uncensored society; it is also relevant in connection to the unrelenting denial of alternative histories and the silencing of atrocities committed during New Order rule. Various historians, anthropologists, and other academics studying Indonesia have argued that Indonesian history is haunted by suppressed stories of violence.[7] In a book on Haitian history, Michel Rolph-Trouillot (1995:48) argued that in history making '[o]ne engages in the practice of silencing. Mentions and silences are thus active, dialectical counterparts of which history is the synthesis.' The New Order was outstandingly skilful in silencing stories of its own bloodshed. In particular the 'active silence' on the brutal aftermath of the coup in 1965-1966 still haunts Indonesia. But also the massacres in East Timor from 1975 up to 1999, the military operations in Aceh (Sears 2005:78-9) and Papua, the *petrus* killings in 1983,[8] the bloody confrontations with Islamic groups in Tanjung Priok, Jakarta, in 1984 and in Lampung, Sumatra, in 1989 (Van Klinken 2005:247), and the widespread practice of silencing individual critics of the regime are not over and done with. Goenawan Mohamad (2005:49), commenting on the silencing and absence of communists in the discourse of history argues that

> It was their absence from the discourse that is disturbing. It inevitably led to further killings, imprisonment, torture, and kidnapping, which is the ugly side of 30 years of Suharto's New Order. It became increasingly clear that in this history of atrocity, silence produces legitimacy. Unfortunately, when free and dissenting expression is muzzled, we can hardly hear the victim scream.

---

7   See, for example, Van Klinken 2005:247; Sears 2005:78-9, Schulte Nordholt 2004: 11-2.
8   *Petrus* is an acronym for '*penembak misterius*' (mysterious killers) or '*penembakan misterius*' (mysterious shootings) that took place in the early 1980s. The 'mysterious killings' were a government operation against a rise in crime rates. Between 1983 and 1985, police and military branches executed some 5,000 suspected criminals in various cities throughout Indonesia without a trial. In many cases the bodies were dumped in public places as a warning to the community (Schwarz 1994:249).

| *Conclusion*

Despite several endeavours by young film-makers to represent 'the voice of the voiceless' and show alternative histories, through documentaries such as *Mass grave* and other productions in, for example, Yogyakarta, among them *Kado untuk ibu* (Present for mother, Syarikat Indonesia, 2005) and *Sinengker* (Concealed, Aprisiyanto, 2007), after the resignation of Soeharto the silence mostly lingers on. Particularly perpetrators of violence are much less eager to face up to their stories. As Laurie J. Sears (2005:95) argues: '[t]he need for some form of truth for the atrocities committed in Indonesia during the 32 years of NO rule seems to be talked about more by Euroamerican or Australian scholars and observers than by Indonesians themselves'. Moreover, Gerry van Klinken has mentioned various negative reactions in Indonesia to revisions of history. When President Abdurahman Wahid in 2000 tried to revoke the ban on communism all factions in parliament rejected his proposition. Also Wahid's unofficial apology on behalf of NU for the violence of its youth organization committed against communists in 1965-1966 resulted in an outrage on all sides of parliamentary politics. Moreover, in several cases members of the military have suppressed dissident accounts of history. For example, under military pressure the memoirs of Soekarno's foreign minister, Subandrio, was barred from publication (Klinken 2005:242-3). In addition to examples of the establishment maintaining a demonization of communism, vigilante groups such as FPI and Aliansi Anti Komunis (AAK, Alliance of Anti-Communists) have also shown their refusal of reform on this part of history. The groups raided publishers and shops which had books with alternative views on communism on their shelves. The same groups publicly burned leftist books, such as those by the writer Pramoedya Ananta Toer. Other negative or even violent reactions have been expressed in response to efforts to exhume and rebury mass grave victims from the period of 1965-1966 (Schreiner 2005:274). Mainly groups of Muslim conviction were active in such protests. In *Mass grave*, Lexy Rambadeta filmed an example of this phenomenon.

It may come as no surprise that also in the context of film-making, endeavours to produce versions of historiography which deviated from the New Order's condemnation of communism have been blocked, mainly by militant right-wing Muslim parties. Particularly the military-sponsored Islamic paramilitary groups have been successful in barring alternative histories. To give just one example: at the end of 2008, under the lead of FPI, inhabitants of Karanganyar near Solo, Central Java, intervened in the production of veteran film-maker Erros Djarot's latest film. *Lastri; Suara perempuan korban tragedi 1965* (Lastri; The voice of women victims of the

1965 tragedy) is a love story, but it also incorporates a different view on the history of 1965.[9] The film was inspired by the book *The voice of women victims of 1965* by Ita Nadia, which includes interviews with former Gerwani members.[10]

With *Lastri*, Djarot tried to propose a reconsideration of New Order historiography. However, when the director wanted to start shooting in Karanganyar, FPI took the lead in staging protests. FPI published a statement that it had read the script and director's notes and rejected *Lastri* on the grounds that the film endeavoured to develop sympathy for communist thinking and denied the history of events at Lubang Buaya.[11] Other groups soon followed suit. Out of fear for unrest the mayor of Karanganyar prohibited Djarot from shooting the film on location. In the end Djarot stopped the production of the film altogether. In many ways the FPI action and their reasoning replicated New Order approaches to silence opposition.[12]

However, while the voices of the 1965 victims are often still muted, memories of the dead, or the dead themselves, emerge from their burial places. When justice has not taken its turn or when scores in society have not been settled, it is widely believed that ghosts will appear. To name a current example, near the Bali bombsite in 2003 many residents of Kuta claimed to see ghostly apparitions and hear strange voices. The ghosts appeared after a state ceremony, which was conducted as an attempt to define and manage anger and violence through a ritual. This ritual was meant to channel emotions in a spiritual way rather than letting feelings of anger and resentment take a political direction such as it did between Hindu Balinese locals and Islamic immigrants. According to Degung Santikarma (2005:321), the enduring manifestation of

---

9   Lastri is a woman's name but according to Djarot, it is also an abbreviation of 'Last Republik Indonesia' (Last Indonesian Republic) (personal communication with Erros Djarot, Jakarta, August 2008).
10   Gerwani, an acronym standing for Gerakan Wanita Indonesia (Indonesian Women's Movement), was a communist women's organization active in the 1950s and 1960s. The organization was closely affiliated with PKI but remained independent. After 30 September 1965, Gerwani was banned. New Order media spread false accusations of Gerwani members having helped to kill the generals, castrating and mutilating them, as well as having danced naked on the site. Thousands of Gerwani members were imprisoned, raped, or killed in the ensuing anti-communist military operation. Not only did the false accusations have a deep impact in Indonesia on creating an image of communists as the source of evil, it also severely crippled the participation of women organizations in politics. For more on Gerwani and New Order sexual politics, see Saskia Wieringa 2002.
11   'FPI menolak keras produksi film LASTRI', http://fpi.or.id/?p=detail&nid=94 (accessed 19-12-2011).
12   Djarot believes that the protesters had been paid by the secret police to stop the shooting of the film. See also Budi 2008.

ghosts near the site testified to the possible ineffectiveness of the ceremony. Not only in Bali, everywhere across Indonesia people admit to seeing ghosts hovering around sites where atrocities have been committed. Fatalities buried in one of the many mass graves of 1965 as well as other victims of torture and murder eventually appear in alternative histories, which take the form of ghost stories. These stories both serve as a means to channel resentment or trauma by giving a voice to those suppressed by formal history, as well as to address perpetrators informing them that scores eventually will be settled in the afterlife.

Strikingly, the resurrection of ghosts in hyper-real Indonesian horror reality-shows and religious soaps is a very literal example of Jean Baudrillard's apprehension (1994:48) of the contemporary loss of history and reality in film. In his view,

> Photography and cinema contributed in large part to the secularization of history, to fixing it in its visible, 'objective' form at the expense of the myths that once traversed it. Today cinema can place all its talent, all its technology in the service of reanimating what itself contributed to liquidating. It only resurrects ghosts, and it itself is lost therein.

All in all, my analysis about what narrative practices have been possible and permissible in the post-Soeharto Indonesian audio-visual media has tied into a struggle over who and what shapes and decides on national popular discourse and the realities of imaginations of society's daily-lived practices. It has highlighted the relationship between mass media, religion, and politics in the construction of post-colonial power relations, and exposed the endeavour to reshape the narratives of regimes of authenticity and the nation-state, thereby opening up new historical possibilities.

Glossary

banser	paramilitary wing (Nahdlatul Ulama)
bupati	regent
Citra	film award handed out at FFI; Indonesian equivalent of the Oscar
Arisan	a regular social gathering whose members contribute to and take turns at winning a collective sum of money
dai	Islamic preacher
dakwah	religious propagation or intensification activities of the Islamic faith
dukun kejawen	Javanese magic specialist
festival arisan	a film festival taking form of a social get-together in which the main focus is on harmonious relations, glamour, and fame.
festival film	film festival
film festival	festival film
film gelora pembangunan	'zeal for development films'; films intended to arouse enthusiasm for modernization among the Indonesian rural masses
film guerilla	guerilla film
film independen	'independent' film
film indie	see film independen
film keliling	'traveling' film screenings
film klenik	'superstitious' film
film mistik	mystical film
film pelarian	fast-track film
film pembangunan	development film
film perjuangan	struggle (for Independence) film
hadits	traditional collection of stories relating to words or deeds of the Prophet Muhammad, the chief source of guidance for understanding religious questions
haram	proscribed in Islam

Glossary

ilmu	spiritual knowledge
ilmu gaib	supernatural powers
jelangkung	a doll made out of a coconut shell and some wooden sticks, which is used as a medium to invite spirits to possess it
jin	genie
kode etik	code of ethics
Komunitas Gardu	Security Post Community
kyai	teacher of Islam
layar tancep	mobile cinema (literally 'screens stuck in the ground')
malam Jumat	Thursday eve
oknum	rotten element of society or its institutions
pantangan	taboo
pejuang	a revolutionary
penjajah	colonial ruler
pesantren	Islamic boarding school
praktek miring	semi-official or illegal practices; 'cursive practices'
selamatan	ceremonial meal, which in the context of film is commonly held at the beginning and end of production in order to pray for a successful outcome
sinema daerah	regional cinema
sinema jemuran	'drying [laundry]' cinema
sinema ngamen	street act cinema
Sineplex	Cineplex; high-end multi-screen movie theatres
sinetron komedi misteri	comedy mystery television series
sinetron misteri	mystery series
sinetron religius	religious soaps
santri	Islamic scholar
tokoh	prominent figure
tuyul	a spirit which obtains wealth for its human master
uang keamanan	safety fees
ulama	Muslim religious teacher or leader
umat	religious community
ustaz	Islamic authority figure
wali	holy man, saint
wali sanga	nine saints; holy men who are believed to have disseminated the teachings of Islam in Java

Bibliography

Abidin, Djamalul
2003 'LSF, waspadai musang berbulu ayam', *Republika*, 26 January.
Abu-Lughod, Lila
1993 'Finding a place for Islam; Egyptian television serials and the national interest', *Public Culture* 5:493-513.
2002 'Egyptian melodrama: Technology of the modern subject?', in: Faye D. Ginsberg, Lila Abu-Lughod and Brian Larkin (eds), *Media worlds; Anthropology on new terrain*, pp. 115-33. Berkeley, CA: University of California Press.
Adityawarman, Enison Sinaro
2007 'Pernyataan sikap dan pendapat KFT-Asosiasi Sineas Indonesia (KFT-ASI) terhadap kondisi perfilman Indonesia masa kini', *Masyarakat Film Indonesia*. http://masyarakatfilmindonesia.wordpress.com/2007/01/ (accessed 19-12-2011).
Adityo
1996 'Program Perfiki tinggal kenangan', *Suara Karya*, 1 September.
1997 'Persaingan layar tancap makin tak sehat', *Suara Karya*, 7 September.
Adjidarma, Seno Gumira
2000 *Layar kata; Menengok 20 skenario Indonesia pemenang Citra festival film Indonesia 1973-1992*. Yogyakarta: Yayasan Bentang Budaya.
Agustin, Ucu
2002 'Sihir *Jelangkung*', *Pantau* II-22:8-9.
Ali, Muhamad
2006 'Power struggle being waged over public morality', *The Jakarta Post*, 1 April.
Anderson, Benedict
1983 *Imagined communities; Reflections on the origin and spread of nationalism*. London: Verso.

1990   'Old state, new society; Indonesia's New Order in comparative historical perspective', in: Benedict R.O'G. Anderson, *Language and power; Exploring political cultures in Indonesia*, 94-120. Ithaca, NY/London: Cornell University Press.

Ang, Ien
1991   *Desperately seeking the audience.* London/New York: Routledge.
1992   'Living room wars; New technologies, audience measurement, and the tactics of television consumption', in: Roger Silverstone and Eric Hirsch (eds), *Consuming technologies; Media and information in domestic spaces.* Foreword by Marilyn Strathren, pp. 74-81. London: Routledge.
1996   *Living room wars; Rethinking media audiences for a postmodern world.* London/New York: Routledge.

Anirun, Suyatna
1989   '"Djakarta '66" atau "Supersemar" menurut para pengamat film', *Pikiran Rakyat*, 18 March.

Antlöv, Hans
1999   'The new rich and cultural tensions in rural Indonesia', in: Michael Pinches (ed.), *Culture and privilege in capitalist Asia*, pp. 189-208. London: Routledge. [The New Rich in Asia Series.]

Anugerah, Eri
2002   'Laris manis tayangan misteri', *Media Indonesia*, 14 April.
2003   'Program hantu dominasi dunia televisi', *Media Indonesia*, 5 January.

Anwar, Joko
2002a   'Movie theater monopoly crippling local film industry', *The Jakarta Post*, 13 July.
2002b   'Kafir, unintentionally hilarious movie', *The Jakarta Post*, 21 December.
2002c   'New directors enter film industry with horror movies', *The Jakarta Post*, 21 December.

Anwar, Rosihan
1999   *Reportase wartawan film, meliput festival film internasional.* Jakarta: Pustaka Antara Utama.

Appadurai, Arjun
1990   'Disjuncture and difference in the global cultural economy', *Public Culture* 2-2:1-23.

1996   *Modernity at large; Cultural dimensions of globalization.* Minneapolis/London: University of Minnesota Press.

Ardan, S.M.

2004   *Setengah abad festival film Indonesia.* Jakarta: Panitia Festival Film Indonesia 2004 and Jaringan Kreatif Independen Workshop Production Network.

Arief, Syarief M.

1996   'Mencari formula film dakwah Islam', *Pelita*, 30 March.

Arifin, Suarif

1989   'Djakarta '66 Super Semar', *Angkatan Bersenjata*, 18 March.

Armbrust, Walter

2006   'Synchronizing watches; The state, the consumer, and sacred time in Ramadan television', in: Birgit Meyer and Annelies Moors (eds), *Religion, media, and the public sphere*, pp. 207-26. Bloomington: Indiana University Press.

Arps, Bernard and Katinka van Heeren

2006.   'Ghosthunting and vulgar news; Popular realities on recent Indonesian television', in: Henk Schulte Nordholt and Ireen Hoogenboom (eds), *Indonesian transitions*, pp. 289-325. Yogyakarta: Pustaka Pelajar.

Ati

2002   'Peringatan empat tahun tragedi Semanggi I; "Student Movement in Indonesia" diputar ulang', *Kompas Online.* http://www.Kompas.com/gayahidup/news/0211/08/065135.htm (accessed 15-1-2003).

Atmowiloto, Arswendo

1986   *Pengkhianatan G30S/PKI.* Jakarta: Pustaka Sinar Harapan.

Barendregt, Bart

2006   'Between m-governance and mobile anarchies; Pornoaksi and the fear of new media in present day Indonesia'. *Mediaanthropology.* http://www.mediaanthropology.net/barendregt_mgovernance.pdf (accessed 7-4-2008).

Baudrillard, Jean

1994   *Simulacra and simulation.* Translated by Sheila Faria Glaser. Ann Arbor: University of Michigan Press. [The Body, in Theory, Histories of Cultural Materialism.] [Originally published as *Simulacres et simulation.* Paris: Galilée, 1981.]

1998   *The consumer society; Myths and structures.* Translated by Chris Turner. London: Sage. [Theory, Culture & Society.] [Originally published as *La société de consummation.* N.p.: Denoël, 1970.]

Bibliography

Baumann, Gerd
1996   *Contesting culture; Discourses of identity in multi-ethnic London.* Cambridge: Cambridge University Press. [Cambridge Studies in Social and Cultural Anthropology 100.]

Bayart, Jean-Francois
1993   *The state in Africa; The politics of the belly.* Translated by Mary Harper, Christopher and Elizabeth Harrison. London: Longman. [Originally published as *L'État en Afrique: La politique du ventre.* Paris: Fayard, 1989.]

Bayat, Asef
2002   'Piety, privilege, and Egyptian youth', *ISIM Newsletter* 10-2:23.

Beyer, Peter
1998   'The modern emergence of religions and a global social system for religion', *International Sociology* 13:151-72.

Bintang Ilham
1983   'Bila ulama & wartawan mendiskusikan film', *Harian Umum*, 20 August.

Buana-R
1985   'Kepala BP-7 Pusat Sarwo Edhie Wibowo; Film Pengkhianatan G30S/PKI penting dilihat masyarakat Indonesia yang berada di luar negeri', *Berita Buana*, 15 October.

Budi, Muchus R.
2008   'Kontroversi film "Lastri" Eros Djarot; Kami berhenti shooting karena tak ada jaminan keamanan', *DetikNews.* http://www.detiknews.com/read/2008/11/17/165342/1038431/10/eros-djarot-kami-berhenti-shooting-karena-tak-ada-jaminan-keamanan (accessed 27-1-2010).

Cahyono, Rachmat H.
1989   'Film sebagai media dakwah', *Terbit Minggu*, 24-30 September.

Calon bintang
1999   '500 calon bintang direkrut; Bonek dan Provokator diangkat ke layar lebar', *Rakyat Merdeka*, 11 June.

Carroll, Noël
1990   *The philosophy of horror; Or paradoxes of the heart.* London: Routledge.

Casanova, José
1994   *Public religions in the modern world.* Chicago: University of Chicago Press.

Chabal, Patrick
1996 'The African crisis; Context and interpretation', in: Richard Werbner and Terence Ranger (eds), *Postcolonial identities in Africa*, pp. 29-54. London: Zed Books.

Christmann, Andreas
1996 'An invented piety; Ramadan on Syrian TV', *Basr.* http://www.basr.ac.uk/diskus/diskus1-6/CHRISTMA.txt (accessed 19-12-2011).

Coates, Paul
1991 *The Gorgon's gaze; German cinema, expressionism, and the image of horror.* London: Cambridge University Press. [Cambridge Studies in Films.]

Creed, Barbara
1995 'Horror and the carnivalesque; The body-monstrous', in: Leslie Devereaux and Roger Hillman (eds), *Fields of vision; Essays in film studies, visual anthropology, and photography*, pp. 127-59. Berkeley, CA: University of California Press.

Croteau, David and William Hoynes
1997 *Media/society; Industries, images, and audiences.* Thousand Oakes, CA: Pine Forge Press.

Dasgupta, Sudeep
2007 'Whither culture? Globalization, media and the promises of cultural studies', in: Sudeep Dasgupta (ed.), *Constellations of the transnational; Modernity, culture, critique*, pp. 139-67. Amsterdam: Rodopi. [Thamyris/Intersecting: Place, Sex, and Race 14.]

Davidson, Neil
2007 'Reimagined communities', *International Socialism.* http://www.isj.org.uk/index.php4?id=401&issue=117 (accessed 19-12-2011).

Dayan, Daniel and Elihu Katz
1992 *Media events; The live broadcasting of history.* Cambridge, MA/London: Harvard University Press.

Desai, Radhika
2009 'The inadvertence of Benedict Anderson; Engaging *Imagined communities*', *Japan Focus.* http://japanfocus.org/-Radhika-Desai/3085 (accessed 19-12-2011).

Diani, Hera
2005 'LSF facing criticism for film poster ban', *The Jakarta Post*, 23 December.

| Bibliography

Dirlik, Arif
1996 'The global in the local', in: Rob Wilson and Wimal Dissanayake (eds), *Global/local; Cultural production and the transnational imaginary*, pp. 21-45. Durham, NC: Duke University Press. [Asia-Pacific: Culture, Politics, and Society.]

Dissanayake, Wimal
1994 (ed.) *Colonialism and nationalism in Asian cinema*. Bloomington: Indiana University Press.
2003 'Rethinking Indian popular cinema', in: Anthony R. Guneratne and Wimal Dissanayake (eds), *Rethinking Third Cinema*, pp. 202-25. New York/London: Routledge.

Duara, Prasenjit
1999 'Transnationalism in the era of nation-states; China, 1900-1945', in: Birgit Meyer and Peter Geschiere (eds), *Globalization and identity; Dialectics of flow and closure*, pp. 47-70. Oxford/ Cambridge, MA: Blackwell.
2008 'The global and regional constitution of nations; The view from East Asia', *Nations and Nationalism* 14-2:323-45.

Dijk, Kees van
2001 *A country in despair; Indonesia between 1997 and 2000*. Leiden: KITLV Press. [Verhandelingen 186.]

Eco, Umberto
1989 *The open work*. Translated by A. Cancogni. With an introduction by David Robey. Cambridge, MA: Harvard University Press. [Originally published as *Opera aperta*. Milano: Bompiani, 1962.]

Eddy
1993 'Kendala film bernafas patriotisme; Memilik ragam pahlawan tak pernah kesampaian', *Pos Film*, 15 August.

Esposito, John
1999 *The Islamic threat; Myth or reality?* Third edition. New York: Oxford University Press. [First edition 1992.]

Fairclough, Norman
1995 *Media discourse*. London: Arnold.

Feith, Herbert
1962 *The decline of constitutional democracy in Indonesia*. Ithaca, NY: Cornell University Press.

Fischer, Johan
2009 *Proper Islamic consumption; Shopping among the Malays in modern Malaysia*. Copenhagen: NIAS Press. [Monograph Series 113.]

Fitrianto, Dahono
2005   'Tontonan religius tanpa mistik', *Kompas*, 9 October.

Forbes, Bruce David and Jeffrey H. Mahan (eds)
2000   *Religion and popular culture in America*. Berkeley, CA: University of California Press.

Friedberg, Anne
1993   *Window shopping; Cinema and the postmodern*. Berkeley, CA: University of California Press.

F.Y.
1993   'PPFI bentuk tim ahli tumpas pembajak film', *Pos Film*, 3 January.

Gaban, Farid
2004   '"Buruan Cium Gue" dan kontroversinya; Surat terbuka buat penandatangan petisi Utan Kayu'. *Groups.yahoo. com*. http://groups.yahoo.com/group/pasarbuku/message/18153 (accessed 19-12-2011).

Gabriel, Teshome
1985   'Towards a critical theory of Third World films', *Teshome Gabriel*. http://teshomegabriel.net/towards-a-critical-theory-of-third-world-films (accessed 19-12-2011).

Garnham, Nicholas
1993   'The mass media, cultural identity, and the public sphere in the modern world', *Public Culture* 5:251-65.

Gibb, H.A.R. and J.H. Kramers
1974   *Shorter encyclopaedia of Islam*. New imprint. Leiden: Brill. [Koninklijke Nederlandse Akademie van Wetenschappen, Amsterdam.] [First edition 1953.]

Gillwald, Alison
1993   'The public sphere, the media, and democracy', *Transformations* 21:65-77.

Gladwin, Stephen
2003   'Witches, spells and politics; The horror films of Indonesia', in: Steven J. Schneider (ed.), *Fear without frontiers; Horror cinema across the globe*, pp. 219-29. Surrey: FAB Press.

Grewal, Inderpal and Caren Kaplan (eds)
1994   *Scattered hegemonies; Postmodernity and transnational feminist practices*. Minneapolis: University of Minnesota Press.

Gus
1997   'Dapat merusak tingkat keimanan dalam masyarakat luas; Stop tayangan sinetron hantu, jin dan tuyul', *Pos Kota*, 13 April.

Hackett, Rosalind I.J.
2005 'Rethinking the role of religion in the public sphere; Local and global perspectives', in: Philip Ostien, Jamila M. Nasir and Franz Kogelmann (eds), *Comparative perspectives on Shari`ah in Nigeria*, pp. 74-100. Ibadan: Spectrum Books. [Available online at http://web.utk.edu/~rhackett/Rethinking_role_religion.pdf (accessed 6-12-2011).]

Hadysusanto, S.
2007 'FPI dukung keberadaan Lembaga Sensor Film', *Bisnis Indonesia*, 18 January.
2008 'Mendulang rupiah dengan membajak produk bajakan', *Jurnal Publik*. http://www.jurnalpublik.com/2008/03/mendulang-rupiah-dengan-membajak-produk.html (accessed 19-12-2011).

Haesly, Richard
2005 'Making the "imagined community" real; A critical reconstruction of Benedict Anderson's concept of "imagined communities"'. Paper, 46th Annual International Studies Association Meeting, Honolulu, Hawaii, 1-5 March.

Hall, Stuart
1980 'Coding and decoding in the television discourse', in: Stuart Hall et al (eds), *Culture, media, language; Working papers in cultural studies, 1972-79*, pp. 197-208. London: Hutchinson.

Hamilton, Mark
2006 'New imaginings; The legacy of Benedict Anderson and alternative engagements of nationalism', *Studies in Ethnicity and Nationalism* 6-3 (December):73-89.

Handiman
1996 'Kisah Ibu Tien difilmkan', *Suara Karya*, 26 May.

Harbord, Janet
2002 *Film cultures*. London: Sage.

Hari, Kurniawan
2007 'Filmmakers want changes in industry', *The Jakarta Post*, 10 January.

Haryanto, Hanibal Wijanta and Sen Tjiauw
1996 'Mengatur agama dan politik lembaga penyiaran', *Forum Keadilan* 5, 17 June.

Hasim, Abdul
1997 'Kembalinya mistis dalam sinema Indonesia', *Pikiran Rakyat*, 8 August.

Hebdige, Dick
1979   *Subculture; The meaning of style.* London: Methuen. [New Accents.]
Heeren, Katinka van
2002   'Revolution of hope; Independent films are young, free and radical', *Inside Indonesia.* http://www.insideindonesia.org/edition-70-apr-jun-2002/default (accessed 6-12-2011).
2007   'Return of the kyai; Representations of horror, commerce, and censorship in post-Suharto Indonesian film and television', *Inter-Asia Cultural Studies* 8-2:211-26.
Hefner, Robert W.
2002   'Globalization, governance, and the crisis of Indonesian Islam'. Paper, Conference on Globalization, State Capacity, and Muslim Self Determination, University of California, Santa Cruz, 7-9 March.
Heider, Karl G.
1991   *Indonesian cinema; National culture on screen.* Honolulu: University of Hawaii Press.
Heryanto, Ariel
1999   'The years of living luxuriously; Identity politics of Indonesia's new rich', in: Michael Pinches (ed.), *Culture and privilege in capitalist Asia*, pp. 159-87. London: Routledge. [The New Rich in Asia Series.]
Hobsbawm, Eric and Terence Ranger (eds)
1983   *The invention of tradition.* Cambridge: Cambridge University Press. [Past and Present Publications.]
Hoeber Rudolph, Suzanne and James Piscatori (eds)
1997   *Transnational religion and fading states.* Boulder, CO: Westview Press.
Hutcheon, Linda
1988   *A poetics of postmodernism; History, theory, fiction.* New York/London:Routledge.
Imanda, Tito
2007   'Kereta malam Reformasi?', *Pikiran Rakyat*, 4 February.
Ismail, Usmar
1983   *Usmar Ismail mengupas film.* Jakarta: New Aqua Press.
Iwan K.
1996   'Sinetron "Terjebak" angkat kerusuhan 27 Juli sebagai latar belakang cerita', *Harian Ekonomi Neraca*, 27 September.

Jacobsen, Michael
2003 'Tightening the unitary state; The inner workings of regional autonomy'. [Southeast Asian Studies Centre, Working Paper 46, May.]

Jasin, Hasbi H.
1985 'Yang porno haram; Bila ulama ramai-ramai menonton film', *Merdeka*, 23 July.

Jhally, Sut and Justin Lewis
1992 *Enlightened racism; The Cosby show, audiences and the myth of the American dream.* Boulder, CO: Westview Press.

Joko, P.
1994 'Film horor punya kans ke pasaran internasional', *Kedaulatan Rakyat*, 2 January.

Junhao Hong
1998 *The internationalization of television in China; The evolution of ideology, society, and media since the reform.* Westport, CT: Praeger.

Kalim, Nurdin and Evieta Fadjar
2005 'Sang ustad di sudut sinetron', *Tempo*, 17 April.

Kayam, Umar
1997 'Tentang neo-feudalisme'. *OHIO University Libraries.* http://www.library.ohiou.edu/indopubs/1997/02/28/0123.html (accessed 19-12-2011).

Khoo Gaik Cheng
2004 'Just-do-it-yourself; Malaysian independent filmmaking', *Aliran Monthly.* http://aliran.com/archives/monthly/2004b/9k.html (accessed 19-12-2011).

Kitley, Philip
2000 *Television, nation, and culture in Indonesia.* Athens, OH: Center for International Studies, Ohio University. [Research in International Studies, Southeast Asia Series 104.]
2002 'Into the thick of things; Tracking the vectors of "Indonesian mediations"; A comment', in: Henk Schulte Nordholt and Irwan Abdullah (eds), *Indonesia in search of transition*, pp. 207-16. Yogyakarta: Pustaka Pelajar.

Klinken, Gerry van
2005 'The battle for history after Suharto', in: Mary S. Zurbuchen (ed.), *Beginning to remember; The past in the Indonesian present*, pp. 233-58. Singapore: Singapore University Press, Seattle, WA: University of Washington Press. [Critical Dialogues in Southeast Asian Studies.]

Knee, Adam
2010 'In (qualified) defense of "Southeast Asian Cinema"'. Keynote speech, 6th Southeast Asian Cinemas Conference, Ho Chi Minh City, 1-4 July.

Kristanto, J.B.
1995 *Katalog film Indonesia, 1926-1995*. Jakarta: Grafiasri Mukti.
2005 *Katalog film Indonesia, 1926-2005*. Jakarta: Grafiasri Mukti and Nalar.

Kusumaputra, Sugianto
2002 'Veven Sp Wardhana; Pengisi acara Ramadhan tak lepas dari popularitas', *Warta Kota*, 10 November.

Lang, Kurt and Gladys Engel Lang
1983 *The battle for public opinion; The president, the press, and the polls during Watergate*. New York: Columbia University Press.

Lasswell, Harold D.
1979 *The signature of power; Buildings, communication, and policy*. With the collaboration of Merritt B. Fox. New Brunswick, NJ: Transaction Press.

Legge, John D.
1972 *Sukarno; A political biography*. Baltimore: Penguin.

Lehmann, David and Batia Siebzehner
2006 'Holy pirates; Media, ethnicity, and religious renewal in Israel', in: Birgit Meyer and Annelies Moors (eds), *Religion, media, and the public sphere*, pp. 91-111. Bloomington: Indiana University Press.

Liddle, William R.
1996 'The Islamic turn in Indonesia; A political explanation', *The Journal of Asian Studies* 55-3:613-34.

Liebes, Tamar and Elihu Katz
1990 *The export of meaning; Cross-cultural readings of Dallas*. New York: Oxford University Press.

Livingstone, Sonia M.
1991 'Audience reception; The role of the viewer in retelling romantic drama', in: James Curran and Michael Gurevitch (eds), *Mass media and society*, pp. 285-306. London/New York: Arnold.

Loven, Klarijn
2008 *Watching Si Doel; Television, language, and cultural identity in contemporary Indonesia*. Leiden: KITLV Press. [Verhandelingen 242.]

Lull, James
1991 *China turned on; Television, reform, and resistance.* London and New York: Routledge.

Mackie, Jamie and Andrew MacIntyre
1994 'Politics', in: Hal Hill (ed.), *Indonesia's New Order; The dynamics of socio-economic transformation,* pp. 1-48. Honolulu: University of Hawaii Press.

Mahmud FR, Nashir M and Agus Suryanto/Bar
1990 'Film dakwah paceklik?', *Jumat,* 2 October.

Manuel, Peter
1993 *Cassette culture; Popular music and technology in North India.* Chicago/London: University of Chicago Press. [Chicago Studies in Ethnomusicology.]

Marjono
1993 'Mengangkat harkat bioskop keliling; Membangun sinema gedeg', *Majalah Film,* 9-22 February.

Mbembe, Achille
1992 'Provisional notes on the postcolony', *Africa* 62-1:3-37.

McGregor, Katharine E.
2002 'Commemoration of 1 October, "Hari Kesaktian Pancasila"; A post mortem analysis?', *Asian Studies Review* 26-1:39-72.
2007 *History in uniform; Military ideology and the construction of Indonesia's past.* Singapore: NUS Press, Leiden: KITLV Press. [Asian Studies Association of Australia, Southeast Asia Publications Series.]

McLuhan, Marshall
1995 *Understanding media; The extensions of man.* Reprint. London: Routledge. [First edition 1964.]

Meyer, Birgit
2000 'Modern mass media, religion and the imagination of communities; Different postcolonial trajectories in West Africa, Brazil and India',http://www2.fmg.uva.nl/media-religion (accessed 6-5-2008.)
2004 'Performativity – "Praise the Lord": Popular cinema and pentecostalite style in Ghana's new public sphere', *American Ethnologist* 31-1:92-110.
2007 'Impossible representations; Pentecostalism, vision, and video technology in Ghana', in: Birgit Meyer and Annelies Moors (eds), *Religion, media, and the public sphere,* pp. 290-312. Bloomington: Indiana University Press.

Mitra, Ananda
1993   *Television and popular culture in India; A study of the Mahabharat.* New Delhi: Sage.

Mohamad, Goenawan
2005   'Kali; A libretto', in: Mary S. Zurbuchen (ed.), *Beginning to remember; The past in the Indonesian present*, pp. 47-73. Singapore: Singapore University Press, Seattle, WA: University of Washington Press. [Critical Dialogues in Southeast Asian Studies.]

Moore, Laurence R.
1994   *Selling God; American religion in the marketplace of culture.* New York: Oxford University Press.

Morley, David
1980   *The 'Nationwide' audience; Structure and decoding.* London: British Film Institute. [Television Monographs 11.]

Mortimer, Rex
1974   *Indonesian communism under Sukarno; Ideology and politics, 1959-1965.* Ithaca, NY: Cornell University Press.

Mosse, George L.
1980   *Masses and man; Nationalist and fascist perceptions of reality.* New York: Fertig.

Muhammad, Aulia
2004   'Ruang hampa Ramadan', *Suara Merdeka*, 17 October.

Mukadis, Sartono
2004   'Buruan cium gue lagi', *Kompas*, 28 August.

My
1993   'Usaha bioskop layar tancap lahan film yang kena peras', *Majalah Film*, 1-17 July.

Naficy, Hamid
1984   *Iran media index.* Westport, CT: Greenwood Press.
2003   'Theorizing "Third World" film spectatorship; The case of Iran and Iranian cinema', in: Anthony R. Guneratne and Wimal Dissanayake (eds), *Rethinking Third Cinema*, pp. 183-201. New York/London: Routledge.

Nichols, Bill
1991   *Representing reality; Issues and concepts in documentary.* Bloomington: Indiana University Press.

Noor, Farish
2009   'Neo-liberalism and the "war on terror" industry', *Aliran*. http://aliran.com/1114.html (accessed 19-12-2011).

Nora, Pierre
1984   *Les lieux de mémoire*. Paris: Gallimard.
Nurhan, Kenedi and Theodore K.S.
1999a   'VCD dari generasi ke generasi', *Kompas*, 9 August.
1999b   'VCD bajakan dan terowongan tanpa lampu', *Kompas*, 9 August.
Nurudin
1997   'Persoalan realitas budaya film horror', *Pikiran Rakyat*, 20 April.
Öncü, Ayse
2006   'Becoming "secular Muslims"; Yasar Nuri Öztürk as a super-subject on Turkish television', in: Birgit Meyer and Annelies Moors (eds), *Religion, media, and the public sphere*, pp. 227-50. Bloomington: Indiana University Press.
Özkırımlı, Umut
2000   *Theories of nationalism; A critical introduction*. Foreword by Fred Halliday. London: Palgrave.
Pandjaitan, Hinca I.P. and Dyah Aryani
2001   *Melepas pasung kebijakan perfilman di Indonesia*. Jakarta: PT Warta Global Indonesia.
Paramaditha, Intan
2007   'Contesting Indonesian nationalism and masculinity in cinema', *Asian Cinema* 18-2:41-61.
2010   'Protectors & provocateurs; Reading the new film law as cultural performance'. Paper, Southeast Asian Cinemas Conference, Saigon, 1-4 July.
Pinches, Michael (ed.)
1999   *Culture and privilege in capitalist Asia*. London: Routledge. [The New Rich in Asia Series.]
Pengkhianatan
1985   'Pengkhianatan G 30 S PKI diedarkan diluar negeri', *Berita Buana*, 5 October.
Prakosa, Gotot
1997   *Film pinggiran*. Jakarta: FFTV-IKJ and YLP Fatma Press.
2001   *Ketika film pendek bersosialisasi*. Jakarta: Yayasan Layar Putih.
2005   *Film pendek independen dalam penilaian*. Jakarta: Komite Film Dewan Kesenian Jakart/Yayasan Seni Visual Indonesia.
Prananto, Jujur
2004   'Surat terbuka buat penandatangan petisi Utang Kayu; "Buruan Cium Gue" dan kontroversinya', posted on Layarkata-Network@yahoogroups.com, 31 August.

Pudjiastuti, Chris and Bre Redana
1997 'Hantu-hantu bergentayangan di televisi...', *Kompas*, 5 July.
Radway, Janice A.
1984 *Reading the romance; Women, patriarchy, and popular literature.* Chapel Hill: University of North Carolina Press.
Ratna, Lulu
2005 'Di bawah radar', *Majalah Film* 2 (October-December):48-50.
Real, Michael R.
1982 'The superbowl; Mythic spectacle', in: Horace Newcomb (ed.), *Television; The critical view.* Third edition, pp. 190-203. New York: Oxford University Press. [First edition 1977.]
Rianto, M.G.
1993 'Perfiki, hidup enggan mati tak mau', *Pikiran Rakyat*, 5 September.
Robertson, Roland
1992 *Globalization; Social theory and global culture.* London: Sage. [Theory, Culture & Society.]
Rodriguez, Robert
1996 *Rebel without a crew; Or, how a 23-year-old filmmaker with $7,000 became a Hollywood player.* New York: Plume.
Ruslani
2005 'Dari sinetron religius ke "emerging reason"', *Kompas*, 1 October.
Salamandra, Christa
1998 'Moustache hairs lost; Ramadan television serials and the construction of identity in Damascus, Syria', *Visual Anthropology* 10 (2-4):227-46.
Samuel, Hanneman and Henk Schulte Nordholt (eds)
2004 *Indonesia in transition; Rethinking 'civil society', 'region', and 'crisis'.* Yogyakarta: Pustaka Pelajar.
Santikarma, Degung
2005 'Monument, document and mass grave; The politics of representing violence in Bali', in: Mary S. Zurbuchen (ed.), *Beginning to remember; The past in the Indonesian present*, pp. 312-23. Singapore: Singapore University Press, Seattle, WA: University of Washington Press. [Critical Dialogues in Southeast Asian Studies.]
Santosa, Novan I
2003 'Antipiracy campaign launched', *The Jakarta Post*, 9 March.

Sanusi, Anwar
1993 'Banyak film lulus sensor tidak sesuai dengan nilai agama', *Harian Terbit*, 7 October.
Sari, Kartika
1993 'Layar tancap panen bila musim penganten', *Suara Karya*, 13 November.
Sarwat, Ahmed H.
2003 'Kajian syariah; Film dalam kacamata syariah Islam'. Paper, Islamic Movie Workshop, June-August.
Sasono, Eric
2007 'Krisis perfilman Indonesia?', *Koran Tempo*, 5 January.
Schneider, Steven J. (ed.)
2003 *Fear without frontiers; Horror cinema across the globe.* Surrey: FAB Press.
Schulte Nordholt, Henk
2004 *De-colonising Indonesian historiography.* Lund: Centre for East and South-East Asian Studies, Lund University. [Working Papers in Contemporary Asian Studies 6.]
2008 *Indonesië na Soeharto; Reformasi en restauratie.* Amsterdam: Bert Bakker.
Schulte Nordholt, Henk and Ireen Hoogenboom (eds)
2006 *Indonesian transitions.* Yogyakarta: Pustaka Pelajar.
Schulz, Dorothea E.
2006 'Morality, community, publicness; Shifting terms of public debate in Mali', in: Birgit Meyer and Annelies Moors (eds), *Religion, media, and the public sphere*, pp. 132-51. Bloomington: Indiana University Press.
Sears, Laurie J.
2005 'The persistence of evil and the impossibility of truth in Goenawan Mohamad's Kali', in: Mary S. Zurbuchen (ed.), *Beginning to remember; The past in the Indonesian present*, pp. 74-98. Singapore: Singapore University Press, Seattle, WA: University of Washington Press. [Critical Dialogues in Southeast Asian Studies.]
Seku, Akhmod
2002 'Religi TV dan peringatan Ramadhan', *Republika*, 3 November.
Sen, Krishna
1994 *Indonesian cinema; Framing the New Order.* London/New Jersey: Zed Books.

2003 'What's "oppositional" in Indonesian cinema?', in: Anthony R. Guneratne and Wimal Dissanayake (eds), *Rethinking Third Cinema*, pp. 147-65. New York /London: Routledge.

Sen, Krishna and David. T. Hill
2000 *Media, culture, and politics in Indonesia.* Melbourne: Oxford University Press.

Shami, Seteney
1999 'Circassian encounters; The self as other and the production of the homeland in the North Caucasus', in: Birgit Meyer and Peter Geschiere (eds), *Globalization and identity; Dialectics of flow and closure*, pp. 17-46. Oxford /Cambridge, MA: Blackwell.

Sharpe, Joanne
2002 'Eliana Eliana; Independent cinema, Indonesian cinema', *Inside Indonesia.* http://www.insideindonesia.org/edition-72-oct-dec-2002/default (accessed 6-12-2011).

Shohat, Ella
2003 'Post-Third-Worldist culture; Gender, nation, and the cinema', in: Anthony R. Guneratne and Wimal Dissanayake (eds), *Rethinking Third Cinema*, pp. 51-78. New York/London: Routledge.

Shohat, Ella and Robert Stam
1994 *Unthinking Eurocentrism; Multiculturalism and the media.* London: Routledge. [Sightlines.]
2003 (eds), *Multiculturalism, postcoloniality, and transnational media.* New Brunswick, NJ: Rutgers University Press. [Rutgers Depth of Field Series.]

Sitorus, Jhony
2001 'Jelangkung mengemas teknologi membetot saraf', *Koran Tempo*, 4 November.

Stacey, Jackie
1994 *Star gazing; Hollywood cinema and female spectatorship.* London: Routledge.

Staiger, Janet
1992 *Interpreting films; Studies in the historical reception of American cinema.* Princeton, NJ: Princeton University Press.

Stam, Robert
1989 *Subversive pleasures; Bakhtin, cultural criticism, and film.* Baltimore: Johns Hopkins University Press. [Parallax.]

Sulistiyo, Hermawan
1997 *The forgotten years; The missing history of Indonesia's mass slaughter (Jombang-Kediri 1965-1966)*. PhD thesis, Arizona State University, Tempe.

Suryana, A'an
2006 'Pornography bill; A serious threat to artists', *The Jakarta Post*, 13 March.

Suryapati, Akhlis
1997 'Tayangan mistik', *Pos Kota*, 13 April.

Suryati
1996 'Film misteri yang menyesatkan', *Pos Film*, 22 September.
1998 'Munafik dan mencari untung sendiri', *Pos Film*, 12 April.

Susanti, Ivy
2001 'United vision for region's cinema', *The Jakarta Post*, 21 October.

Sutara, Yaya
1994 'Kerja Badan Sensor Film digugat masyarakat', *Suara Pembaruan*, 25 July.

Suyono, Joko Seno and Dwi Arjanto
2003 'Dari Babi Ngepet hingga Jelangkung', *Tempo* (23 February):69-72.

Syah, Firman H.
1997 'Persaingan pengusaha film keliling langgar peraturan pemerintah', *Pos Film*, 31 August.
1998 'Pembajak VCD main kucing-kucingan', *Pos Film*, 24 May.

Taufiqurrahman, M.
2005 'Indonesia; Be goodod is on television', *The Jakarta Post*, 16 July.
2007 'Young filmmakers give back awards to protest FFI', *The Jakarta Post*, 4 January.

Taussig, Michael
1997 *The magic of the state*. New York/London: Routledge.

Tim SP
2000 'Mafia Glodok cukongi pembajak VCD', *Sinar Pagi*, 17 May.

Tranggono, Indra
2004 'Sinetron Ramadan; Memihak kepentingan modal atau sosial?', *Kedaulatan Rakyat*, 4 November.

Trinh T. Minh-ha
1993 'All-owing spectatorship', in: Hamid Naficy and Teshome H. Gabriel (eds), *Otherness and the media; The ethnography of the*

imagined and the imaged, pp. 189-204. Chur, Switzerland: Harwood Academic Publishers. [Studies in Film and Video 3.]

Turner, Graeme
1988 *Film as social practice*. London: Routledge. [Studies in Communication.]

Ukadike, Frank N.
2003 'Video booms and the manifestations of "First" cinema in Anglophone Africa', in: Anthony R. Guneratne and Wimal Dissanayake (eds), *Rethinking Third Cinema*, pp. 126-43. New York/London: Routledge.

Unidjaja, Febiola D.
2004 'Local teen flick withdrawn after Muslim leaders protest', *The Jakarta Post*, 21 August.

Usman, Syaikhu
2001 'Indonesia's decentralization policy; Initial experiences and emerging problems', *Smeru*. http://www.smeru.or.id/report/workpaper/euroseasdecentral/euroseasexperience.pdf (accessed 6-12-2011).

Veer, Peter van der
1994 *Religious nationalism; Hindus and Muslims in India*. Berkeley, CA: University of California Press.

Wardhana, Veven
2001a *Televisi dan prasangka budaya massa*. Jakarta: PT Media Lintas Inti Nusantara.
2001b. 'Sekawan sensor dalam cinema Indonesia'. Paper, Seminar 'Mencari Format Undang-Undang Perfilman Yang Ideal', Yogyakarta, 24 July.

Wark, McKenzie
1994 *Virtual geography; Living with global media events*. Bloomington: Indiana University Press. [Arts and Politics of the Everyday.]

Wasko, Janet
1994 *Hollywood in the information age; Beyond the silver screen*. Cambridge: Polity Press.

Watson, Rubie S.
1994 *Memory, history, and opposition under state socialism*. Santa Fe, NM: School of American Research Press.

Werbner, Richard
1996 'Multiple identities, plural arenas', in: Richard Werbner and Terence Ranger (eds), *Postcolonial identities in Africa*, pp. 1-26. London: Zed Books. [Postcolonial Encounters.]

White, Hayden
1999 *Figural realism; Studies in the mimesis effect*. Baltimore: Johns Hopkins University Press.

Wieringa, Saskia
2002 *Sexual politics in Indonesia*. Houndmills, Basingstoke: Palgrave Macmillan. [Institute of Social Studies Series.]

Willemen, Paul
1994 *Looks and frictions; Essays in cultural studies and film theory*. London: British Film Institute, Bloomington: Indiana University Press.

Wilson, Rob and Wimal Dissanayake (eds)
1996 *Global/local; Cultural production and the transnational imaginary*. Durham, NC: Duke University Press. [Asia-Pacific: Culture, Politics, and Society.]

Witte, Marleen de
2003 'Altar media's living word; Televised Christianity in Ghana', *Journal of Religion in Africa* 33-2:172-202.

Yordenaya, Ine
2004a 'MUI imbau "Buruan Cium Gue" diturunkan dari bioskop', *Detik.com*. http://m.detik.com/read/2004/08/13/171735/191182/115/mui-imbau-buruan-cium-gue-diturunkan-dari-bioskop (accessed 6-12-2011).
2004b 'Alasan LSF loloskan "Buruan Cium Gue"', *Detik.com*. http://m.detik.com/read/2004/08/18/150714/192982/115/alasan-lsf-loloskan-buruan-cium-gue (accessed 6-12-2011).

Zoso
2004 'Kiss me quick, please, for I'm indecent', *The Jakarta Post*. http://www.thejakartapost.com/news/2004/08/22/kiss-me-quick-please-i039m-indecent.html (accessed 6-12-2011).

Zurbuchen, Mary S. (ed.)
2005 *Beginning to remember; The past in the Indonesian present*. Singapore: Singapore University Press, Seattle, WA: University of Washington Press. [Critical Dialogues in Southeast Asian Studies.]

Filmography

Films

Ada apa dengan Cinta, 2002, dir. Rudi Soedjarwo.
Aku ingin menciummu sekali saja, 2003, dir. Garin Nugroho.
Antara masa lalu dan masa sekarang, 2001, dir. Eddie Cahyono.
Arisan, 2003, dir. Nia Dinata.
Bad wolves, 2005, dir. Richard Buntario.
Bangungnya Nyai Roro Kidul, 1985, dir. Sisworo Gautama.
Berbagi suami (Love for share), 2006, dir. Nia Dinata.
Beth, 2001, dir. Aria Kusumadewa.
Blair Witch project, the, 1999, dir. Daniel Myrick, Eduardo Sànchez.
Bonex
Bukan isteri pilihannya, 1981, dir. Eduart P. Sirait.
Bulan tertusuk ilalang, 1994, dir. Garin Nugroho.
Buruan cium gue! (satu kecupan), 2004, dir. Findo Purwono.
Cemeng 2005 (The last prima donna), 1995, dir. N. Riantiarno.
Cinta dalam sepotong roti, 1991, dir. Garin Nugroho.
Coyote ugly, 2000, dir. David McNally.
Darah dan doa, 1950, dir. Usmar Ismail.
Death of a nation, 1994, dir. John Pilger.
Denias; Senandung di atas awan, 2006, dir. John de Rantau.
Desa di kaki bukit, 1972, dir. Asrul Sani.
Detik-detik revolusi, 1959, dir. Alam Surawidjaja.
Detik terakhir, 2005, dir. Nanang Istiabudi.
Di antara masa lalu dan masa sekarang, 2001, dir. Eddie Cahyono.
Djakarta 1966, 1982, dir. Arifin C. Noer.
Doea siloeman oeler poeti en item, 1934, dir. The Teng Cun.
Dr. Siti Pertiwi kembali ke desa, 1979, dir. Ami Prijono.
Dunia kami, duniaku, dunia mereka, 1999, dir. Adi Nugroho.
Ekskul, 2006, dir. Nayato.

| *Filmography*

El-Mariachi, 1992, dir. Robert Rodriguez.
Enam jam di Yogya, 1951, dir. Usmar Ismail.
Fatahillah, 1996, dir. Imam Tantowi, Chaerul Umam.
Fright night, 1985, dir. Tom Holland.
Ghostbusters, 1984, dir. Ivan Reitman.
Gie, 2005, dir. Riri Riza.
Harry Potter and the sorcerer's stone, 2001, dir. Chris Colombus.
Jaka Sembung sang penakluk, 1981, dir. Sisworo Gautama.
Janur kuning, 1979, dir. Alam Surawijaya.
Jelangkung, 2001, dir. Rizal Mantovani.
Joe turun ke desa, 1989, dir. Chaerul Umam.
Kado buat rakyat Indonesia, 2003, dir. Daniel Indra Kusuma.
Kado untuk ibu, 2005, prod. Syarikat Indonesia.
Kadosh, 1999, dir. Amos Gitai.
Kafir (Satanic), 2002, dir. Mardali Syarief.
Kameng gampoeng nyang keunong geulawa, 1999, dir. Aryo Danusiri.
Kepada yang terhormat titik 2, 2002, dir. Dimas Jayasrana.
Kereta api terakhir, 1981, dir. Mochtar Soemodimedjo.
Kiamat sudah dekat, 2003, dir. Deddy Mizwar.
Kisah cinta Nyi Blorong, 1989, dir. Norman Benny.
Kuldesak, 1997, dir. Mira Lesmana, Riri Riza, Rizal Mantovani, Nan Achnas.
Kutunggu di sudut Semanggi, 2004, dir. Lukmantoro.
Lahir di Aceh, 2003, dir. Ariani Djalal.
Last communist, the (Lelaki komunis terakhir), 2006, Amir Muhammad.
Lastri; Suara perempuan korban tragedi 1965.
Lentera merah, 2006, dir. Hanung Bramantyo.
Lebak membara, 1982, dir. Imam Tantowi.
Lung boonmee raluek chat (Uncle Boonmee who can recall his past lives), 2010, dir. Apichatpong Weerasethakul.
Marsinah, 2002, dir. Slamet Rahardjo.
Mass grave, 2001, dir. Lexy Rambadeta.
Mistik (punahnya rahasia ilmu Iblis leak), 1981, dir. Tjut Djalil.
Novel tanpa huruf R, 2003, dir. Aria Kusumadewa.
Opera Jawa, 2006, dir. Garin Nugroho.
Operasi X, 1968, dir. Misbach Yusa Biran.
Pena pena patah, 2002, dir. Sarjev Faozan.

Penumpasan pengkhianatan G30S/PKI, 1982, dir. Arifin C Noer.

Penumpasan sisa-sisa PKI Blitar Selatan (Operasi Trisula), 1986, dir. BZ Kadaryono.

Pembalasan Ratu Laut Selatan, 1988, dir. Tjut Djalil.

Penyair negeri Linge, 2000, dir. Aryo Danusiri.

Perawan di Sektor Selatan, 1971, dir. Alam Surawidjaja.

Perempuan di wilayah konflik, 2002, dir. Gadis Arivia.

Perempuan; Kisah dalam guntingan, 2007, dir. Ucu Agustin.

Peronika, 2004, dir. Bowo Leksono.

Peti mati (The coffin), 2003, dir. Mardali Syarief.

Puisi tak terkuburkan (A poet), 1999, dir. Garin Nugroho.

Pulp fiction, 1994, dir. Quentin Tarantino.

Putri Kunti'anak, 1988, dir. Atok Suharto.

Ramadhan dan Ramona, 1992, dir. Chaerul Umam.

Ranjang Setan, 1986, dir. Tjut Djalil.

Ratu ular, 1972, dir. Lilik Sudjio.

Rembulan dan matahari, 1979, dir. Slamet Rahardjo.

Revolusi harapan, 1997, dir. Nanang Istiabudi.

Sangat laki-laki, 2004, dir. Fajar Nugroho.

Satria bergitar, 1983, dir. Nurhadie Irawan.

Satu nyawa dalam denting lonceng kecil, 2002, dir. Abiprasidi.

Saur sepuh (Satria Madangkara), 1988, dir. Imam Tantowi.

Schindler's list, 1993, dir. Steven Spielberg.

Sembilan wali, 1985, dir. Djun Saptohadi.

Serangan fajar, 1982, dir. Arifin C. Noer.

Sinengker, 2007, dir. Aprisiyanto, 2007.

Si Pitung beraksi kembali, 1981, dir. Lie Soen Bok.

Snatch (Dukot (Desaparecidos)), 2009, dir. Joel Lamangan.

Soerabaia 45, 1990, dir. Imam Tantowi.

Soul, the, 2003, dir. Nayato Fio Nuala.

Student movement in Indonesia, 1998, dir. Tino Saroengallo.

Sunan Kalijaga, 1983, dir. Sofyan Sharna.

Sunan Kalijaga & Syeh Sitijenar, 1985, dir. Sofyan Sharna.

Thirteen, 2003, dir. Catherine Hardwick.

Titian serambut dibelah tujuh (The narrow bridge), 1982, dir. Chaerul Umam.

Titik hitam, 2002, dir. Sentot Sahid.

| *Filmography*

Topeng kekasih, 2000, dir. Hanung Bramantyo.
True lies, 1994, dir. James Cameron.
Tusuk jelangkung, 2003, dir. Dimas Djayadiningrat.
Virgin, 2004, dir. Hanny Saputra.

Television films

Bang bang you're dead, 2002, dir. Guy Ferland.
Bukan sekadar kenangan Kasih ibu selamanya Pedang keadilan (Indosiar).
Terjebak, 1996, dir. Dedi Setiadi.

Television series

Anak Baru Gedhe (RCTI)
Astaghfirullah (SCTV)
Azab Ilahi (Lativi)
Baywatch (RCTI; first broadcast on NBC, United States of America)
Beverly Hills 90210 (RCTI; first broadcast on Fox, United States of America)
Ceramah Ramadhan AA Gym (Trans TV)
Cowok cowok keren (RCTI)
Dua dunia (Indosiar)
Dunia lain (Trans TV)
Esmeralda (SCTV; first broadcast on Televisa Mexico)
Gema Ramadhan (SCTV)
Gema takdir (SCTV)
Hantu sok usil (SCTV)
Hidayah (Trans TV)
Indahnya kebersamaan (SCTV)
Insyaf (Trans TV)
Janda kembang (SCTV)
Jin dan Jun (RCTI)
Kembalinya Si Manis Jembatan Ancol (RCTI)
Kisah2 teladan (Indosiar)
Kismis (RCTI)
Kismis; Arwah penasaran (RCTI)
Layar tancep (Lativi)
Manajemen qulbu spesial Ramadhan (RCTI)
Melrose Place (SCTV; first broadcast on Fox Network, United States of America)

Membuka pintu langit (SCTV)
Misteri (Anteve)
Misteri sinden (RCTI)
Nah ini dia (SCTV)
O seraam (Anteve)
Pemburu hantu (Lativi)
Percaya nggak percaya (Anteve)
Rahasia Ilahi (TPI)
Sambut Ramadhan (SCTV)
Sebuah kesaksian (Lativi)
Sentuhan qolbu Ramadhan (TPI
Si Manis Jembatan Ancol (RCTI)
Takdir Ilahi (TPI)
Taubat (Trans TV)
Three in one (SCTV)
Tuyul dan Mbak Yul (RCTI)
VIP (RCTI, American syndicated television series)

Index

Abiyoga, Budiyati 140, 185
Aceh 55, 108-9, 159, 199
Achnas, Nan 53
Acup, Nya Abbas 87
Ada apa dengan Cinta 172, 179
Adjidarma, Seno Gumira 68, 185, 190
Africa 15
Aku ingin menciummu sekali saja 171
Ali, Muhamad 160, 183
Aliansi Anti Komunis (AAK) 200
Aliansi Masyarakat Aniti Porno-Aksi (AMAP) 164, 172
Allah Maha Besar 173
Amidhan 187-8
Amini, Aisyah 142
Anak Baru Gedhe 161
Anderson, Benedict 7, 11, 21, 65, 135
Angkatan Bersenjata Republik Indonesia (ABRI) 93
Angriawan, Ferry 140
Anteve 142, 150-1
Arisan 172
Asshiddiqie, Jimly 185
Astaghfirullah 174
Australia 45, 113, 120, 200
Azab Ilahi 174
Azis, Abuh 193

Badan Pertimbangan Perfilman Nasional (BP2N) 176, 178, 185
Badan Sensor Film (BSF) 30, 139-40, 168, 188
Bang bang you're dead 177
Bangkok International Film Festival 15
Banyuwangi 27, 58
Batam 58, 70
Batu 18, 56
Baudrillard, Jean 128, 202
Baywatch 172
Berau 58
Berbagi suami (Love for share) 177
Berlinale 16
Beth 20, 59-78
Bilbina, Arzeti 150
Biran, Misbach Yusa 93
Bisiri, Ahmad Mustofa 167-8
Bonex 26, 29
Brazil 15, 75-6, 105
Buchory, Jeffry al- 174
Bukan sekadar kenangan (BSK) 124
Bulan tertusuk ilalang 46
Burma 105
Buruan cium gue! 157, 161-7, 172-84, 194-8

Cairo 120
celebrity *kyai* 132, 157-84, 198
Cemeng 2005 46
Cianjur 159
Cilacap 58

Cinema 21 (Group 21) 36, 54, 58-64, 77-8, 124-5, 179
Cinemanila 15
code of ethics 95, 139-41, 148, 153
Coyote ugly 164

Danusiri, Aryo 55, 108
Darah dan doa 84
Daraista, Inul 157, 167
Darul Islam 95
Dayan, Daniel 97, 100, 113
Denias; Senandung di atas awan 177
Denpasar 45
Desa di kaki bukit 86
Dewa 19 158
Dewan Film Nasional (DFN) 85, 139
Dewan Gereja-Gereja di Indonesia (DGI) 168
Dinata, Nia 185
Direktorat Pembinaan Film Rekaman Video 27
Dirlik, Arif 11, 66, 194
Dissanayake, Wimal 10-1, 194-5
Djakarta 1966 97
Djamaluddin Malik 45
Djarot, Erros 119, 200
Doea siloeman oeler poeti en item 136
Dr. Siti Pertiwi kembali ke desa 86
Dua dunia 142
Duara, Prasenjit 20, 182, 197-8
Dunia lain 150
Dwipayana, Brigadier General 89, 92-3

East Timor 8, 39, 199
Eddendi, Mahadjir 109
Egypt 15, 75, 123, 130, 132, 173
Ekskul 177, 189

Fairclough, Norman 2, 5-6, 107
Febriono, CC 151
Festival Arisan 20, 46-9, 189-9
Festival Film Asia Pasifik (FFAP) 40, 44-7
Festival Film Bandung 40-1
Festival Film dan Video Independen Indonesia (FFVII) 54
Festival Film Documenter (FFD) 68
Festival Film Indonesia (FFI) 40, 47-8, 176-200
Festival Film Perdamaian 67
Festival Sinetron Indonesia (FSI) 44
Film Censor Board (BSF) 139-40
film discourse practices 5, 107, 147, 196
film independen 17, 52-9, 64-7, 78, 104, 190-4
film indie 57-9, 62, 64, 67, 177, 195
film Islami 20, 115, 122, 130-1, 160, 190, 192, 194-5
film keliling 26, 54
film mediation practices 2-3, 9-13, 25, 28, 30, 48-53, 65, 76, 78, 121-2, 130, 189, 194
film mistik 135-45, 147-8, 155
film narrative practices 6, 12-4, 135
film pembangunan 81, 85-8, 94, 104
film perjuangan 81-2, 84-5, 88, 94, 103-4
Ford Foundation 108
Forum Komunikasi Lembaga Dakwah (FKLD) 169
Forum Lingkar Pena (FLP) 119
Foucault, Michel 2

Fright night 60
Front Pembela Islam (FPI) 158, 170, 197, 200
Fu:n Community 119-20

Gaban, Farid 166
Gabungan Perusahaan Bioskop Seluruh Indonesia (GPBSI) 30
Gabungan Studio Film Indonesia (Gasfi) 30
Gabungan Subtitling Indonesia (Gasi) 30
gelora pembangunan films 87-8, 114
Gerakan Perempuan Hindu Muda Indonesia (GPHMI) 171
Gymnastiar, Abdullah (AA Gym) 126-7, 157-67, 183-4, 197-8

Habibie, B.J. 147, 159, 165
Hackett, Rosalind 190
Hari Film National 84
Hari Peringatan Kesaktian Pancasila (Hapsak) 96-102, 105, 111-3, 124
Harmayn, Shanty 67, 178, 185
Harmoko 43-4, 141
Harry Potter and the sorcerer's stone 61
Hartono 118, 146, 155
Hatta, Muhammad 189
Hebdige, Dick 128
Hefner, Robert 191
Heider, Karl 136
Hello;fest 68-9
Heryanto, Ariel 130
Hidayah 173
Hidayatullah, Utstaz Aziz 153
Hill, David 89
Himpunan Artis Film dan Sinetron Indonesia (Hafsi) 28
Himpunan Artis Film dan Televisi (Hafti) 28
Himpunan Film Keliling Indonesia (Hifki) 26
Himpunan Mahasiswa Islam (HMI) 169
Himpunan Pengusaha Bioskop Indonesia (HPBI) 26
Hizbut Tahri (HT) 167, 175
Hollywood 15, 20, 33
Hong Kong 45, 70, 121, 146
horror film 135-45, 147-8, 155
Hucheon, Linda 81
hyperreal ghosts 135-55, 202

Ikatan Karyawan Film dan Televisi (KFT) 28, 54
Ilham, Arifin 127, 173
Imam Tantowi 145
Imanjaya, Ekky 82
India 33, 45, 71, 73, 75, 121, 137, 146, 167, 173, 191, 195
Indonesian Documentary Film Festival (FFD) 112
Indonesian Institute for the Study of Human Rights and Advocacy Elsham 108
Indonesian Mediation Project (IMP) 17
Institut Kesenian Jakarta (IKJ) 59, 119-20
International Film Festival Rotterdam 16
International Monetary Fund (IMF) 65, 73
Irama, Rhoma 118, 127, 157, 167
Iran 88, 105

I-Sinema 10, 57-8, 193
Ismail, Taufiq 185, 187-8, 190
Ismail, Usmar 45, 83-4, 87, 90, 129

Jakarta 41, 44, 70, 90, 94, 98, 112-4, 116, 119-20, 125, 127, 144, 147, 150, 152, 154-8, 185, 198-9
Jakarta International Film Festival (Jiffest) 15, 19, 61, 67
Jakarta Post, The 164
Janur kuning 90, 97, 102
Japan 45, 65, 84, 88, 137
Japan Foundation 17
Jayakusuma 87
Jayapura 19
Jayasrana, Dimas 181
Jelangkung 59-78, 147
Jenderal Soedirman University 52
Jin dan Jun 141-6
Joe turun ke desa 86

Kado buat rakyat Indonesia 108
Kado untuk ibu 200
Kafir (Satanic) 148-9
Kameng gampoeng nyang keunong geulawa 55, 108
Kammi 120
Karanganyar 200-1
Karyawan Film Television - Asosiasi Sineas (KFT-ASI) 179
Katz, Elihu 97, 100, 113
Kayam, Umar 20, 96, 128
Kembalinya Si Manis Jembatan Ancol 142
Kepada yang terhormat titik 2 52
Kiamat sudah dekat 175
Kismis 149-50
Kitley, Philip 6-7

Knee, Adam 15
Kode Etik Produksi Film Nasional 139
Komisi Penyiaran Indonesia (KPI) 185
Komite Indonesia untuk Solidaritas Dunia Islam (KISDI) 169
Komite Peduli Perfilman Nasional (KP2N) 26
komunitas film dokumenter 68
Komunitas Film Independen (Konfiden) 19, 54-5, 67, 75, 192
Komunitas Gardu 61
Konferensi Wali Gereja Indonesia (KWI) 168
Kuldesak 10, 52-4, 57, 178, 193
Kus, Doni 64
Kusumadewa, Aria 19, 61, 63, 182
Kutunggu di sudut Semanggi 109
Kuwait 45

Lahir di Aceh 108
Lampung 199
Last communist (Lelaki komunis terakhir), The 17
Last prima donna, The 46
Lastri; Suara perempuan korban tragedi 1965 200
layar tancep 33, 48, 164, 190
Lefebvre, Henry 128
Lembaga Kebudayaan Rakyat (LEKRA) 84
Lembaga Sensor Film (LSF) 27, 176-200
Lesmana, Mira 53, 185
Lung Boonmee raluek chat (Uncle Boonmee who can recall his past lives) 17

Maarif, Ahmad Syafii 131
McGregor, Katharine 81, 91, 95, 101
Mafin 53
Majalengka 29
Majelis Mujahiddin Indonesia (MMI) 166
Majelis Ulama Indonesia (MUI) 116, 128, 168, 175, 187
Mak, Hariry 153
Makarim, Nono Anwar 185
Malang 18, 56, 58
Malaysia 16-7, 45, 70-1, 173, 123, 189
Malyati Ws, Tatiek 173
Manila 45
Mantovani, Riza 53
Markuzi, Ismail 100
Marsinah 109
Masaichi Nagata 45
Mass grave 110-3, 129, 200
Masyarakat Anti Pembajakan dan Pornografi Indonesia (MAPPI) 70
Masyarakat Film Indonesia (MFI) 176-200
Mataram 58
Medan 58, 70
Media Cipta Utama, PT 119
media jujitsu 21, 75-6
Mediarta, Agus 192
Melrose Place 172
Mer-C 119
Mexico 75
Miftah, Fetty Fajriati 85
Minh-ha, Trinh 81, 197
Misteri 142
Mistik (punahnya rahasia ilmu Iblis leak) 139

Mistiri sinden 142
Mizwar, Deddy 175
modes of engagement 13-4, 20-1, 81, 86, 95, 104, 107, 110, 129
Mohamad, Goenawan 101, 185, 187, 199
Morality Audio Visual Network (MAV-Net) 120-1
Motion Picture Association (MPA) 73
moving-image technologies 15
MQTV Bandung 120, 127
M-Screen Indonesia 119-20
Mudzakir 185
Muhammad, Ali 159, 166
Muhammad, Aulia 128-31
Muhammadiyah 109, 118-9, 168, 173
Muhir, Fadloli El 192-3
Mukadis, Sartono 167
Munir 189, 199
Murtopo, Ali 43, 85, 139
Muslim Movie Education (MME) 119
Mutiara Film, PT 29
Mutiara Industri Perfilman Rakyat, PT 26

Naficy, Hamid 86-8
Nahdlatul Ulama (NU) 167-8
Nasution, Abdul Haris 111
National Indie Film Festival 55
Nayato 148, 177
New Order 11-4, 17, 26, 30-2, 37, 40, 45, 47, 49, 53-4, 57, 65-7, 69, 81, 83-114, 125, 129-31, 136, 139-43, 153-4, 157, 166-8, 172, 176-8, 184, 186, 188, 191, 194, 196, 199-200

New Zealand 45, 47
Nichols, Bill 110
Noer, Arifin C. 90-1, 170
Noor, Farish 195-7
Notosusanto, Nugroho 92
Nugroho, Garin 9, 20, 46-7, 171

O seraam 150
Offstream Production 108
Opera Jawa 172
Operasi X 93

Padang 159
Padang Panjang 58
Pancasila 92, 94, 99, 159
Panitia Persiapan Kemerdekaan Indonesia (PPKI) 189
Pantja, Harry 151
Papua 19, 171, 177, 199
Paramaditha, Intan 188, 192
Parisada Hindu Dharma Indonesia (PHDI) 168
Partai Bintang Reformasi (PBR) 127
Partai Demokrasi Indonesia (PDI) 94
Partai Keadilan Sejahtera (PKS) 167, 170
Partai Komunis Indonesia (PKI) 82-4, 91-3, 98, 100, 110
Parwez, Chand 198
Pembalasan Ratu Laut Selatan 170
Pemburu hantu 152
Pena pena patah 108
Pendidikan Sejarah Perjuangan Bangsa (PSPB) 93
Penumpasan pengkhianatan G30s-PKI 91-4, 97-8, 100-7, 109-13

Penumpasan sisa-sisa PKI Blitar Selatan (Operasi Trisula) 93-4
Penyair negeri Linge 108
Percaya nggak percaya 150
Perempuan di wilayah konflik 108
Perfini-Persari 45
Peronika 56
Persatuan Artis Film Indonesia (Parfi) 28, 30, 185
Persatuan Perusahaan Film Indonesia (PPFI) 28
Persatuan Wartawan Indonesia (PWI) 40
Perusahaan Film Negara (PFN) 87-8
Perusahaan Jawatan Kereta Api (PJKA) 29
Pesantren Darunnajah 120
Pesta Sinema Indonesia (PSI) 68
Peti mati 148
Philippines 45, 71, 73
Pinches, Michael 25-6
Prakosa, Gotot 51, 89
praktek miring (cursive practices) 21, 31, 48-9, 76, 78
Prananto, Jujur 167, 184
Provokator 25-32, 48
Puisi tak terkuburkan (A poet) 108
Pulp fiction 193
Punjabi, Raam 198
Purwokerto 52-3, 68
Pusat Perfilman Haji Usmar Ismail (PPHUI) 19, 90
Pusat Produksi Film Negara (PPFN) 89-90, 93
Putih, Ki Gusti Candra 153

Q Festival 19
Queer Film Festival (QFF) 68

Rahasia Ilahi 173
Rahman, Fadjoel 185
Rajawali Citra Televisi Indonesia (RCTI) 141, 149, 151, 161, 164
Ramadan 122-32, 169
Rambadeta, Lexy 200
Ranjang Setan 139
Ratna, Lulu 20, 75
Ratu ular 136
Rebel without a crew 193
Reformasi 8-9, 12-3, 30, 32, 51, 53-4, 67, 104, 107, 114, 123-4, 147-9, 153-7, 159, 170, 178, 187-8
Revolusi harapan 17, 55
Riza, Riri 53, 185
Rohis Mimazah 120
Roisamri, Lalu 185
Rolph-Trouillot, Michel 199
Run Shaw 45

Sahab, Ali 125
Said, Titie 163, 179-80
Salman Film-maker Club 119
Sangat laki-laki 19
Sani, Asrul 87
Sanusi, Anwar 169
Sari, Masna 185
Saroenggalo, Tino 182
Sarwat, Ahmed 121
Sastrowardoyo, Dian 185
Satu nyawa dalam denting lonceng kecil 148
Schindler's list 170
SCTV's Festival Film Independen Indonesia 58
Sears, Laurie J. 200
Sejarah Orde Baru (SOB) 92
selamatan 28

Semarang 19, 70-1, 162
Sembilan wali 116
Sen, Krishna 8, 11, 33, 42, 44, 66, 83, 86-7, 89, 140
Serangan fajar 90, 97, 102
Shohat, Ella 1-2, 20, 64-5, 76
Si Manis Jembatan Ancol 141-6
Siagian, Bachtiar 83
Sidik, Ustaz Jafar 180
Sihab, Quraish 127
Sihombing, Wahyu 87
Sinengker 200
sinetron 54
sinetron komedi misteri 141
sinetron misteri 141
sinetron religius 160
Singapore 15-6, 45, 61, 70-1, 73
Singapore International Film Festival 70
Sinta obong 171
Snatch 17
Soeharto 2, 12 , 17, 20, 25, 30-2, 37, 40, 45, 49, 53, 57, 65-9, 77, 81-114, 125, 129-31, 136, 139-43, 153-4, 166-9, 172, 176, 178, 184, 186, 188, 191, 194, 196, 199-200
Soekarno 45, 81-2, 90-1
Soekarnoputri, Megawati 98, 124, 165
Soemardjono 87
Sophiaan, Sophan 188
Soul, The 148
North Korea 45
South Korea 45, 47, 73
South Sulawesi 159
Southeast Asian Cinemas Conference 15
Southeast Asian Film Festival 44-5

Stam, Robert 20, 64-5, 76
State Islamic University, Jakarta 159
Student movement in Indonesia 112-3, 124-5, 129, 131
Suaidy, Ahmad 169
Sudjono, Dondy 174
Sudwikatmono 66
Sunan Kalijaga 116
Sunan Kalijaga & Syeh Sitijenar 116
Surabaya 43, 58, 70-1
Surya Citra Televisi (SCTV) 58, 67, 142, 161, 164, 171, 173, 195
Syamsudin, Din 175
Syarief, Mardali 25, 28, 148

Taiwan 45, 47, 73
Takdir Ilahi 174
Tangerang 159
Taufiqurrahman 175
Teater Bening 119
Teater Kanvas 119
Technical Cooperation Administration (TCA) 87
Technical University of Bandung 119
Televisi Pendidikan Indonesia (TPI) 29, 173-4
Televisi Republik Indonesia (TVRI) 42, 44, 88, 98
Tentara Nasional Indonesia (TNI) 28
Terjebak 94
Thailand 16-7, 45, 73
The Teng Cun 136
Third Cinema discourse 64-7, 115

Third Cinema theories 20, 52, 75, 121
Thirteen 164
Three in one 19
Tien, Ali 139
Tifa Foundation 108
Titian serambut dibelah tujuh 116
Titik hitam 148
Toer, Pramoedya Ananta 200
Topeng kekasih 116
Trans TV 150-1
Trisakti and Semanggi affairs 29
Trisakti University 29
True lies 170
Truman, Harry S. 85
Tusuk jelangkung 148
Tuyul dan Mbak Yu 142-6

Umam, Chaerul 86, 116, 120, 174, 179
Umar, Husein 169
underground cinema 51-78
United Kingdom 83, 120
United States 15, 18, 36, 39, 59, 83, 85-6, 88, 130
United States Information Agency (USIA) 85, 196
Universitas Muhammadiyah Malang (UMM) 18, 109
Utan Kayu 164, 166

Veer, Peter van der 191
Vietnam 15-6, 45
VIP 172
Virgin 10, 164-5, 198

Wahid, Abdurrahman 98, 147, 165, 167, 176, 200

Wark, McKenzie 1, 197
White, Hayden 81
Wilson, Rob 10
Wonogiri 58

Yayasan Jurnal Perempuan 108
Yayasan Nasional Festival Film Indonesia (YFI) 41

Yogyakarta 17-9, 43, 45, 55-6, 58, 64, 68, 90, 97, 114, 200
Yogyakarta Muhamadiyah University film club 18
Yusanto, Ismail 75

Zachri, Caroline 149
Zoso 164, 166

www.ingramcontent.com/pod-product-compliance
Lightning Source LLC
Chambersburg PA
CBHW052032300426
44117CB00012B/1796